SILVER
OPPORTUNITY

SILVER
OPPORTUNITY

Building Integrated Services for Older Adults around Primary Health Care

**Edited by Xiaohui Hou,
Jigyasa Sharma, and
Feng Zhao**

WORLD BANK GROUP

Contents

Chapter 5. Designing Integrated Care for an Aging Population: Regulation and Governance for Healthy Aging   113

Naoki Kondo, Koryu Sato, and Yuiko Nagamine

Chapter 6. Evaluating Care of Older Adults in Low- and Middle-Income Countries   133

Zhanlian Feng, Guadalupe Suarez, and Elena E. Glinskaya

Chapter 7. Community-Based Integrated Care in Japan   159

Japan International Cooperation Agency (JICA), summarized by Risa Nakayama and Xiaohui Hou

Box

Figures

Maps

Tables

Foreword

Like many diseases, COVID-19 (coronavirus disease 2019) has had a sharply disproportionate impact on older people. During the first year of the pandemic, people age 65 years and older in high-income countries accounted for 89 percent of official and excess COVID-19 deaths, and in low- and middle-income countries, they accounted for nearly half.

The strain on health systems worldwide from the burden of both infectious and chronic diseases is growing by the day, in part because populations are rapidly aging. In 2018, for the first time in history, people age 65 years and older outnumbered children under five worldwide. By 2050, the number of older people is projected to more than double from 2019.

Why does this matter?

A failure by countries to improve the capacity of their health systems to care for their aging populations will have a devastating ripple effect on older people and their families, communities, and economies.

When medical care does not meet older people's needs, population aging can cause health and social care costs to balloon, government deficits to rise, and economic growth to decline—and, of course, can have deleterious effects on older people themselves.

Moreover, in communities where formal long-term care infrastructure is weak, the burden of care for older adults often falls on family members, who may have to forgo employment to care for their relatives, with consequences for their own health and well-being and for human capital accumulation in their countries.

It does not have to be this way.

As our report title suggests, governments have a "silver opportunity" to improve health by reimagining primary health care (PHC) and integrating it with other forms of person-centered care, including long-term care, to better address the health needs of older populations.

Longevity gains reflect hard-won progress in human development. Now we need to redesign health care systems and link PHC to broader forms of social care and support—including community care, secondary and tertiary care, and long-term care facilities—to maintain and accelerate this progress.

However, PHC delivery systems in most countries have yet to fulfill their promise, and most systems do not regularly provide the range of quality services that meet the needs of older populations.

Addressing the high burden of disease among seniors, especially epidemics of chronic disease, will require reforming PHC systems to make them more agile and responsive to the needs of this growing population.

This book presents an original framework to show how core policy levers—health financing, innovation in service delivery and digital technology, regulation, and evaluation, which we call the FIRE framework—can help countries make their PHC systems more responsive to the needs of older people, coordinate care across different types of medical and social support, and uplift older people's health.

The ultimate result will be more integrated care systems that link different facets of people's health and well-being across their lifespans.

If governments can improve the supply-side levers outlined in the FIRE framework to meet the needs of their surging populations of older adults swiftly and at scale, they can usher in a silver age of healthier people and societies.

Doing so will pay other dividends. Providing integrated care centered in PHC systems not only will have a positive impact on individual health and allow people to thrive in old age but also will speed progress toward achieving two critical goals—universal health coverage and health equity.

This book weaves together a collection of studies and thought leadership contributed by research groups from different backgrounds and with varied domains of expertise at the World Bank, universities, think tanks, and research institutes. The diversity of backgrounds, perspectives, and skill sets among contributors enriches the book's treatment of a complex and evolving topic.

We are publishing it during the United Nations Decade of Healthy Ageing, designed to bring together governments, civil society, international agencies, academia, and the private sector to improve the lives of older people, their families, and the communities in which they live. We hope this book makes a vital contribution to these efforts.

Juan Pablo Uribe
Global Director
Health, Nutrition and Population Global Practice
The World Bank

Acknowledgments

The editors would like to extend their appreciation to the individuals, organizations, and institutions that provided their knowledge and expertise to the development of this report.

This report was led by Xiaohui Hou (senior economist, Global Engagement, Health, Nutrition and Population Global Practice) and Jigyasa Sharma (health economist, Global Engagement, Health, Nutrition and Population Global Practice), under the supervision and guidance of Feng Zhao (practice manager, South Asia Region, Health, Nutrition and Population Global Practice), Juan Pablo Uribe (global director, Health, Nutrition and Population Global Practice), Monique Vledder (practice manager, Global Engagement, Health, Nutrition and Population Global Practice), and David Wilson (program director, Global Engagement, Health, Nutrition and Population Global Practice). Sana Haider, Risa Nakayama, and Mengxiao Wang provided technical support; Jocelyn Haye and Marize de Fatima Santos provided administrative support; Naoko Ohno and Kyoko Tokuda provided Trust Fund administration guidance and support. The report was edited by Alexander Irwin and Karen Ann Schneider. The report was copyedited by Sherrie Brown and proofread by Ann O'Malley. The authors also thank Carissa Qin and Daniel Yustos for design work.

The editors also thank Mickey Chopra, Elena E. Glinskaya, Naoko Ohno, and Sameera Maziad Al Tuwaijri for their reviews and comments. The editors also thank Bushra Binte Alam, Kathryn Gilman Andrews, Xi Chen, Zhanlian Feng, Pagma Genden, Atia Hossain, Roberto F. Iunes, Kate Mandeville, Vikram Rajan, Sameh El-Saharty, Sevil Kamalovna Salakhutdinova, and Jeremy Veillard for providing feedback on the framework and for their contributions to the country case studies.

The team also thanks the Japan International Cooperation Agency for multiple discussions on the topic and for their contributions to the Japan case study and Professor Haruko Noguchi of Waseda University for contributions to the regulation chapter.

The team is grateful to the Japan Policy and Human Resources Development Fund Trust Fund for support of this report.

However, PHC delivery systems in most countries have yet to fulfill their promise, and most systems do not regularly provide the range of quality services that meet the needs of older populations.

Addressing the high burden of disease among seniors, especially epidemics of chronic disease, will require reforming PHC systems to make them more agile and responsive to the needs of this growing population.

This book presents an original framework to show how core policy levers—health financing, innovation in service delivery and digital technology, regulation, and evaluation, which we call the FIRE framework—can help countries make their PHC systems more responsive to the needs of older people, coordinate care across different types of medical and social support, and uplift older people's health.

The ultimate result will be more integrated care systems that link different facets of people's health and well-being across their lifespans.

If governments can improve the supply-side levers outlined in the FIRE framework to meet the needs of their surging populations of older adults swiftly and at scale, they can usher in a silver age of healthier people and societies. Doing so will pay other dividends. Providing integrated care centered in PHC systems not only will have a positive impact on individual health and allow people to thrive in old age but also will speed progress toward achieving two critical goals—universal health coverage and health equity.

This book weaves together a collection of studies and thought leadership contributed by research groups from different backgrounds and with varied domains of expertise at the World Bank, universities, think tanks, and research institutes. The diversity of backgrounds, perspectives, and skill sets among contributors enriches the book's treatment of a complex and evolving topic. We are publishing it during the United Nations Decade of Healthy Ageing, designed to bring together governments, civil society, international agencies, academia, and the private sector to improve the lives of older people, their families, and the communities in which they live. We hope this book makes a vital contribution to these efforts.

Juan Pablo Uribe
Global Director
Health, Nutrition and Population Global Practice
The World Bank

Foreword

Like many diseases, COVID-19 (coronavirus disease 2019) has had a sharply disproportionate impact on older people. During the first year of the pandemic, people age 65 years and older in high-income countries accounted for 89 percent of official and excess COVID-19 deaths, and in low- and middle-income countries, they accounted for nearly half.

The strain on health systems worldwide from the burden of both infectious and chronic diseases is growing by the day, in part because populations are rapidly aging. In 2018, for the first time in history, people age 65 years and older outnumbered children under five worldwide. By 2050, the number of older people is projected to more than double from 2019.

Why does this matter?

A failure by countries to improve the capacity of their health systems to care for their aging populations will have a devastating ripple effect on older people and their families, communities, and economies.

When medical care does not meet older people's needs, population aging can cause health and social care costs to balloon, government deficits to rise, and economic growth to decline—and, of course, can have deleterious effects on older people themselves.

Moreover, in communities where formal long-term care infrastructure is weak, the burden of care for older adults often falls on family members, who may have to forgo employment to care for their relatives, with consequences for their own health and well-being and for human capital accumulation in their countries.

It does not have to be this way.

As our report title suggests, governments have a "silver opportunity" to improve health by reimagining primary health care (PHC) and integrating it with other forms of person-centered care, including long-term care, to better address the health needs of older populations.

Longevity gains reflect hard-won progress in human development. Now we need to redesign health care systems and link PHC to broader forms of social care and support—including community care, secondary and tertiary care, and long-term care facilities—to maintain and accelerate this progress.

About the Editors and Authors

Xiaohui Hou is a senior economist in the World Bank's Health, Nutrition and Population Global Practice. She has more than 15 years of experience in development and specializes in health financing, service delivery, and health systems strengthening. Throughout her career, Xiaohui has led policy dialogues, lending operations, flagship analytical projects, and program development in various countries across Africa, East Asia and the Pacific, Eastern Europe, and South Asia. Her work has been published in books and peer-reviewed journals in the field of economics and health and has earned her recognition as a respected expert in her field. She has served as a visiting scholar at several universities. Xiaohui holds a PhD in health services and policy analysis and a master's degree in economics from the University of California, Berkeley; a master's degree in health policy and administration from Washington State University; and a bachelor's degree in biochemistry and molecular biology from Beijing University.

Jigyasa Sharma is a health economist in the World Bank's Health, Nutrition and Population Global Practice. She joined the World Bank in September 2019 in the Office of the Chief Economist for Human Development. Her areas of expertise include health systems strengthening and measurement of health system quality and primary care performance. A population health and health system researcher, she has coauthored dozens of journal articles and reports on health system quality and measurement of quality of care, contributed to the Lancet Global Health Commission for High Quality Health Systems, and worked as a consultant for the Department of Reproductive Health and Research at the World Health Organization. Jigyasa holds an ScD degree in global health and population from Harvard University and an MSc in epidemiology and biostatistics from McGill University.

Feng Zhao serves as the World Bank's South Asia practice manager in the Health, Nutrition and Population Global Practice. He has more than 20 years of experience in public health, medicine, economics, and demography at the global, regional, and country levels. Previously, he oversaw the World Bank's Global Health Engagement program and led the COVID-19 (coronavirus) health response program as the manager for Global Health Engagement. He has served in different positions at the World Bank, including program leader for the human development programs for Belarus, Moldova, and Ukraine and task manager for a number of African countries. From August 2009 to July 2011, he was based in the World Bank's Ethiopia country office and served as chair of the Health Partner Group in Ethiopia. He was health manager at the African Development Bank, responsible for health operations in 54 African countries from 2011 to 2014. Feng serves as a faculty member at a number of universities, including the Harvard Finance Minister Executive Leadership Program. He holds a PhD in population and health economics from Johns Hopkins University; an MPH from the University of California, Berkeley; and a medical degree from China.

Contributing Authors

Gabriel Catan Burlac	Digital health specialist, World Bank
Victoria Y. Fan	Senior fellow, Center for Global Development, Washington, DC, and associate professor, University of Hawaii at Manoa, Honolulu, HI
Zhanlian Feng	Senior researcher, RTI International
Elena E. Glinskaya	Lead economist, World Bank, Social Protection and Labor
Sana Haider	Consultant, World Bank
Xiaohui Hou	Senior economist, World Bank, Health, Nutrition and Population Global Practice
Alexander Irwin	Consultant, World Bank
Naoki Kondo	Professor, Department of Social Epidemiology, Graduate School of Medicine and School of Public Health, Kyoto University
Margaret E. Kruk	Professor of Health Systems, Department of Global Health and Population, Harvard T.H. Chan School of Public Health, Boston, MA
Todd P. Lewis	Postdoctoral fellow, Department of Global Health and Population, Harvard T.H. Chan School of Public Health, Boston, MA
Yuiko Nagamine	Adjunct lecturer, Department of Global Health Promotion, Tokyo Medical and Dental University
Risa Nakayama	Consultant, World Bank
Koryu Sato	Assistant professor, Department of Social Epidemiology, Graduate School of Medicine and School of Public Health, Kyoto University
Jigyasa Sharma	Health economist, World Bank, Health, Nutrition and Population Global Practice
Guadalupe Suarez	Research analyst, RTI International
Feng Zhao	Practice manager, World Bank South Asia Region, Health, Nutrition and Population Global Practice

Abbreviations

AARP	American Association of Retired Persons
ACOVE-3	Assessing Care of Vulnerable Elders-3
ADL	activity of daily living
AHRQ	Agency for Healthcare Research and Quality
AI	artificial intelligence
CDEs	common data elements
CICS	Community-Based Integrated Care System
FIRE	financing, innovation, regulation, evaluation
GDP	gross domestic product
GP	general practitioner
HICs	high-income countries
HIV	human immunodeficiency virus
IADL	instrumental activity of daily living
JICA	Japan International Cooperation Agency
LMICs	low- and middle-income countries
LTC	long-term care
LTCI	long-term care insurance
MDS	minimum data set
NCD	noncommunicable disease
OECD	Organisation for Economic Co-operation and Development
OPA	Older People's Association
PACE	Program of All-Inclusive Care for the Elderly
PHC	primary health care
PRISMA	Program of Research to Integrate the Services for the Maintenance of Autonomy
RAI	Resident Assessment Instrument
SCH	SingHealth Community Hospitals
UHC	universal health coverage
WG-SS	Washington Group Short Set on Functioning
WHO	World Health Organization

Overview and Framework for Action

Xiaohui Hou, Jigyasa Sharma, Feng Zhao, and Alexander Irwin

Introduction

We live in a rapidly aging world. In 2018, for the first time in history, people age 65 years and older outnumbered children under five worldwide. By 2050, one in six people in the world will be older than 65. The trends affect all global regions: between 2017 and 2050, Africa's population age 60 and older is projected to rise threefold, the fastest growth rate of any continent (UN DESA 2017). In all countries, aging populations and rising burdens of chronic disease are creating higher health care demand and costs, even as global economic uncertainty tightens resources for health spending (Kämpfen, Wijemunige, and Evangelista 2018). But the demographic transformation also brings fresh opportunities—to tap new sources of productivity, reinforce social inclusion, advance long-needed health system reforms, and speed progress toward health and development goals, including universal health coverage (UHC).

This book shows how countries can turn the aging challenge into a chance to transform their health systems, making them more responsive to the needs of all populations. The volume addresses policy makers and implementers in health, social protection, and public finance, along with a broad community of practitioners, researchers, and advocates concerned with healthy aging. Marshaling fresh evidence on health and long-term care (LTC) needs and provision for older people around the world, the book reveals large and rapidly growing old-age care gaps in countries at all income levels. How can societies close these gaps and leverage aging as an opportunity for health gains and shared prosperity? The book argues that the best approaches will anchor integrated services for older people in primary health care (PHC). Surveying current research and country experiences, the analysis identifies levers that policy makers and implementers can use to design person-centered, PHC-driven care for older people and deliver it sustainably at scale. As they transform

1

care models for older adults, countries will build critical health stewardship capacity, achieve greater integration and efficiency across their health systems, increase synergies between health care and social protection, and improve outcomes for people at every stage of life.

A Challenge That Will Not Wait

Statistics highlight the unprecedented aging of the global population (figure O.1). The number of persons age 65 or older globally is projected to more than double between 2019 and 2050, translating to 1.5 billion people 65 or older worldwide, whereas the total number of adolescents and youth age 15 to 24 years in 2050 will stand at 1.3 billion (UN DESA 2019).

These trends appear on every continent and in practically every country, though with regional variations. In recent decades, the speed of population aging has been fastest in eastern and southeastern Asia, while the largest gains in life expectancy have come in Sub-Saharan Africa (UN DESA 2019). Patterns of mortality and morbidity are also changing, as low- and middle-income countries (LMICs) increasingly face a double burden of disease, including high rates of both infectious and chronic illnesses (WHO 2015). In LMICs, as of 2011, 75 percent of deaths from noncommunicable diseases (NCDs) were in people older than 60, and

FIGURE O.1 Estimated and Projected Global Population, by Age Group, 1950–2100

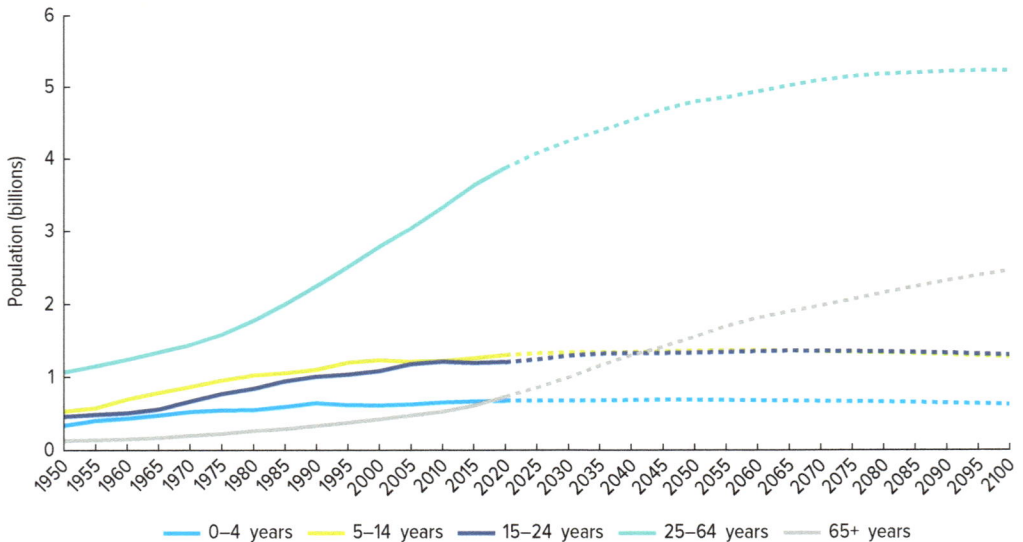

Source: UN DESA 2022.
Note: Medium-variant projection. (In projecting future levels of fertility (2020–2100), UN DESA uses probabilistic methods based on historic variability of changes in each country. The medium-variant projection corresponds to the median of several thousand distinct trajectories of each demographic component derived using this probabilistic model.)

disability among older adults was four times higher than for their younger counterparts (Williamson 2019). The trends pose a daunting challenge for the health and social care systems tasked with meeting care needs among aging populations.

Diverse Populations with Complex Needs

Older populations are highly diverse. Although many older people enjoy vibrant health, large numbers of older adults face growing burdens of multimorbidity. Among the causes of ill health in older populations, chronic illnesses have grown in importance. In 2016, almost half (48 percent) of deaths among people age 70 and older were due to cardiovascular diseases, followed by cancers, chronic respiratory diseases, and diabetes (Bennett et al. 2018). Many NCD deaths in older adults can be averted through primary or secondary prevention and treatment, which have boosted longevity in high-income countries (HICs) but remain undersupplied in LMICs (Bennett et al. 2018). Other burdensome conditions among older adults include cognitive and neurological conditions, such as dementia. The health and economic impact of dementia, for instance, merits attention: as of 2016, an estimated 43.8 million adults age 60 and older had dementia (Nichols et al. 2019), and the estimated global economic cost of dementia care in 2015 was approximately US$818 billion (Wimo et al. 2017). Among country groups, LMICs are projected to experience the largest rise in dementia prevalence by 2050 (Dominguez et al. 2021).

Meanwhile, as average longevity rises globally, there is wide variability in the settings where older people live and receive care and in the type of care they need. Such differences are marked, not only between countries but also within them, and often within the same community. Although some older adults are able to extend their healthy lifespans by accessing high-quality, community-based PHC, many will eventually lose their ability to live independently and will require specialized LTC, such as residential, hospital-based, rehabilitative, palliative, or end-of-life care options (He, Goodkind, and Kowal 2016; Suzman et al. 2015; WHO 2021).[1] When formal LTC infrastructure is not accessible, family members may have to give up employment or education to care for older relatives, with consequences for household welfare, human capital accumulation, and, ultimately, national economies. In HICs, per capita health spending is high in older age groups, because they often need more and alternative types of care (He, Goodkind, and Kowal 2016).

Aging in the Time of COVID-19

High mortality among older people during COVID-19 (coronavirus) has shone a stark light on unmet health needs in this population and the failure of existing care systems to adequately protect older people during health crises, but also between crises. Numerous studies show high rates of COVID-related hospitalization, intensive care unit admission, and death among older persons compared with other population groups (Dong, Du, and Gardner 2020).

Increased longevity coupled with elevated comorbidity among older people results in a high prevalence of medical frailty, particularly among older people living in nursing homes and other LTC facilities (Burgaña Agoües et al. 2021). Such persons often require complex interventions when they become ill. Even in the wealthiest countries, most LTC establishments were unprepared to manage a lethal infectious epidemic spreading rapidly among frail residents. The toll of COVID-19 in LTC settings has underscored the life-or-death consequences of shortfalls in integrated, person-centered care for older adults and made clear that finding and implementing solutions is urgent. Drawing lessons from the crisis, leaders need to seize the opportunity to act boldly, anticipate future risks, and better prepare health systems for the challenges ahead, as population aging, chronic disease burdens, and emerging infectious threats increasingly converge in deadly "syndemics"—crises in which two or more diseases reinforce each other in populations that are made more vulnerable by socioeconomic exclusion and disparities (Singer et al. 2017; *The Lancet* 2017; World Bank, forthcoming b). Hitting hardest among older people and those with preexisting chronic conditions such as cardiovascular diseases, diabetes, and obesity, COVID-19 was the most destructive syndemic in decades, but it will not be the last.

What This Book Contributes

This book has been written to support policy makers, their advisers, and other health and development stakeholders in advancing an agenda for healthier aging. The book does the following:

- Compiles the latest evidence on care needs and care gaps for aging populations around the world
- Synthesizes the literature on evaluation tools to provide a better understanding of older adults' care preferences and measure the quantity and quality of available services
- Presents an original framework for policy action to advance PHC-centered, integrated care for aging populations
- Formulates health financing options for countries at different income levels for their "silver age" populations
- Marshals evidence on how innovation in technology and care delivery can help countries meet growing older adult care needs, and how countries can foster senior-centric innovation
- Sheds fresh light on how regulation and governance can improve results in care for older adults
- Documents the experiences of pioneering countries, including Japan, in delivering community-based care for older populations
- Provides actionable recommendations for decision-makers, including in LMICs.

The book explores how countries can successfully link PHC-centered health services with broader forms of social care and support for older people. As it does, the book's central focus remains on health service delivery. It emphasizes how health policy makers, system managers, and service providers can contribute to realizing the person-centered, integrated care that older people want. As such, the volume's supply-side focus complements the expansive vision advanced by the United Nations Decade of Healthy Ageing and aims to deepen operational knowledge in a circumscribed but crucial field.[2] The book's concentration on health service delivery similarly complements new research emerging from the Healthy Longevity Initiative, whose contributors are clarifying relationships between healthy aging, human capital, and inclusive economic growth; bolstering the economic case for multisectoral NCD prevention and control; and analyzing the impacts of healthy longevity on labor market outcomes and economic opportunity, notably for women.[3] This book sheds light on stubborn supply-side challenges that are a key part of this overall picture to improve results in countries.

Investing in Healthy Aging: Toward a "Triple Dividend" for Health Systems and Societies

The United Nations 2030 Agenda for Sustainable Development aims to ensure that the Sustainable Development Goals are met for everyone, notably by "ensuring healthy lives and well-being at all ages" (Sustainable Development Goal 3) (UNDP, HelpAge International, and AARP 2017). Under the Sustainable Development Goals, all countries have committed to achieve UHC by 2030. UHC means that people have access to the health services they need, when and where they need them, and without financial hardship.[4] The UHC agenda presents a unique opportunity for health systems to meet the chronic conditions and complex care needs of the growing number of older people (Williamson 2019). As this agenda advances, age-responsive UHC reforms will increasingly yield a "triple dividend" for health systems and societies, enabling older people to lead thriving lives, cost less, and contribute more (He, Goodkind, and Kowal 2016).

Fulfilling the UHC Promise: PHC-Centered, Integrated Care for Aging Populations

In turn, health systems prepared to provide PHC-centered integrated care responsive to the needs of older people will be critical to speeding progress toward UHC in many settings. PHC has been recognized as the cornerstone of UHC and the foundation of sustainable health systems in the twenty-first century (Baris et al. 2021; Stenberg et al. 2019; WHO and UNICEF 2018). As the first level of medical services, PHC serves as a linchpin in the coordination and integration of person-centered care across the life course.

PHC can provide proactive preventive care and interventions to manage the burden of NCDs and other chronic illnesses associated with aging. PHC has a critical role in early diagnosis, referral, and postspecialist or posthospitalization care. In this way, strong PHC can reduce the high costs of inpatient and specialist care.

Countries' PHC reform priorities will reflect their diverse population age structures, epidemiological profiles, current health system conditions, and other country-specific factors. But by building and strengthening PHC services for older adults, all countries have an opportunity to accelerate progress in the service coverage, financial protection, and equity dimensions of UHC.

Today's Reality: Shortfalls in Age-Responsive Care Worldwide

Today, however, shortfalls in the availability and quality of PHC and related care modalities for older people persist across regions. The problems span HICs and LMICs, though the specific challenges in these settings are often different.

A robust PHC system should provide accessible, affordable, and timely care to users, but many older adults face a disconnect between their large health needs and care utilization. In many HICs, service utilization increases with age, commensurate with need. Among adults in LMICs, similar correlations are not observed, suggesting that many older adults are not accessing the care they need (WHO 2015). Even in countries where health services for older adults are available, they are not always efficient or effective. Care competence for older adults is inadequate in today's health systems. Multiple conditions and poor coordination introduce opportunities for suboptimal management, such as missed diagnoses, inadequate treatment, and poor user experience (Zulman et al. 2015). A 2017 study looks at the effectiveness and patient-centeredness of care in six countries that together account for more than half of the global population. The researchers find that, of 11 effectiveness indicators related to the prevention and management of chronic conditions common among older people, none surpassed 80 percent in any country. Less than 38 percent of respondents with known hypertension had been prescribed hypertension medication in the past 12 months in five of the six countries (Alshamsan et al. 2017).

Meanwhile, across LMICs, familial (or informal) care remains the dominant form of LTC for older persons. Because publicly financed LTC is limited, paid care is funded primarily by older persons and their families out of pocket. Availability of, and access to, formal home care services, community-based services (such as community care and adult day care centers), and institutional services (such as nursing and residential care facilities) are generally limited.

Tackling PHC Gaps for Healthier Aging

PHC delivery systems in most countries have yet to fulfill their promise. Most are not able to consistently deliver the range of quality services that older people need and want. Addressing the high burden of disease among aging populations, especially epidemics of chronic disease, will require focusing efforts and resources on age-dependent conditions. Achieving this focus will mean boosting primary and secondary prevention and improving clinical management of multiple morbidities, for example, through closer coordination among providers and the creation of multidisciplinary care teams (Baris et al. 2021; OECD 2020).

PHC will also need to extend beyond traditional health facilities to mesh with LTC to adequately serve aging populations. Because older adults receive care at home and in institutional settings from both formal and informal caregivers, there are multiple ways to deliver primary care services and improve connectivity across care systems. However, the variable quality of older adult care, especially residential care, warrants urgent attention. Shoring up these platforms for care will also require supporting informal caregivers, including families.

Closing Care Gaps: Where Do Countries Start?

Where can countries start to tackle this complex challenge? This volume argues that the first step needs to be understanding older people's needs and preferences for care. When developing health care policies and prioritizing investments during COVID-19 and beyond, decision-makers will get the best results through a collaborative approach to building resilience and avoiding preventable inequalities and burdens. This approach will only be possible if they first aim to understand and address the needs that older people themselves identify as priorities. Consultative processes that ensure a strong voice for older people in decision-making, and that engage older adults as actors in their own health care, will be fundamental.

Understanding the Care Needs and Preferences of Diverse Older Populations

In a rapidly changing world, older people's health care needs, expectations, and preferences are also quickly evolving. Older adults' care preferences are influenced by such factors as individual health needs, national old-age care policies, health care infrastructure, societal values and traditions, and demographic differences within older adult populations. By disentangling the key factors that influence care preferences and understanding where client preferences best fit in the sequencing of integrated care delivery, policy makers can plan and implement a locally workable model of integrated, person-centered care.

It is not surprising that older people's individual health care needs substantially affect their preferences regarding care types and delivery mechanisms. For example, older adults with greater health care needs often appear to prefer formal care (institutionalized or paid care) rather than informal care provided by family or friends (Mair, Quiñones, and Pasha 2016). The quality of existing national health care infrastructure, policies, and welfare regimes also appears to influence older adults' preferences for publicly provided care versus family-based care. Thus, middle-age and older adults in countries that invest strongly in government-based health and social care may be more likely to prefer publicly provided care, whereas older people in countries with weaker health care infrastructure may prefer family-based care because of the lack of reliable government-based care options (Mair, Quiñones, and Pasha 2016; Pinquart and Sörensen 2002).

Values and traditions in a person's society also affect their preferences for care settings and caregivers. In China, for example, a country with a deep-rooted tradition of children assuming responsibility for aging parents, recent surveys and academic studies find that family care remains the cornerstone of LTC preferences among older adults (Lu, Zhang, and Zhang 2021; You, Fung, and Vitaliano 2020). Such cultural links are not simple, however. A recent study examines the intersection between formal and informal care in the Arab sector of northern Israel, a setting with a strong tradition of respect and care for older family members and intergenerational solidarity. Older adult respondents in this context criticized the inadequacy of family care and favored paid care, with their ideal situation being a mix of formal and informal care, in which the caregiver should be a familiar person who also receives financial compensation for care work (Ayalon 2018).

Care preferences vary by demographics across diverse populations of older adults. Preferences and expectations among 80-year-olds are likely to differ from those among 60-year-olds, for example, and gender, socioeconomic status, education, and other demographic variables will also affect people's views about care. In a study from the United States, for example, older adults with more education, higher incomes, and from white, non-Hispanic ethnic backgrounds were most likely to select assisted living or continuing care retirement communities as their preferred LTC options, as opposed to family-based care (Kasper, Wolff, and Skehan 2019). Importantly, too, older people's care preferences are not static but dynamic and evolving. Thus, some studies have suggested that older adults living in formal, professionally staffed LTC facilities may increasingly value the advantages of these arrangements over time (Degenholtz, Kane, and Kivnick 1997).

In recent years, person-centeredness has received increasing attention as a key feature of quality older adult care, accompanying the greater emphasis on "aging in place" and "treating in place," rather than relying on frequent, often disruptive transitions of patients through various care providers and settings. To date, these discussions have mainly taken place in HICs, but LMICs will be increasingly concerned, given growing awareness of and demand for quality of care and accountability from populations. Person-centered care is planned according to individuals' personal preferences, values, and goals. Person-centeredness is especially crucial in older adult care systems because the prevalence of multimorbidity and long-term health problems among these patients requires care from multiple providers and a more deliberate focus on patient autonomy and preferences. To achieve person-centered care, documenting older adults' care preferences in the specific context is fundamental, and policy makers need to be clear about where user preferences fit in the sequence of decisions and implementation steps required to deliver person-centered care.

Person-centered PHC forms the organizing hub of an integrated holistic care system able to support healthy aging. Primary care professionals can act as the first point of contact in identifying older people's needs, including physical, psychological, and sociocultural needs, while supporting disease prevention and managing chronic conditions. Effectively implementing PHC within older adult care systems requires involvement from national and local governments, service providers, civil society, the private sector, organizations for older people, academia, and older individuals and their families and friends.

PHC-Centered Integrated Care for Aging Populations: A Framework for Action

Older populations are surging worldwide, their health needs are complex, and their preferences for care are also multifaceted and evolving. Numerous institutions and stakeholders will share responsibility for planning and delivering the comprehensive care that older people need to thrive. How can health systems navigate this new landscape and exercise appropriate stewardship of the processes involved? This book argues that PHC provides the cornerstone for that work. But in most settings, PHC itself needs to adapt to demographic change. PHC networks must rapidly build their capacity to respond to older adults' health needs, integrating age-appropriate primary care with specialty medicine and broader human services, in line with older people's care preferences and goals.

Levers for Age-Responsive Health System Change: Presenting the FIRE Framework

This book presents an original framework for country action to deliver age-responsive health systems (figure O.2). The framework embodies a vision for PHC-centered integrated care for all people, including older adults, and identifies levers countries can use to realize that vision. The framework reflects the book's primary focus on health service delivery while highlighting the connections between service provision and other health system functions, between levels of care within the health service architecture, and between the health system as a whole and its demographic, socioeconomic, cultural, and political context. The framework supports a whole-of-life approach to care design and aims to ensure that health systems are prepared to meet aging populations' needs while promoting older people's ability to continue contributing to their communities.

Supply-side pillars. Age-responsive care design and delivery face a range of constraints, many of them context-specific, and leaders in different countries will need to engage different policy mechanisms to overcome these barriers. However, a core set of policy tools will be critical across settings. The framework presented here identifies four supply-side policy levers to advance PHC-centered integrated care for older people in all countries. These are financing, innovation, regulation, and evaluation and measurement (FIRE).

FIGURE O.2 PHC-Centered Integrated Care for an Aging Population: The FIRE Framework

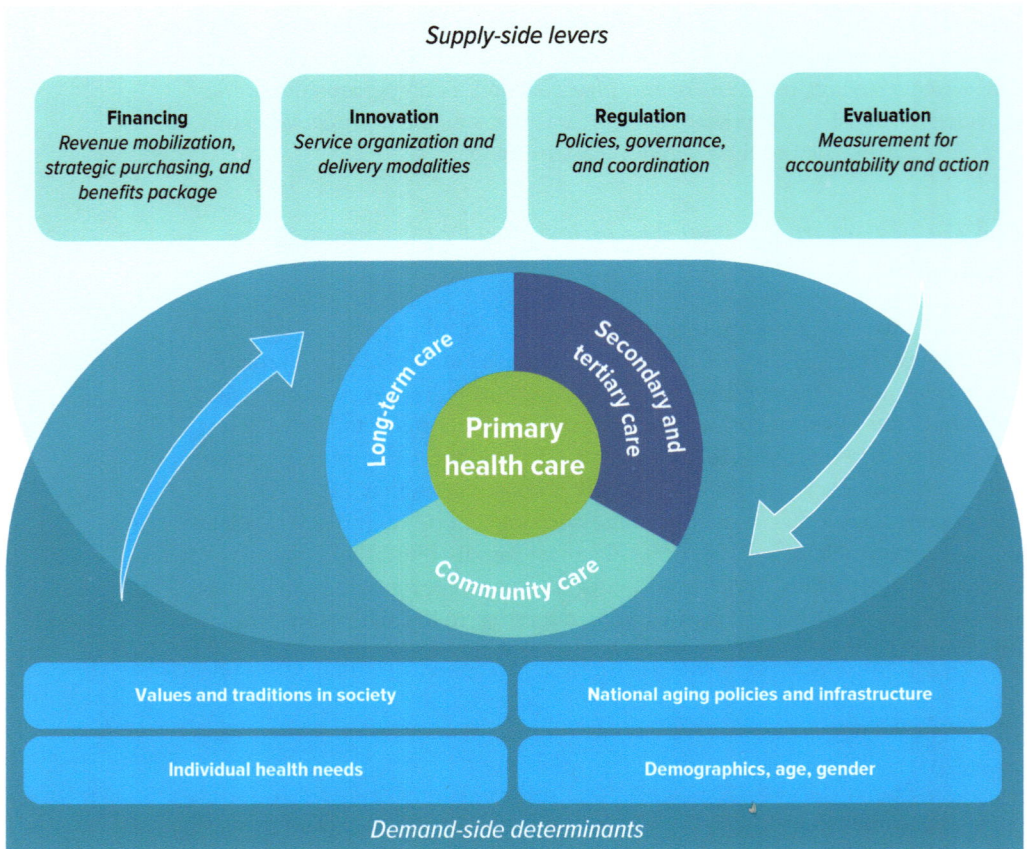

Supply-side levers

Financing
Revenue mobilization,
strategic purchasing, and
benefits package

Innovation
Service organization and
delivery modalities

Regulation
Policies, governance,
and coordination

Evaluation
Measurement for
accountability and action

Long-term care

Secondary and
tertiary care

Primary
health care

Community care

Values and traditions in society

National aging policies and infrastructure

Individual health needs

Demographics, age, gender

Demand-side determinants

Source: World Bank.
Note: FIRE = financing, innovation, regulation, and evaluation and measurement; PHC = primary health care.

These four functions define critical change domains for health systems entering the silver age. They structure the core chapters of this book and shape its analysis and policy recommendations. FIRE as a framework for action seeks to inform global dialogue on aging and health service delivery and to support transformative policies toward healthier aging for all.

PHC at the center. This book makes the case that activating the FIRE levers in line with specific local conditions can facilitate the design and implementation of PHC-centered care models able to work synergistically with other forms and levels of care, including secondary and tertiary clinical services, and home-based, community-based, and institutional LTC, resulting in better health outcomes and higher quality of life for diverse populations of older adults.

PHC alone is not meant to deliver every form of care and support that older people may require. But quality PHC addresses older adults' most common health concerns and connects them efficiently to other types of care that can help them lead their healthiest and best lives. In concert with other parts of health and social care systems, PHC offers a care delivery model that can be adapted to meet diverse and dynamic needs in aging populations, improve a broad range of outcomes, and better control health system costs.

Care integration across multiple dimensions. Recent proposals for PHC reform have emphasized the importance of service integration (Baris et al. 2021; OECD 2020). The concept of care integration adopted in this book includes two main dimensions. First, it concerns the person-centered integration of clinical services for older patients over time and across providers and levels of care within the health system.[5] Second, it incorporates links between health care and other human service systems, including LTC and social protection (Leutz 1999; Shortell 2021).[6] Both types of integration have historically proven difficult to achieve, including in wealthy countries, but successful models exist, and promising new approaches are emerging.

Practical strategies to advance PHC-centered service integration are reviewed in chapter 1 of this book and discussed in relation to the specific FIRE pillars in the book's core technical chapters. Strengthening links between PHC and LTC recurs as a specific concern in several chapters, given that this agenda will be both crucial and challenging for countries. As recently framed by the World Health Organization (WHO), "integrated long-term care" entails "integration of health and social services along the whole spectrum from information systems to care delivery, so that long-term care can be provided and received in a non-fragmented way" (WHO 2021, v). Core chapters of this volume explore opportunities and obstacles for PHC-LTC synergies in relation to the respective FIRE pillars.

FIRE and supporting frameworks. FIRE anchors the overall vision that the book sets forth. Within individual chapters, the contributing researchers propose granular subframeworks that add richness to FIRE and that the authors have found useful for analyzing specific challenges, policy solutions, and delivery strategies that show promise, based on current research and country experience, within the action domains delineated by FIRE. Thus, for example, in tracing directions for PHC reform oriented to the needs of older adults, chapter 1 incorporates a health systems framework adapted from the Lancet Global Health Commission on High Quality Health Systems (HQSS Commission) (Kruk et al. 2018). Subsequent discussions of the innovation dimension of FIRE (chapters 3 and 4) use health system factors highlighted in the High Quality Health Systems framework to organize policy proposals around service delivery innovation and digital health for older adults. In this way, technical subframeworks help bring the broad FIRE categories into sharper focus and clarify specific entry points for policy change in countries.

Informing Action through the FIRE Framework

The four supply-side domains highlighted in FIRE represent opportunities to reform health systems to meet the needs of an aging population. The book's core chapters explore each of these areas in detail. This section briefly describes the FIRE levers and indicates some of the main policy directions that subsequent chapters will discuss.

Financing. Financing is one of the main tools available to policy makers for shaping the accessibility, quality, and efficiency of health care services and for providing incentives for care integration. Health spending was rising steadily in most countries even before COVID-19, with population aging being a major driver. In the wake of the pandemic's health and economic "double shock," subsequent inflation, and ongoing instability in the global economy (Kurowski et al. 2021, 2022), financing health care for older populations has become an increasingly urgent policy concern for countries at all income levels.

Policy makers working to develop health financing options need to consider at least three questions that are critical for meeting the health needs of older adults and advancing toward UHC: First, who is covered (or will be covered) by the country's set of essential health services? Second, which services are people covered for? Third, how are health system resources raised, and how much is publicly financed? Put differently, health financing options must specify population eligibility, a benefits package, and revenue mobilization mechanisms.

This book proposes an original technical framework for health financing policy decisions. The framework builds on previous work on countries' health financing transition, highlighting the critical role of public financing as countries move toward UHC (Fan and Savedoff 2014; Savedoff et al. 2012). As countries grow richer and age, they tend toward greater public financing as a share of total health care spending. Importantly, this measure is a crude proxy for the financial risk protection provided to citizens as a key goal of the health system.

Applying the health financing framework, this book develops case studies of seven countries that span global regions and are diverse in national income, population size, and health-expenditure variables. Based on the case studies and a literature review, the analysis identifies priority health financing strategies countries can use to adapt their health systems as populations age. Results highlight, for example, how some countries have successfully leveraged health financing reforms to strengthen PHC gatekeeping and care coordination functions.

Further findings presented in the book underscore that countries where public sector health service provision has been dominant need to proceed cautiously as private sector care expands, managing system changes to accommodate private sector growth through an appropriately regulated insurance model. Recent experiences in China, Colombia, and Saudi Arabia suggest that well-managed health insurance models can help balance access and benefits for system users while providing incentives for care coordination and efficient referrals within provider networks, a crucial part of strengthening PHC-centered care for older adults.

Innovation. Fostering innovation in multiple dimensions will be vital as health systems confront the aging challenge. Today, the rapid advance of digital and virtual technologies is transforming health care delivery in countries at all income levels. Technological advances and the exponential growth of data provide an unprecedented opportunity for countries to leapfrog stages of health system development, improve care quality, reinforce evidence-based decision-making, and optimize resource management and utilization. At the same time, wide gaps in access to digital health tools and other innovative care resources for older adults persist between and within countries. Service-delivery innovations and digital health solutions potentially relevant to older adults raise urgent questions of accessibility, acceptability, and equity.

This book reviews the available evidence on country-level innovation in two key dimensions of health and social care systems: (1) integrated care delivery models for older adults and (2) creative digital health solutions. A shortage of published evidence from LMICs limits the strength of conclusions in both domains, but important lessons can still be drawn. These lessons show promising directions for policy action in countries.

In care delivery, innovative service models emerging in both HICs and some LMICs show common features that promote person-centered integrated care tailored to the unique needs of older adults. High-yield strategies include the deployment of multidisciplinary teams; reinforced care coordination among providers across settings, facilitated by tools such as electronic medical records; and care planning and case management based on individualized comprehensive geriatric assessment. Current resource constraints need not prevent policy makers and practitioners in LMICs from "aiming high" toward delivery models that reflect these and other desirable system features. Aided by intercountry learning and a growing knowledge base from international health care and LTC research, countries have opportunities to leapfrog by adopting and adapting international best practices.

Digital health technologies hold growing promise to transform care options and quality of life for the older adults who can access them. To date, however, socioeconomic, generational, and gender-based digital divides limit uptake and results. The utilization of digital health needs to be reframed in ways that can benefit all older adults and boost the responsiveness and efficiency of health systems across global regions. Promising policy solutions to these challenges are emerging. A key opportunity for transformative health stewardship would be facilitating the engagement of the private health technology sector in older adult health. Burgeoning interest in digital technology for older people has fueled an increasing number of start-ups and growing investment in home health care and old-age care as part of the "silver economy," currently most evident in HICs. Technology hubs and other regulatory and investment measures to foster an enabling environment for senior-focused digital health innovation can expand opportunities in LMICs. Some public-private partnerships and other innovative business models have begun to show promising results.

Regulation. Regulation of care systems for older adults is the responsibility of governments. Core values that inform the governance of PHC-led care systems include maintaining the dignity and autonomy of older persons, meeting the diverse needs that exist within this population, and facilitating integration among diverse stakeholders under government oversight.

This book draws lessons for regulation and governance from diverse country experiences. Although published evidence from LMICs remains scant, results in multiple contexts suggest that care systems for older people work best when they adopt a whole-of-government regulatory approach. Robust whole-of-government models align the strengths of central, regional, and local governments. Priority domains for coordinated action include stewardship, financing, human resources, and infrastructure. A key stewardship task is facilitating the engagement of local communities and the private sector in care, which highlights the pivotal frontline role of local governments.

The book's analysis shows how some countries have scored successes by balancing "hard" legal regulations with "soft" incentives that reward collaboration and good performance among system actors. Japan's Community-Based Integrated Care System offers a promising care coordination model from a high-income setting, and Thailand's community-based LTC approach provides regulatory lessons that may be applicable in a wide range of countries. The Thai government has focused on strengthening community-based or home-based LTC services. Through features such as its hybrid service delivery approach, incorporating both professional caregivers and volunteers, Thailand's LTC strategy may be especially well suited to middle-income countries experiencing rapid increases in their older adult populations (Chanprasert 2021).

Evaluation and measurement. Evaluation and measurement are key to understanding older people's care needs and ensuring that the supply of services matches demand. Today's care landscape for older adults in LMICs is marked by deficits in research, validated tools, and empirical evidence relevant to evaluation. This book's treatment of evaluation synthesizes findings from a literature review on the current older adult care landscape across LMICs. Placing a strong focus on LTC, the analysis pinpoints existing gaps and barriers to the development of integrated, person-centered care systems for aging populations, along with the creative solutions that some countries have found. Based on the literature and drawing policy lessons from selected HICs and pioneering LMICs, the book recommends practical strategies for assessing older adult care needs and service availability and for building the information, monitoring, and evaluation systems that can improve the health and quality of life of their older populations.

On the demand side, countries need to obtain reliable estimates of the number of older people with disabilities that prevent them from living independently. Standard assessment tools for this purpose measure people's ability to carry out activities of daily living, for example, feeding oneself and bathing, and instrumental activities of daily living, for example, managing money. Where the costs of frequent large-scale data collection are a concern, as in many LMIC settings, researchers and government agencies can consider shortened yet validated data instruments.[7] On the supply side, streamlined models are available to measure health care and LTC availability and quality. LMICs can learn from countries such as Sweden that have developed robust yet nimble and cost-effective strategies for quality measurement and control in their older adult care systems.

Drawing on recent normative work from the WHO (2015, 2021), along with findings from independent research, this book identifies evidence-based operational steps countries can take to build and reinforce LTC evaluation systems. Whereas policy makers understandably prioritize investments in infrastructure and service delivery, countries working to upgrade their old-age care systems also have an interest in creating effective information, monitoring, and evaluation systems from the start. Doing so is the best way to ensure that investments in care for older adults remain cost-effective while delivering the benefits that people want.

Methods and Limitations

The core chapters of this volume use literature reviews and country case studies as their primary analytic tools. Specific methodologies are described in the chapters. The dearth of published information available for LMICs limits the scope of some discussions, the richness of country comparisons, and the strength of evidence available to support recommendations. A forthcoming companion volume to this book will contribute to bridging LMIC data gaps (World Bank, forthcoming b). The companion volume comprises specially commissioned country and regional case studies assessing care needs and PHC-centered reform measures for aging populations in Bangladesh, Mongolia, the United Arab Emirates, Eastern European countries, and some African countries, notably LMICs. Findings from those studies will help strengthen the evidence base for future policy making and implementation as health systems across all regions navigate swift demographic change.

This book maintains a primary focus on health service delivery, even as it analyzes LTC needs and options and brings forward evidence on how some countries are working to integrate health services for older adults more effectively with social care, including in LTC settings.[8] As noted, by drilling down on quality routine health service delivery and the policies that can enable it in the FIRE domains, this book complements the expansive vision of older people's well-being advanced by the United Nations Decade of Healthy Ageing. This approach also dovetails with Healthy Longevity Initiative research designed to clarify the economic and social determinants of healthy aging, including gender impacts; reinforce the economic case for investing in healthy longevity through NCD prevention and control; and analyze policy options across sectors, notably fiscal, education, and labor market strategies, and in medical care.[9]

This volume seeks to analyze country experiences with PHC-centered health service delivery for older adults at a more granular level and to highlight operationally relevant details and decision points for policy makers, program managers, and implementers. This book does not repeat or seek to replace the detailed analyses of PHC service delivery reform options developed in landmark publications, including Baris et al. (2021), National Academies of Sciences, Engineering, and Medicine (2021), and OECD (2020) and advanced through collaborations such as the Primary Health Care Performance Initiative that is now completing its work.[10] Instead, this approach aims to complement and extend those contributions through analysis and policy proposals focused on the FIRE domains.

There are good reasons to view the four FIRE levers as foundational for all countries' efforts to build sustainable PHC-based care models for older populations. However, an approach that relies on these levers is far from exhaustive. For example, health and human resources in geriatric care are an essential building block for meeting population needs. This book touches on workforce issues from several angles but does not systematically examine the range of options for bolstering country geriatric-care workforces. Similarly, consistent with its focus on public financing options, the book does not assess some countries' efforts to foster private sector engagement in LTC to leverage more capital into this market. Such topics are important priorities for future research.

Finally, this book is not a publication produced by a single author or small team, but rather a collection of studies contributed by research groups from different backgrounds and with varied domains of expertise. This approach brings benefits but also involves trade-offs. The diversity of backgrounds, perspectives, and skill sets among contributors enriches the book's treatment of a complex and evolving topic. At the same time, contributors have applied different analytic methods and conceptual subframeworks across chapters to clarify issues and policy options in their respective areas of interest. As previously noted, those individual technical subframeworks enrich the FIRE model that organizes the book as a whole.

Structure of the Volume

The book's core chapters follow the FIRE domains: financing, innovation, regulation, and evaluation. Together, the chapters marshal empirical evidence to inform policies for healthier aging around these four health-reform leverage points.

As overall background, chapter 1 introduces the evolving health and service needs of aging populations and explains the urgency of building PHC-centered care models for older people. The chapter documents the global trend toward increased longevity and concurrent growth in chronic disease burdens. It proposes a whole-of-health-system analysis that shows how PHC can operate in concert with other parts of the health system to improve outcomes for older people. It also discusses current performance shortfalls and missed opportunities in many PHC systems worldwide. The chapter distinguishes between care models for healthy older people living at home and other models designed for persons with greater medical needs in home or institutional care settings. This discussion offers a starting point for considering the diversity of care needs in aging populations and how PHC-led systems can respond.

Chapter 2 analyzes financing solutions for PHC oriented to the needs of older people. The chapter proposes an original technical framework for age-responsive PHC financing. This model integrates two typologies widely used in the health financing literature: the WHO's classic "health financing cube" (WHO 2015) and a previous model from Roberts et al. (2008) that analyzes public financing mechanisms for health systems. The chapter applies its hybrid analytic framework to a series of country case studies. It compares the financing schemes used for PHC in seven countries at different income levels and stages of population aging and distills lessons and policy options. Three high-income countries (Canada, the Netherlands, and Saudi Arabia), three middle-income countries (China, Colombia, and Sri Lanka), and one low-income country (Ethiopia) are studied. The exercise highlights the different approaches that countries can adopt to finance PHC services for aging populations by adjusting population eligibility, benefits packages, and the means of financing.

Chapters 3 and 4 consider the topic of innovation from two distinct angles. Chapter 3 discusses innovations in models of care for older people and surveys the current LTC landscape worldwide. It shows rapidly rising demand for formal LTC in many LMICs, even as familial or informal care remains the predominant care source. The chapter describes innovative LTC models, mostly from HICs, analyzing the population served, governance, workforce, and tools to promote continual innovation. To date, integrated service provision models remain rare in LMICs. However, the chapter identifies promising approaches from a number of lower-income countries with potential for wider application. Aided by intercountry learning and a growing knowledge base from international health care and LTC research, more countries can grasp opportunities to "leapfrog" by adapting innovative care practices—and sharing their own.

Chapter 4 documents how digital health innovations may improve health and well-being for older people, including in lower-income settings. The chapter surveys global trends in older adults' use of digital health technologies, revealing surprising attitudes toward some digital health options in this population. It examines a series of domains in which digital health shows potential to transform living arrangements, care options, and health service delivery models adapted to older people's needs. The chapter assesses digital divides between and within countries and considers ways to tackle them, analyzes digital health implementation challenges and solutions for older populations, and formulates recommendations for policy makers and practitioners.

Chapter 5 examines issues of regulation and governance. The chapter argues that appropriately regulated PHC systems for older adults can help create an inclusive society for all generations. It discusses the distinct and complementary roles of central or federal, regional, and local or municipal governments in regulating PHC systems for healthy aging. Both binding regulation and incentives for voluntary action by diverse stakeholders can improve governance and outcomes. Choices will reflect a country's political economy, administrative organization, and the development stage of its PHC systems. The chapter discusses specific strategies for promoting organized community engagement in older adult care and facilitating intersectoral and interorganizational partnerships, drawing on in-depth analyses of care governance in Japan and Thailand.

Chapter 6 explores evaluation and measurement. It synthesizes the limited available evaluation literature on older adult care across LMICs and reviews methods used by researchers to assess LMIC care systems from both the demand and supply sides. On the demand side, to measure needs or disability, aging studies commonly assess functional status, namely, a person's ability to perform activities of daily living or instrumental activities of daily living. On the supply side, the chapter reviews multiple instruments used to measure service delivery for older populations and evaluate the person-centeredness of care, including recent methods crafted to facilitate intercountry comparison. The chapter closes with recommendations for how countries at all income levels can best use evaluation and measurement tools to locate and tackle barriers to PHC-driven, integrated, person-centered care for older adults.

Finally, chapter 7 offers an extended case study of Japan's Community-Based Integrated Care System for older adults. The chapter describes the underlying philosophy of the system and its progressive integration into national laws and health financing models since the 1960s. It highlights the system's core agendas, including (1) collaborating to optimize regional resources, (2) enhancing self-support and mutual support among older adults and across the community, (3) realizing dignified lives, and (4) adapting to local contexts. The chapter discusses three local examples that showcase integrated medical care, LTC, and comprehensive living-support services under the Community-Based Integrated Care System. The examples focus on self-management support for stroke patients, measures to realize an "inclusive society" based on community mutual support in an urban setting, and an enhanced medical collaboration system spanning inpatient care and home care for older rural residents. The chapter concludes with recommendations adapted to developing countries based on the Japanese experience. Despite important differences, substantive joint learning across these contexts is possible.

Notes

1. This book adopts the comprehensive definition of LTC developed by the WHO (2015, 2021). LTC in this sense addresses "health, personal care, and social needs." It includes diverse activities across a range of settings designed to ensure that people "with or at risk of a significant ongoing loss of intrinsic capacity can maintain a level of functional ability consistent with their basic rights, fundamental freedoms and dignity" (WHO 2015, 127). The principle of a "continuum of long-term care" emphasizes "coordination across health and social sectors through effective governance, seamless transition across settings (home-based, community, facility care, and acute care), and coordinated provision and collaboration across various care roles" (WHO 2021, 9).
2. "Decade of Healthy Ageing: The Platform," https://www.decadeofhealthyageing.org.
3. See World Bank (forthcoming a).
4. "Universal Health Coverage," https://www.who.int/health-topics/universal-health-coverage#tab=tab_1.
5. This is an area in which many health systems currently fall short, and in which reimagined PHC can make a strong contribution (Baris et al. 2021). See the discussion in chapter 1.
6. Valentijn et al. (2013) note the need to move beyond clinical integration (coordination of care for a specific health need of an older individual) to professional, institutional, and system integration, although they acknowledge the difficulty of

doing so. See chapter 1. Chapter 7 presents a detailed case study of an ambitious integrative model linking medical and social care for older adults—Japan's Community-Based Integrated Care System.

7. Such user-friendly data collection tools include the Washington Group Short Set on Functioning (Washington Group on Disability Statistics 2020).
8. See, in particular, the detailed study of Japan's Community-Based Integrated Care System in chapter 7.
9. See World Bank (forthcoming a).
10. "A Message from the Steering Committee of the Primary Health Care Performance Initiative (PHCPI)," https://improvingphc.org/transition.

References

Alshamsan, R., J. T. Lee, S. Rana, H. Areabi, and C. Millett. 2017. "Comparative Health System Performance in Six Middle-Income Countries: Cross-Sectional Analysis Using World Health Organization Study of Global Aging and Health." *Journal of the Royal Society of Medicine* 110 (9): 365–75.

Ayalon, L. 2018. "Family Relations and Elder Care among Arabs in the North of Israel." *Research on Aging* 40 (9): 839–58. doi:10.1177/0164027517749612.

Barış, E., R. Silverman, H. Wang, F. Zhao, and M. Ali Pate. 2021. *Walking the Talk: Reimagining Primary Health Care after COVID-19.* Washington, DC: World Bank. https://openknowledge.worldbank.org/handle/10986/35842.

Bennett, J. E., G. A. Stevens, C. D. Mathers, R. Bonita, J. Rehm, M. E. Kruk, L. M. Riley, et al. 2018. "NCD Countdown 2030: Worldwide Trends in Non-Communicable Disease Mortality and Progress towards Sustainable Development Goal Target 3.4." *The Lancet* 392 (10152): 1072–88.

Burgaña Agoües, A., M. Serra Gallego, R. Hernández Resa, B. Joven Llorente, M. Lloret Arabi, J. Ortiz Rodriguez, H. Puig Acebal, et al. 2021. "Risk Factors for COVID-19 Morbidity and Mortality in Institutionalized Elderly People." *International Journal of Environmental Research and Public Health* 18 (19): 10221. https://www.ncbi.nlm.nih.gov/pmc/articles/PMC8507792/.

Chanprasert, P. 2021. "Long-Term Care Policy and Implementation in Thailand." In *Coping with Rapid Population Ageing in Asia,*" edited by O. Komazawa and Y. Saito, 36–44. Jakarta: Economic Research Institute for ASEAN and East Asia (ERIA).

Degenholtz, H., R. A. Kane, and H. Q. Kivnick. 1997. "Care-Related Preferences and Values of Elderly Community-Based LTC Consumers: Can Case Managers Learn What's Important to Clients?" *Gerontologist* 37 (6): 767–76. doi:10.1093/geront/37.6.767.

Dominguez, J., L. Jiloca, K. C. Fowler, Ma. Fe De Guzman, J. K. Dominguez-Awao, B. Natividad, J. Domingo, et al. 2021. "Dementia Incidence, Burden and Cost of Care: A Filipino Community-Based Study." *Frontiers in Public Health* 9: 628700.

Dong, E., H. Du, and L. Gardner. 2020. "An Interactive Web-Based Dashboard to Track COVID-19 in Real Time." *Lancet Infectious Diseases* 20 (5): 533–34.

Fan, V. Y., and W. D. Savedoff. 2014. "The Health Financing Transition: A Conceptual Framework and Empirical Evidence." *Social Science & Medicine* 105: 112–21.

He, W., D. Goodkind, and P. Kowal. 2016. "An Aging World: 2015, International Population Reports." U.S. Government Printing Office, Washington, DC.

Kämpfen, F., N. Wijemunige, and B. Evangelista. 2018. "Aging, Non-Communicable Diseases, and Old-Age Disability in Low- and Middle-Income Countries: A Challenge for Global Health." *International Journal of Public Health* 63: 1011–12. https://doi .org/10.1007/s00038-018-1137-z.

Kasper, J. D., J. L. Wolff, and M. Skehan. 2019. "Care Arrangements of Older Adults: What They Prefer, What They Have, and Implications for Quality of Life." *Gerontologist* 59 (5): 845–55. doi:10.1093/geront/gny127.

Kruk, M. E., A. D. Gage, C. Arsenault, K. Jordan, H. H. Leslie, S. Roder-DeWan, O. Adeyi, et al. 2018. "High-Quality Health Systems in the Sustainable Development Goals Era: Time for a Revolution." *Lancet Global Health* 6 (11): e1196–e1252. https:// doi.org/10.1016/S2214-109X(18)30386-3.

Kurowski, C., D. B. Evans, A. Tandon, P. Hoang-Vu Eozenou, M. Schmidt, A. Irwin, J. Salcedo Cain, E. S. Pambudi, and I. Postolovska. 2021. "From Double Shock to Double Recovery: Implications and Options for Health Financing in the Time of COVID-19." Health, Nutrition and Population Discussion Paper, World Bank Group, Washington, DC.

Kurowski, C., D. B. Evans, A. Tandon, P. Hoang-Vu Eozenou, M. Schmidt, A. Irwin, J. Salcedo Cain, E. S. Pambudi, and I. Postolovska. 2022. "From Double Shock to Double Recovery: Implications and Options for Health Financing in the Time of COVID-19. Second Technical Update. Old Scars, New Wounds." Health, Nutrition and Population Discussion Paper, World Bank Group, Washington, DC.

The Lancet. 2017. "Syndemics: Health in Context." Editorial. *The Lancet* 389 (10072): 881.

Leutz, W. N. 1999. "Five Laws for Integrating Medical and Social Services: Lessons from the United States and the United Kingdom." *Milbank Quarterly* 77 (1): 77–110, iv–v. https://doi.org/10.1111/1468-0009.00125.

Lu, J., L. Zhang, and K. Zhang. 2021. "Care Preferences among Chinese Older Adults with Daily Care Needs: Individual and Community Factors." *Research on Aging* 43 (3–4): 166–76. doi:10.1177/0164027520939321.

Mair, C. A., A. R. Quiñones, and M. A. Pasha. 2016. "Care Preferences among Middle-Aged and Older Adults with Chronic Disease in Europe: Individual Health Care Needs and National Health Care Infrastructure." *Gerontologist* 56 (4): 687–701. doi:10.1093/geront/gnu119.

National Academies of Sciences, Engineering, and Medicine. 2021. *Implementing High-Quality Primary Care: Rebuilding the Foundation of Health Care*. Washington, DC: National Academies Press.

Nichols, E., C. E. Szoeke, S. E. Vollset, N. Abbasi, F. Abd-Allah, J. Abdela, M. Taki Eddine Aichour, et al. 2019. "Global, Regional, and National Burden of Alzheimer's Disease and Other Dementias, 1990–2016: A Systematic Analysis for the Global Burden of Disease Study 2016." *The Lancet Neurology* 18: 88–106.

OECD (Organisation for Economic Co-operation and Development). 2020. *Realising the Potential of Primary Health Care*. OECD Health Policy Studies. Paris: OECD.

Pinquart, M., and A. Sörensen. 2002. "Older Adults' Preferences for Informal, Formal, and Mixed Support for Future Care Needs: A Comparison of Germany and the United States." *International Journal of Aging and Human Development* 54 (4): 291–314. doi:10.2190/1FVT-24T3-Y1V3-57A5.

Roberts, M., W. Hsiao, P. Berman, and M. Reich. 2008. *Getting Health Reform Right: A Guide to Improving Performance and Equity*. Oxford: Oxford University Press.

Savedoff, W. D., D. de Ferranti, A. L. Smith, and V. Fan. 2012. "Political and Economic Aspects of the Transition to Universal Health Coverage." *The Lancet* 380 (9845): 924–32.

Shortell, S. M. 2021. "Reflections on the Five Laws of Integrating Medical and Social Services—21 Years Later." *Milbank Quarterly* 99 (1): 91–98. https://doi.org /10.1111/1468-0009.12495.

Singer, M., N. Bulled, B. Ostrach, and E. Mendenhall. 2017. "Syndemics and the Biosocial Conception of Health." *The Lancet* 389 (10072): 941–50.

Stenberg, K., O. Hanssen, M. Bertram, C. Brindley, A. Meshreky, S. Barkley, and T. Tan-Torres Edejer. 2019. "Guideposts for Investment in Primary Health Care and Projected Resource Needs in 67 Low-Income and Middle-Income Countries: A Modelling Study." *The Lancet Global Health* 7 (11): e1500–e1510.

Suzman, R., J. R. Beard, T. Boerma, and S. Chatterji. 2015. "Health in an Ageing World— What Do We Know?" *The Lancet* 385 (9967): 484–86.

UN DESA (United Nations Department of Economic and Social Affairs, Population Division). 2017. *World Population Ageing 2017*. New York: UN DESA.

UN DESA (United Nations Department of Economic and Social Affairs, Population Division). 2019. *World Population Prospects 2019: Highlights*. ST/ESA/SER.A/423. New York: UN DESA.

UN DESA (United Nations Department of Economic and Social Affairs, Population Division). 2022. World Population Prospects 2022. Data files. https://population .un.org/wpp/.

UNDP (United Nations Development Programme), HelpAge International, and AARP (American Association of Retired Persons). 2017. "Ageing, Older Persons and the 2030 Agenda for Sustainable Development." Issue brief. UNDP, New York. https:// www.un.org/development/desa/ageing/wp-content/uploads/sites/24/2017/07 /UNDP_AARP_HelpAge_International_AgeingOlderpersons-and-2030 -Agenda-2.pdf.

Valentijn, P. P., S. M. Schepman, W. Opheij, and M. A. Bruijnzeels. 2013. "Understanding Integrated Care: A Comprehensive Conceptual Framework Based on the Integrative Functions of Primary Care." *International Journal of Integrated Care* 13: e010. https:// doi.org/10.5334/ijic.886.

Washington Group on Disability Statistics. 2020. "The Washington Group Short Set on Functioning (WG-SS)." Washington Group on Disability Statistics, Hyattsville, MD.

WHO (World Health Organization). 2015. *World Report on Aging and Health*. Geneva: WHO. https://apps.who.int/iris/handle/10665/186463.

WHO (World Health Organization). 2021. *Framework for Countries to Achieve an Integrated Continuum of Long-Term Care*. Geneva: WHO.

WHO and UNICEF (World Health Organization and the United Nations Children's Fund). 2018. "Declaration of Astana." WHO and UNICEF. https://www.who.int /docs/default-source/primary-health/declaration/gcphc-declaration.pdf.

Williamson, C. 2019. "Universal Health Coverage Fit for an Ageing World." UHC2030 Partner Insight blog. October 24, 2019. https://www.uhc2030.org/blog-news-events /uhc2030-news/partner-insights/universal-health-coverage-fit-for-an-ageing -world-555311/.

Wimo, A., M. Guerchet, G.-C. Ali, Y.-T. Wu, A. M. Prina, B. Winblad, L. Jönsson, Z. Liu, and M. Prince. 2017. "The Worldwide Costs of Dementia 2015 and Comparisons with 2010." *Alzheimer's & Dementia* 13 (1): 1–7.

World Bank. Forthcoming a. *Promoting Healthy Longevity and Enhancing Human Capital by Tackling Noncommunicable Diseases: Findings from the World Bank Healthy Longevity Initiative*. Washington, DC: World Bank.

World Bank. Forthcoming b. *Transforming Health Systems: Investing in Health System Resilience*. Washington, DC: World Bank.

You, J., H. Fung, and P. Vitaliano. 2020. "The Pattern of Social Support Seeking and Its Socio-Demographic Variations among Older Adults in China." *European Journal of Ageing* 17 (3): 341–48. doi:10.1007/s10433-019-00550-w.

Zulman, D. M., S. B. Martins, Y. Liu, S. W. Tu, B. B. Hoffman, S. M. Asch, and M. K. Goldstein. 2015. "Using a Clinical Knowledge Base to Assess Comorbidity Interrelatedness among Patients with Multiple Chronic Conditions." *AMIA Annual Symposium Proceedings 2015*: 1381–9.

CHAPTER 1

High-Quality Health Systems for an Aging Population: Primary Care Models with Users at the Center

Todd P. Lewis, Margaret E. Kruk, Jigyasa Sharma, and Xiaohui Hou

Key Messages

- The world is aging rapidly. By 2050, one in six people worldwide will be over age 65.

- To meet the needs of older populations while controlling costs, health systems must harness the potential of primary health care (PHC).

- Multimorbidity and rising chronic disease burdens among older adults demand better clinical management, including coordination between providers and integration of care teams. Strong PHC incorporates these features, but PHC systems in most countries are underresourced and underperforming.

- Age-responsive PHC will need to extend beyond traditional clinical facilities to encompass home-based care and institutional care settings, with improved systemwide connectivity.

- The preferences of older people and their families can inform new, PHC-led care models, starting from a robust assessment of current system assets and deficits.

The Health and Service Needs of an Aging Population

Increased Longevity, but a Growing Burden of Chronic Illness

The world is rapidly growing older. People today are living longer. In 2018, for the first time in history, individuals age 65 and older outnumbered children under five globally (UN DESA Population Division 2019a). As average life expectancy grows and fertility levels decline, older adults will continue to be the fastest-growing age group in the world (map 1.1). By 2050, one in six people,

MAP 1.1 Life Expectancy at Age 60 for Men and Women, 2019

Years

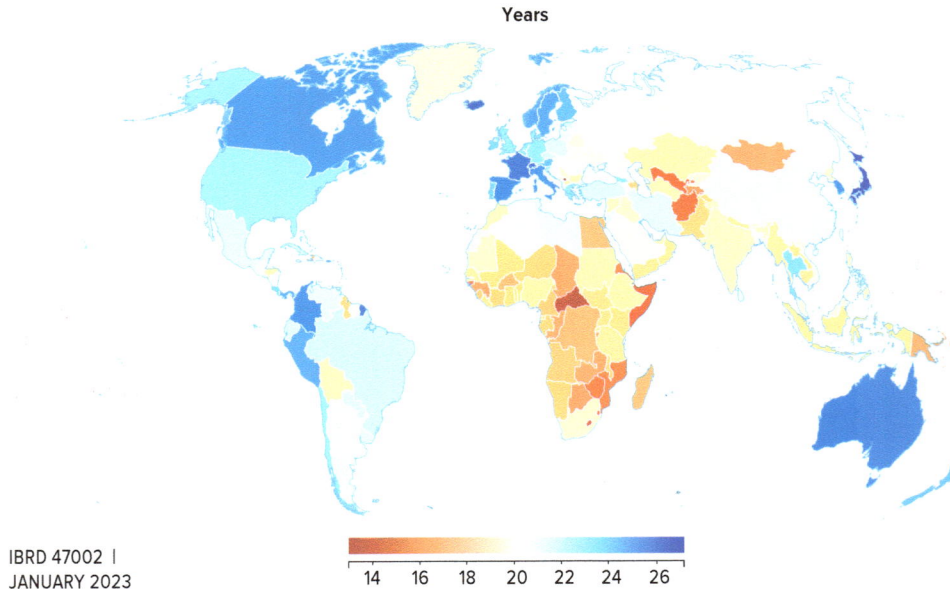

IBRD 47002 |
JANUARY 2023

14 16 18 20 22 24 26

Source: Map compiled using the Institute for Health Metrics and Evaluation's GBD [Global Burden of Disease] Compare tool. Visualizations and data available at https://vizhub.healthdata.org/gbd-compare.

approximately 16 percent of the world's population, will be over age 65 (they currently make up about 9 percent), and it is expected that by 2050 the number of people older than 80 will have tripled (UN DESA Population Division 2019b). These increases are occurring across regions: the proportion of the population over age 65 is projected to double by 2050 in northern Africa and western Asia, central and southern Asia, eastern and southeastern Asia, and Latin America and the Caribbean, and is projected to reach 25 percent of the population in Europe and North America (UN DESA Population Division 2019b).

The growth of the older population can be attributed to improved survival at older ages (Mathers et al. 2015). Life expectancy at age 65—the average number of additional years a 65-year-old person would live if they were to be subjected to the age-specific mortality risks of a given period throughout the remainder of his or her life—increased from 16 years for women and 13 years for men between 1990 and 1995, to 18 years for women and 16 years for men between 2015 and 2020 (UN DESA Population Division 2019b). These gains stem in part from advances in medicine and socioeconomic development, which have reduced mortality and morbidity from infectious diseases and some chronic diseases. The greatest decreases in mortality and morbidity have occurred in high-income countries (HICs), where populations have benefited from effective strategies for reducing tobacco use and managing hypertension. Improved coverage of health interventions, their greater effectiveness, and improved health systems have also contributed to reducing mortality (Bloom et al. 2011; Mathers et al. 2015).

These benefits, however, are not evenly distributed: in many lower-income countries, social changes, such as urbanization and accompanying changes in dietary and activity patterns, have increased the prevalence of chronic conditions, especially among older people (Suzman et al. 2015). Still, the sharp decline in overall global mortality rates at higher ages is a striking and hopeful change. It is, however, not likely to lessen the pressure on primary care health systems around the world to meet the increasingly complex and variable health needs of older people and to undertake the organizational transformations and structural redesigns that will enable this response.

Even as chronic conditions rise, older people are generally healthier. Overall, the age-related disease burden has declined globally since 1990, with large decreases in the case fatality and disease severity of age-related diseases (Chang et al. 2019). As of 2015, 23 percent of the total global burden of disease was attributable to disorders in people age 60 and older (Prince et al. 2015). The leading contributors were cardiovascular diseases (30.3 percent of the total burden in people age 60 and older), malignant neoplasms, chronic respiratory diseases, diabetes and kidney diseases, musculoskeletal diseases, and neurological and mental disorders (figure 1.1) (Prince et al. 2015).

FIGURE 1.1 Global Disability-Adjusted Life Years Burden, by Cause, for Adults Age 60 and Older, 2019

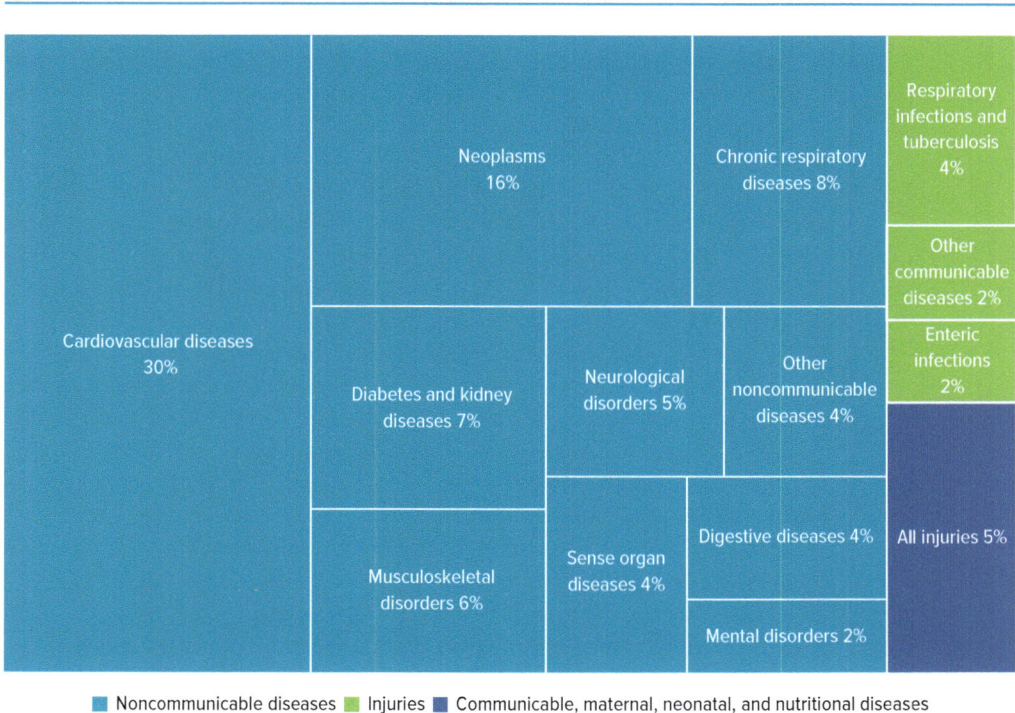

- Noncommunicable diseases Injuries Communicable, maternal, neonatal, and nutritional diseases

Source: Data from the Institute for Health Metrics and Evaluation's GBD [Global Burden of Disease] Results Tool. Data available at http://ghdx.healthdata.org/gbd-results-tool.

However, there is substantial regional variation in disease burden. Although the proportion of the burden contributed by older people is highest in high-income regions, disability-adjusted life years per capita are 40 percent higher in low- and middle-income countries, largely from cardiovascular diseases and sensory, respiratory, and infectious disorders (Prince et al. 2015). The onset of disease burden also varies across countries; for example, people in their mid-70s in Japan and those in their mid-40s in Papua New Guinea have the same disease burden as the average person in their mid-60s globally (Chang et al. 2019).

Among causes of ill health in older populations, chronic illnesses have grown. In 2016, an estimated 40.5 million (71 percent) of the 56.9 million deaths globally were from noncommunicable diseases. Of these, an estimated 23.6 million (58 percent) occurred in people age 70 and older (Bennett et al. 2018). Almost half (48 percent) of the deaths among people age 70 and older were due to cardiovascular diseases, followed by cancers, chronic respiratory diseases, and diabetes (Bennett et al. 2018). Many noncommunicable disease deaths in older adults can be delayed through primary or secondary prevention and treatment, which have contributed to increases in longevity in HICs (Bennett et al. 2018).

Hypertension is a primary contributor to morbidity at older ages (figure 1.2). Although coverage of treatment remains low, it increases with age and is highest in older adults (Zhou et al. 2021). The Oceania, Sub-Saharan Africa, and South Asia regions have the highest proportion of older individuals with undiagnosed or untreated hypertension (Zhou et al. 2021). Cancer, the second-largest contributor to the disease burden in older people, is also growing in prevalence, especially in less-developed regions. In 2012, 6.7 million new cancer cases occurred in older adults globally, with a projected 14 million new cases among older people by 2035 (60 percent of the global cancer incidence at all ages) (Pilleron et al. 2019). Musculoskeletal conditions, which affect mobility, contributed to an increase in disability-adjusted life years of nearly 20 percent between 2006 and 2016 (Briggs, Woolf, et al. 2018). These conditions, such as back and neck pain, osteoarthritis, rheumatoid arthritis, and fractures, are growing threats to healthy aging.

Other high-burden conditions that affect older adults include cognitive and neurological conditions, such as dementia. Approximately 43.8 million adults age 60 and older had dementia as of 2016 (Nichols et al. 2019). Globally, the estimated annual economic cost of dementia care was US$818 billion as of 2015 (Wimo et al. 2017). Sensory disorders, such as vision impairment and hearing loss, are risk factors for dementia and are common among older people (Burton et al. 2021; Wilson et al. 2019). The prevalence of vision impairment is increasing because of population aging and changes in disease patterns, with an expected increase from 700 million to 1.5 billion people age 65 and older over the next 30 years (Burton et al. 2021). Vision impairment is also a risk factor for falls among older people, although the risk of falls can be mitigated through timely interventions such as cataract surgery. As of 2019, one in five people had hearing loss globally. Of these, 62 percent were older than 50 (Haile et al. 2021). Treatment and prevention of hearing loss for middle-age people could significantly reduce the incidence of dementia and other conditions.

FIGURE 1.2 Percentage of Adults with Hypertension Who Were Undiagnosed, Reported a Diagnosis, Who Used Treatment, and Whose Blood Pressure Was Effectively Controlled, by Region and Age Group, 2019

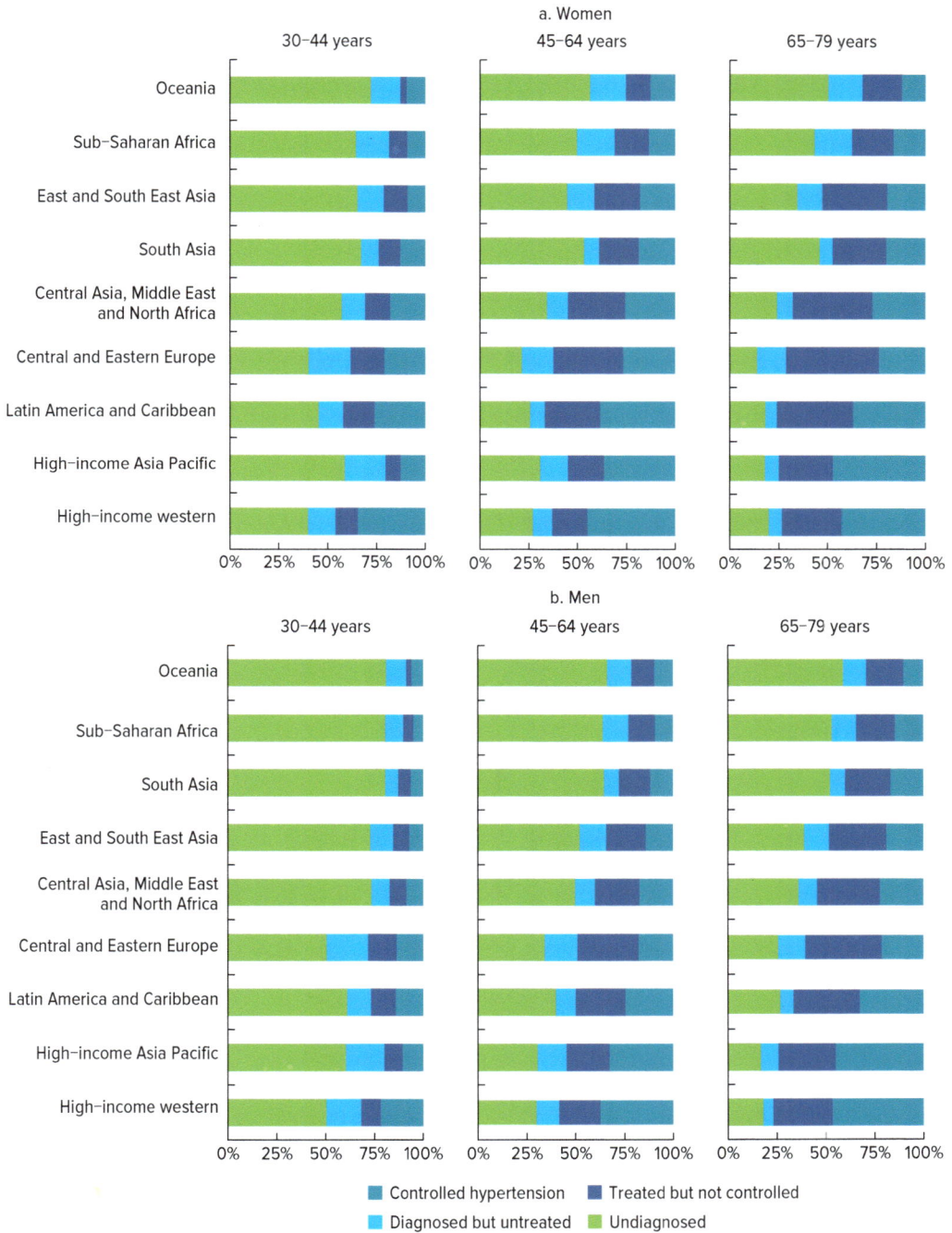

Source: Zhou et al. 2021.

Context Matters: Health Services at Home and in Institutional Settings

Older people frequently require long-term care (LTC), including a range of medical and personal care. LTC is frequently provided through institutions such as nursing and residential care facilities, which may provide residents with health care ranging from basic primary care to highly specialized services. Across Organisation for Economic Co-operation and Development (OECD) countries with available data, an average of 3.7 percent of people age 65 and over received LTC in nonhospital institutions in 2019 (figure 1.3). Adults age 80 and over comprise the majority of LTC recipients in OECD countries: on average, 10 percent of adults in this age group received LTC in institutions in 2019. There are, nevertheless, large differences by setting: in the Netherlands, more than 7 percent of people age 65 and older received LTC services, compared with less than 1 percent in Poland.

Differences in the formal provision of LTC among countries may stem from structural factors, such as publicly funded services, and cultural norms, such as the extent to which families look after older people by providing informal care or inviting them to live with them (OECD 2021). It is worth noting that updated data on the number of older people living in institutions are not

FIGURE 1.3   Percentage of Adults Age 65 and Older Receiving Long-Term Care in Institutions, 2005 and 2019 (or Nearest Year)

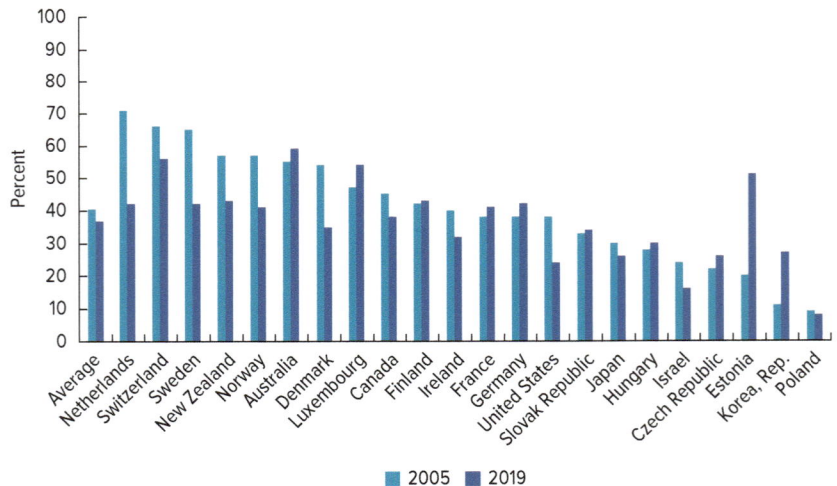

Source: Data retrieved from the OECD.Stat database available at https://stats.oecd.org.
Note: Long-term care (LTC) recipients are defined as people receiving LTC by paid providers, including nonprofessionals receiving cash payments under a social program. They also include recipients of cash benefits such as consumer-choice programs, care allowances, or other social benefits granted with the primary goal of supporting people with LTC needs. LTC institutions refer to nursing and residential care facilities that provide accommodation and LTC as a package. However, there are variations in data coverage across countries. Several countries include only beds in publicly funded LTC facilities, while others also include private facilities (both for profit and not for profit). Some countries also include beds in treatment centers for addicted people, psychiatric units of general or specialized hospitals, and rehabilitation centers. Selected countries were included if they reported data within three years of 2005 or 2019. The "average" category is the mean for all countries represented in the figure.

widely available and are likely underreported, especially in low-income countries and settings where many people are receiving care outside public systems.

Unfortunately, the quality of care in residential facilities is often poor. Few countries collect data on the quality of LTC services and facilities, which may include falls, fractures, bed sores, poor quality of life, and abuse (OECD and European Union 2013). These issues are often attributed to staffing shortages, high resident-to-staff ratios, and supply shortages, though structural solutions to these problems have been elusive (Davidson and Szanton 2020). The COVID-19 (coronavirus) pandemic highlighted the poor quality of care in many residential facilities, including the frequency of inadequate infection prevention and control measures (Davidson and Szanton 2020; Ouslander and Grabowski 2020). These challenges notwithstanding, demand for institutional settings is likely to increase globally as the older population grows, and countries must rise to the challenge of providing better quality care and catering to older adults who increasingly demand control over their lives and care (OECD and European Union 2013). The cost of LTC services, estimated at 1.6 percent of gross domestic product across OECD countries in 2010, is expected to double by 2050 (OECD and European Union 2013).

Older people who live at home are more likely than younger people to live alone, which presents its own health challenges (figure 1.4). Globally, 16 percent

FIGURE 1.4 Percentage of Adults Age 60 and Older Living in a Solo Household, 2010–18

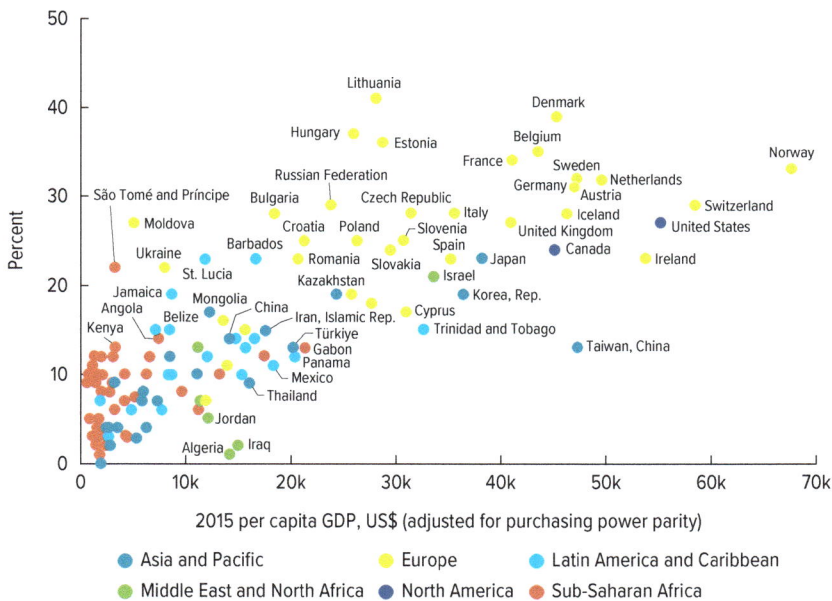

Source: Pew Research Center 2020.
Note: Data are from a Pew Research Center analysis of 2010–18 census and survey data. GDP data are in US dollars and come from the International Monetary Fund. Not all dots are labeled due to space constraints; refer to the original figure for any missing labels. GDP = gross domestic product.

of adults age 60 and older live in solo households, compared with just 4 percent of adults ages 18 to 59 (Pew Research Center 2020). In Europe, more than 30 percent of adults 60 and older live alone, while in other parts of the world, living alone is rarer. In China, only 5 percent of individuals of any age occupy solo households (Pew Research Center 2020). Living alone has been linked to an increased risk of accidents, injury, and mental health conditions, including loneliness, among older adults (O'Suilleabhain, Gallagher, and Steptoe 2019). These issues have grown particularly acute during the pandemic, which inhibited both formal and informal caregiving and discouraged in-person socialization (Pew Research Center 2020).

In some countries, older adults receive assistance services at home to counter these and other health issues. In 2019, 68 percent of LTC recipients age 65 and over in 20 OECD countries received at-home care (OECD 2021). Many older people who need LTC wish to live at home for as long as possible. This preference, combined with the high cost of institutional living, has led many countries to develop home-based support services for older adults. However, home-based care depends on informal caregivers, such as family members, who may lack the knowledge and resources to adequately manage complex illnesses. In 2017, family caregivers in the United States provided approximately 34 billion hours of care to adults who had limitations to daily activities (Reinhard et al. 2019). Overreliance on informal caregivers can result in a high physical, psychological, emotional, behavioral, and financial burden on families and poor-quality care (Chiao, Wu, and Hsiao 2015; Grant and Graven 2018).

Primary Care for Older Adults: Frameworks and Functions

Primary Care Frameworks

Several scientific and policy communities have developed frameworks for high-quality primary care for older adults. Chief among these are the conceptual frameworks for primary care advanced since the 1978 Alma-Ata Declaration on Primary Health Care (Veillard et al. 2017; Walley et al. 2008; WHO 1978, 2017). The provisions of Alma-Ata and its subsequent revisions that are most relevant to the concerns of older adults are the following:

- Health includes physical, mental, and social well-being and not merely the absence of disease, and attaining it requires actions by the social and economic sectors along with the health sector.

- People have the right to participate in the planning and implementation of their health care.

- Governments have a responsibility to provide adequate health and social measures.

- PHC is the first element and central function of the health system and the first level of contact with the national health system, bringing care closer to people.

- PHC addresses the main health problems in the community, providing promotive, preventive, curative, and rehabilitative services.

Subsequently, Barbara Starfield, a professor of health policy who championed PHC, defined PHC as care characterized by first contact, accessibility, longitudinality, and comprehensiveness (Starfield 1992). In 1996, the Institute of Medicine (now the National Academies of Sciences, Engineering, and Medicine) similarly emphasized the provision of integrated, accessible health care services; the ability to address a large majority of health care needs; and a sustained partnership between patients, family, and community as the core components of PHC (Donaldson et al. 1996).

In 2018, the Astana Conference of the World Health Organization (WHO) revisited the Alma-Ata Declaration and noted that in a well-functioning PHC system with comprehensive services, "PHC will also be accessible, equitable, safe, of high-quality, comprehensive, efficient, acceptable, available and affordable, and will deliver continuous, integrated services that are people-centered and gender-sensitive. We will strive to avoid fragmentation and ensure a functional referral system between primary and other levels of care" (WHO 2019, 6).

In the same time frame, a new initiative—the Primary Health Care Performance Initiative, funded by the Bill and Melinda Gates Foundation and working with the World Bank and the WHO—defined the PHC system as "the totality of the system, inputs and service delivery components that contribute to high-quality primary care services and achieve the four functions of PHC described by Barbara Starfield—first contact accessibility, continuity, comprehensiveness, and coordination—as well as person-centeredness" (Bitton et al. 2019, 2).

In 2021, the National Academies of Sciences, Engineering, and Medicine, in a study it published on the implementation of high-quality primary care, stressed that it "provides comprehensive person-centered, relationship-based care that considers the needs and preferences of individuals, families, and communities" (National Academies of Sciences, Engineering, and Medicine 2021, 3).

In 2021, the World Bank published a strategic paper on reimagining PHC after COVID-19, reflecting a renewed understanding of global and local vulnerabilities and opportunities in the post-COVID world (World Bank 2021). The report outlines priorities for reimagining PHC and structural shifts in how PHC is designed, financed, and delivered.

Taken together, the number and scope of these efforts to redefine primary care illustrate strong demand for a clear, effective primary care approach—one that capitalizes on the efficiencies of close-to-patient, cost-effective care while demonstrating value to users and measurably improving health outcomes. The above primary care frameworks identify a number of cardinal features of primary care, including the following:

- Readily accessible services (short wait time, short distance, low cost)
- Ability to serve as the first point of contact with the health system
- Comprehensive range of services
- Integration of care
- Continuity of care

- Consideration of medical, psychological, and social dimensions of health
- Consideration of the needs and preferences of users, their families, and their communities.

The next section incorporates these features into a new framework for a high-quality health system with primary care as the engine—a critical provider and coordinator—of care.

A New Framework for a High-Quality, Primary Care–Powered Health System for Older Adults

Rather than a primary care framework, this section presents a whole-of-health-system framework to highlight the fact that primary care functions in concert with other parts of the health system. Neither primary care alone, nor a health system that marginalizes primary care, is effective in improving the health of older adults (or, for that matter, the rest of the population). The starting point is the Lancet Global Health Commission on High Quality Health Systems in the Sustainable Development Goals Era (HQSS Commission) developed in 2018 (Kruk et al. 2018). The HQSS Commission defined a high-quality health system as one that optimizes health in a given context by consistently delivering care that maintains or improves health, is valued and trusted by all people, and responds to changing population needs (Kruk et al. 2018). The commission noted that health systems rest on societal values and that high-quality systems require broad-based agreement on the values of equity, efficiency, resilience, and well-being for people.

The HQSS Commission framework—shown in figure 1.5, with the key health system domains and subdomains that are particularly salient for older-age groups—consists of foundations, processes, and outcomes. Linked together in a self-enclosed flow chart (indicated by the three arrows), the processes and outcomes are intended to guide measurement, while the foundations indicate initial points of entry for improvement. The foundations are used later in this book (chapters 3 and 4) to organize policy recommendations for countries seeking to strengthen innovation in age-responsive health service delivery and social support. In this way, the framework can help clarify policy priorities and options within key domains of the FIRE model (financing, innovation, regulation, evaluation and measurement) that structures this book.

Each of the framework's three components—outcomes, processes, and foundations—is looked at in turn.

First, the *outcomes* of a high-quality health system include better health, confidence in the health system, and economic benefits. For older adults, health goals may include greater life expectancy at age 60 and a focus on healthy longevity that includes low levels of multimorbidity and hospitalization and optimal physical and social function. The greater health needs of older people demand a strong therapeutic relationship between patients and providers. This dynamic rests on, and is enabled by, trust—users and their families must have confidence in the system to trigger appropriate care seeking and to comply with clinical advice.

FIGURE 1.5 Conceptual Framework for a High-Quality Health System for Older Adults

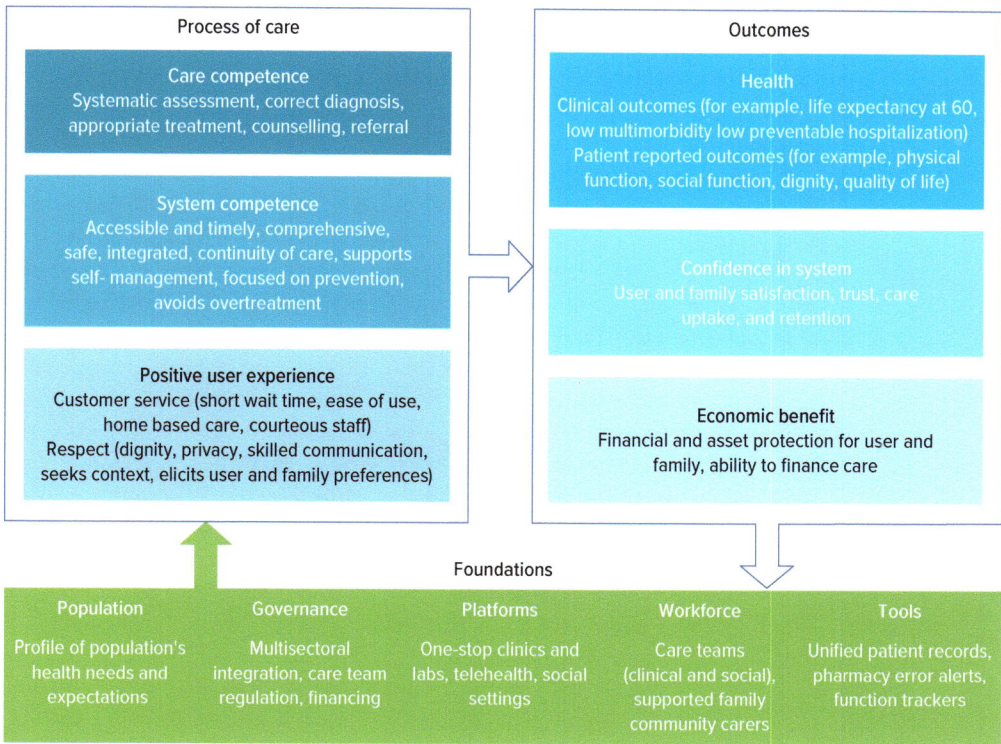

Process of care

Care competence
Systematic assessment, correct diagnosis, appropriate treatment, counselling, referral

System competence
Accessible and timely, comprehensive, safe, integrated, continuity of care, supports self- management, focused on prevention, avoids overtreatment

Positive user experience
Customer service (short wait time, ease of use, home based care, courteous staff) Respect (dignity, privacy, skilled communication, seeks context, elicits user and family preferences)

Outcomes

Health
Clinical outcomes (for example, life expectancy at 60, low multimorbidity low preventable hospitalization) Patient reported outcomes (for example, physical function, social function, dignity, quality of life)

Confidence in system
User and family satisfaction, trust, care uptake, and retention

Economic benefit
Financial and asset protection for user and family, ability to finance care

Foundations

Population	Governance	Platforms	Workforce	Tools
Profile of population's health needs and expectations	Multisectoral integration, care team regulation, financing	One-stop clinics and labs, telehealth, social settings	Care teams (clinical and social), supported family community carers	Unified patient records, pharmacy error alerts, function trackers

Source: Original figure for this publication.

Finally, financial protection, and the protection of older people's often meager assets, should be key goals of a well-designed health system. Outcomes are key measures of health system performance, although time lags, and the difficulty of accurately attributing outcomes to specific health care choices, can make such measurement technically challenging.

Second, *care processes* reveal the function of the health system in real time, and carefully identified metrics in this domain can be used as signals of performance. Care competence refers to provision of care that reflects current best practices and the latest evidence. System competence goes beyond the individual provider or visit and includes the ability of the system to co-manage the care of individuals longitudinally. The geriatric and family medicine communities have highlighted the particular importance of continual, integrated care for older adults (Briggs, Valentijn, et al. 2018; Lawless et al. 2020; Uijen et al. 2012; Valentijn et al. 2013).

Continuity is typically defined as the patient's experience of a coordinated and seamless progression of care (Threapleton et al. 2017; Uijen et al. 2012). Continuity includes care coordination between providers and case management. Continuity has three domains: (1) interpersonal continuity—a personal care provider in every separate care setting who knows and follows the patient;

(2) informational continuity—communication of relevant patient information from one care provider to the next; and (3) cooperation among care providers (for example, discharge planning and primary and specialty care coordination) (Uijen et al. 2012). Integration is the notion of forging connections between the health care system and other human service systems (for example, LTC, education, housing, and vocational services) with the aim of improved health outcomes (Leutz 1999; Shortell 2021).

Literature on community health and health promotion describes the desirable features of social systems for preventing and detecting health problems in aging populations (Leutz 1999; Saito et al. 2019; Shortell 2021; Threapleton et al. 2017). Valentijn et al. (2013) note the need to move beyond clinical integration (coordination of care for a specific health need of an older individual) to professional, institutional, and system integration, although they acknowledge the difficulty of doing so given the wide variation in existing governance, payment, and professional models. A more modest and implementable vision of integration might include examples such as Japan's *ikoino saron*, salons for older adults that provide social interaction along with health screenings and counseling (Saito et al. 2019).

Positive user experience is integral to good-quality care and is both an intrinsic feature of, and an essential prerequisite for, good outcomes. Systems should also be client-focused—easy to navigate, with short wait times and attention to people's values and preferences. People's values and preferences should not be passively assumed but actively ascertained. Providers need to treat older people with dignity, communicate with them clearly, and provide the desired degree of autonomy and confidentiality. Disrespectful and discriminatory behavior are serious quality failures that result from ageism— the discriminatory stereotyping of individuals or groups based on their age— and more generally from a poorly managed, inadequately compensated, or undermotivated workforce (WHO 2015).

Foundations of health systems—population, governance, platforms, workforce, and tools—are structures that can generate good or poor performance and the levers of improvement. Attention to population begins with assessing the needs and preferences of the population because these are the critical substantive inputs that should shape care models. Governance begins with effective health system leadership at central, subnational, and facility levels. It includes effective regulation of providers in both the public and private sectors, accountability mechanisms, and financing to promote appropriate access to health care and to limit financial hardship through fund pooling, insurance, contracting, and appropriate payment arrangements.

The third foundation, care platforms, or the place from which care is provided, should reflect the specific needs of the various groups that comprise the older population, from independent, healthy adults to institutionalized older adults with multiple health problems. The workforce includes health workers and managers with appropriate preparation, professionalism, and motivation. Clinical education that emphasizes team care, patient-centered care, and ethics, together with a supportive work environment once providers are in practice, is essential for achieving high performance. Health systems also require the right tools—hardware (for example, equipment, medicines, and supplies) and software (for example, performance mindset, supervision and feedback, and willingness to learn from data).

Finally, high-quality health systems need to have a learning culture, with the timely production of information on performance, evaluation of new ideas, and organizational off-ramps to retire ineffective approaches.

Applying the Framework: How Well Are Primary Care Systems Performing?

As the HQSS Commission notes, outcomes and processes of care should be the primary basis for the assessment of health system performance. This chapter earlier described shortcomings in health outcomes of older adults globally. This section describes the performance of primary care systems in terms of care processes, including system competence, care competence, and user experience.

When performing as intended, high-quality health systems should produce better health in an equitable manner, build user confidence in the system, and protect users and families financially. However, health system performance varies from country to country and is often suboptimal. By one estimate, in low- and middle-income countries, poor-quality health systems result in the deaths of more than 8 million people a year, many with conditions treatable in primary care services (Kruk et al. 2018). Primary care systems, as a foundational platform underpinning health system functions, are currently inadequate to the challenge of a growing aging population.

A competent primary care system should provide accessible, timely care to users, but many older adults face a disconnect between their demonstrated high health needs and care utilization. In many HICs, service utilization rises with increasing age, making it commensurate with need. But among adults in low- and middle-income countries, a similar correlation is not observed, suggesting underprovision (WHO 2015).

Two key barriers to utilization include costs of health care visits and transportation to health facilities. According to the WHO *World Report on Ageing and Health*, which draws upon survey data from 2002 to 2014, more than 60 percent of older people in low-income countries did not access health care because of the cost of the visit, lack of transportation, or inability to pay for transportation (WHO 2015). Affordability is also a challenge for older adults in HICs, though it is highly dependent on the structure of the health system. Studies shows that almost 20 percent of older adults in the United States miss health care treatments because of cost, compared with only 3 percent of older adults in France (figure 1.6) (WHO 2015).

For older adults who can access care, effective care coordination is a cornerstone of competent primary care. Health systems have historically been designed to diagnose and treat acute illnesses using a disease-specific, biomedically based approach, with less attention paid to long-term health and functioning. They therefore frequently fail to coordinate care over time, among providers, and across settings (figure 1.7). Older adults, who often have multiple chronic conditions and high health needs, may rely on more than one health care provider in different settings, which introduces complex

FIGURE 1.6 Percentage of Adults Age 65 and Older in 11 Countries Who Had Problems Accessing Health Care Services Because of Their Cost, 2014

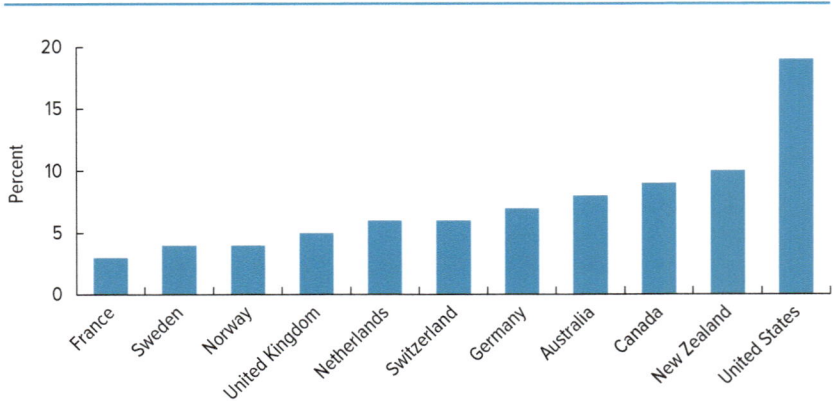

Source: WHO 2015.
Note: Because of cost, respondents with a medical problem did not visit a doctor, missed a medical test or treatment recommended by a doctor, did not fill a prescription, or missed a dose of medicine, or a combination of these.

FIGURE 1.7 Percentage of Adults Age 65 and Older in 11 Countries Who Experienced Problems with the Coordination of Their Care, 2013–14

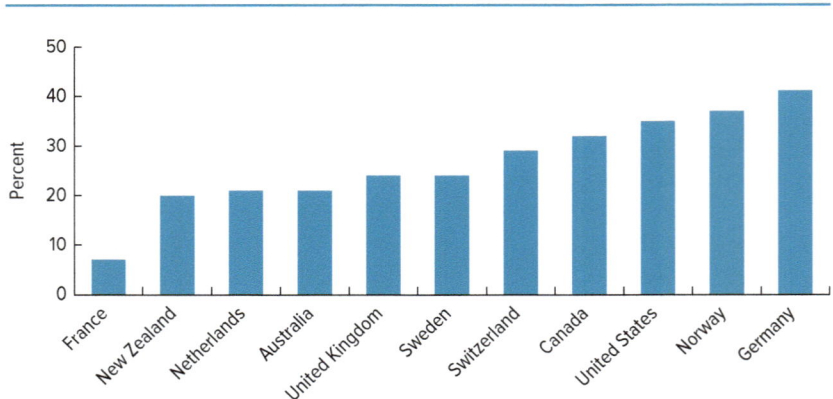

Source: WHO 2015.
Note: Problems with care coordination included test results or records not being available at the time of an appointment, duplicate tests being ordered, receiving conflicting information from different doctors, a specialist lacking the patient's medical history, the regular doctor not being informed about specialist care, or a combination of these.

dynamics into their health care and places them at higher risk of receiving fragmented care (MacLeod et al. 2018). One study of older adults in the United States finds that the median patient saw two primary care physicians and five specialists in four different practices (Pham et al. 2007). Use of multiple providers increases the likelihood of conflicting health advice, provision of unnecessary or duplicative tests and services, and uncoordinated treatments (Zulman et al. 2015).

In Germany, an HIC with an internationally lauded health system, up to 41 percent of surveyed older adults reported having problems with care coordination during the previous two years (WHO 2015). This problem is not Germany's alone; poor care coordination ranges across high- and low-income countries. Poor coordination is visible in the high prevalence of polypharmacy, defined as the use of multiple drugs or more drugs than are medically necessary (Maher, Hanlon, and Hajjar 2014). More than half of the older population is estimated to experience polypharmacy in some settings, including regions of Ireland, Italy, and Sweden, where data on polypharmacy prevalence is available (Wastesson et al. 2018). Polypharmacy can have significant negative consequences such as falls, mortality, frailty, and complications stemming from drug interactions (Wastesson et al. 2018). Addressing polypharmacy will likely require an interprofessional approach that better coordinates older patients' treatments across settings.

Care competence for older adults is similarly inadequate in today's health systems. Multiple conditions and poor coordination introduce opportunities for suboptimal management, such as missed diagnoses, inadequate treatment, and poor user experience (Zulman et al. 2015). Quality deficits for acute illness and communicable diseases are common—analysis of basic primary care services for younger people, such as sick-child care, indicates poor adherence to clinical guidelines among health care workers and frequent incorrect diagnoses for serious conditions (Kruk et al. 2017; Lewis et al. 2019). But similar multicountry analyses for older adults are rare, and older populations remain less visible than other age groups in the available data.

An analysis by Alshamsan et al. (2017) of the World Health Organization Study on Global AGEing and Adult Health, which includes nationally representative data on the health and well-being of adults age 50 and older in six countries that account for more than half of the global population, assesses care quality indicators in domains such as the effectiveness and patient-centeredness of care. Of the 11 effectiveness indicators, which related to the prevention and management of common chronic conditions, none surpassed 80 percent in any country. For example, fewer than 38 percent of respondents with known hypertension had been prescribed hypertension medication in the past 12 months in five of the six countries, and the share of respondents with undiagnosed hypertension ranged from 27 percent in the Russian Federation to 76 percent in Ghana. Performance on important preventive interventions, such as breast and cervical screening coverage, was also very low. In India, performance on these two indicators was less than 1 percent (Alshamsan et al. 2017).

Positive user experience, another core aspect of care processes, falls short for older adults. Whereas older people in low-income countries report issues with accessibility and affordability as key barriers to greater utilization, the greatest barriers reported in HICs stem from users having been treated poorly by health care professionals (WHO 2015). In the WHO Study on Global AGEing and Adult Health analysis, patient-centeredness indicators were lowest for inpatient involvement in decision-making (range: 62–73 percent) and outpatient promptness of attention (range: 58–73 percent) (Alshamsan et al. 2017). These problems may be compounded by ageism in primary care services that discourages older adults from using health care services or inhibits the provision of high-quality, age-appropriate care. Ageism within health care can take multiple forms, including "health-care workers having negative attitudes towards older people or the aging process, engaging in patronizing behaviour, failing to consult older people about their preferences for care, and discouraging or restricting access to otherwise-indicated medical interventions" (WHO 2015, 94–95).

Ageism may also manifest through low usability for older people, who may struggle with accessibility in poorly designed health facilities, the increased use of technology in the administration of health care, and long wait times at health facilities. Over time, persistent poor experience and ageism in health care can erode trust and confidence in health services.

Many of these issues are underpinned, reinforced, or aggravated by an underprepared health workforce. The shortage of health workers with training specific to the needs of older people, including specialists such as geriatricians, contributes to poor health system performance. Health workers are trained primarily to identify and treat symptoms and conditions using an episodic approach to care. This training does not prepare them well to adopt the holistic perspective that has been shown to be the most effective when caring for older people or to control and manage the consequences of chronic conditions in ways that meet an older person's priorities.

Existing medical and nursing school curricula frequently overlook gerontological and geriatric knowledge and training, and may lack guidance on managing common problems, such as multimorbidity and frailty. For example, a survey of 36 countries finds that 27 percent of medical schools did not conduct any training in geriatric medicine, which included 19 percent of schools in HICs, 43 percent of schools in transition economies,[1] and 38 percent of all schools in other countries (Keller et al. 2002; WHO 2015). Ample opportunity exists to improve the quality of care available to older adults by upskilling the health care workforce and preparing workers to adequately serve this population.

It is important to highlight the dearth of cross-national data on health system performance for older people. Two surveys that sample older adults regarding their health care include the WHO Study on Global AGEing and Adult Health survey described above, which samples adults 50 and older in six countries, and the OECD Patient-Reported Indicator Survey of Patients with Chronic Conditions, which surveys patients age 45 and older. These examples notwithstanding, timely, cross-national data on care and system competence for aging populations are urgently needed.

Toward a Fit-for-Purpose Primary Care Model with Older Users at the Center

Care Models for Older Adults

The complex health needs of older populations, and the diversity of settings in which they receive care, present a challenge for today's PHC systems. Care delivery models and settings as currently structured may be inadequate for the task and will require adaptation.

Addressing the high burden of disease among aging populations, especially the epidemic of chronic disease, will require focusing efforts and resources on the most age-dependent conditions. This will involve improving primary and secondary prevention, including strong disease detection functions, to manage the growing disease burden in older people, which will be particularly important in low- and middle-income countries that have little access to essential diagnostics (Fleming et al. 2021). Multimorbidities, common in older adults, and the high proportion of disease burden from chronic diseases, demand better clinical management, including coordination between providers and integration of care teams. A diverse array of primary care clinicians will be essential to support these services, although there is a dearth of primary care practitioners, especially those skilled in the care of older adults, in many settings (Bodenheimer and Pham 2010). These clinicians must be adequately prepared to provide age-appropriate care, especially for chronic diseases, and must be distributed geographically according to need. Retention of skilled health workers, especially in low-income settings, is a growing problem (Botezat and Ramos 2020).

PHC will also need to extend beyond traditional health facilities to adequately serve aging populations. Because older adults receive care at home and in institutional settings from both formal and informal caregivers, there are multiple platforms with which to deliver primary care services and improve older adults' connections to the health system. However, the variable quality of this care, especially that of residential care, warrants specific attention. Shoring up these platforms will also require supporting informal caregivers, such as family members, who are a significant source of care for older adults. Even as tasks performed by family caregivers are growing in scope and complexity, the declining proportion of working-age people in many countries is putting pressure on social protection systems. The potential support ratio, which compares the numbers of people age 25 to 64 to those age 65 and older, is falling globally. In Japan, this ratio is 1.8, the lowest in the world (UN DESA Population Division 2019b). These demographic changes will increase the burden on caregivers and on social protection systems broadly.

The particular needs of older adults demand a reexamination of primary care delivery models. This reexamination should begin with confronting the ageist attitudes prevalent among the general population and among health professionals, which may lead to care underprovision, particularly in low-income settings, but also for some health conditions in high-income countries (Prince et al. 2015; WHO 2015). On the other hand, overtreatment and polypharmacy that lead to adverse drug interactions and overspending are also common signals of poor-quality care, resulting from the failure to consider multimorbidity and people's care needs and preferences (Prince et al. 2015).

Care delivery should be guided by the health and social needs of the older adult population. Indeed, it may be more useful to regard the population as several subpopulations with different health needs and preferences, living contexts, and support systems. These subpopulations will require somewhat different service models. A fit-for-purpose primary care approach could be informed by model practices gleaned from the differentiated care employed in HIV management and from the notion of integrated, people-centered health services (Hagey et al. 2018; Roy et al. 2019; WHO 2016). In HIV programs, for example, elements of differentiation include customized appointment spacing, fast-track medication refills, facility- and community-based adherence clubs, and self-management support groups that can be accessed by users according to their needs and circumstances.

For primary care for older people, this chapter proposes differentiated care models for healthy older populations living at home versus those with medical needs in home care or institutional care settings (table 1.1). In all care models, the emphasis should be on managing the major modifiable risk factors (for example, hypertension, dyslipidemia, diabetes, smoking, and obesity) (Prince et al. 2015). This care can be provided through a combination of clinic visits, outreach, and social or community-based programs, depending on user profiles. For individuals with multimorbidity, care coordination is the cardinal function of primary care. Frailty, the state of vulnerability to health stressors brought on by a cumulative decline in physical and cognitive functions over a lifetime, afflicts 4 to 25 percent of people older than 65, rising with age, and requires a highly attuned, integrated, and sensitive model of primary care (Clegg et al. 2013).

Decisions on care models need to be based on the existing health care system, including financing models and the human resource mix. A primary care design assessment that measures the demographic and epidemiologic context, health system assets, social and community assets, current utilization pattern, and experience with any local experiments or initiatives in this space can help guide the intentional development of updated models of care. Health promotion, socialization, and instilling a sense of purpose to avert loneliness and depression are critical for all aging subpopulations.

TABLE 1.1 Elements of Differentiated Primary Care with Older Users at the Center

	Living at home	Living in care settings
Healthy	• Existing medical care model • Active health promotion, prevention, and socialization via community platforms • Home visits, especially for those living alone	• Institutional[a] plus regular medical care model • Institutional health promotion • Promotion of socialization, intellectual stimulation, and a sense of purpose
Moderate illness or disability	• Aggressive management of early disease and risk factors • Multispecialty coordination and holistic (vs. single disease) treatment approach • Active health promotion, prevention, and socialization via community platforms • Social and functional team assessment • Support for family and informal caregivers	• Institutional care coordination • Link to external specialists • Promotion of socialization, intellectual stimulation, and a sense of purpose
Frail	• Specialized team care, including geriatric specialists and social and palliative care professionals • Active health promotion, prevention, and socialization via community platforms	• Advanced care facilities and teams • Protection from abuse or severe quality deficits • Links to palliative or hospice care, or both

Source: Original table for this publication.
a. Institutional models refer to care provided in residential facilities such as nursing homes and long-term care facilities.

Conclusions

As the population of older adults grows across the world, health systems will be under increasing pressure to meet their unique health and service needs. Current models of care are poorly equipped for this challenge. Major deficits are present in key areas of performance, including system competence and user experience. What is needed is nimble and robust primary care capable of managing complex health needs among a diverse population that ranges from active older adults with minimal needs to frail older adults living alone or in care settings. Growing user expectations will put further pressure on health systems to respond to these diverse needs with competence and care. Although many countries struggle to provide high-quality primary care to older adults, these pressures will be particularly intense for countries with underfunded primary care systems.

These challenges require fresh thinking. Although international commitments to support high-quality primary care are manifold, few countries have actually implemented primary care that fulfills these aspirations. The COVID-19 pandemic, which has revealed widespread inadequacies in primary care infrastructure, presents a clear opportunity to redesign primary care. Next-generation primary care services should be tailored to needs, focused on age-appropriate care (younger vs. older adults), health status (healthy vs. frail), key modifiable risk factors, and optimal delivery platforms. New care models are urgently needed and should be developed using a robust assessment of current system deficits and assets and the preferences of users and their families.

Such an assessment can help tailor innovations such as differentiated care models, integration with social systems, programs to empower caregivers, and the development of digital platforms. New approaches should be carefully monitored and rigorously evaluated to guide smart investments that strengthen primary care for all older adults.

Note

1. In the survey, the transition economies were Bulgaria, Croatia, the Czech Republic, Estonia, Latvia, Lithuania, Poland, the Slovak Republic, and Ukraine.

References

Alshamsan, R., J. T. Lee, S. Rana, H. Areabi, and C. Millett. 2017. "Comparative Health System Performance in Six Middle-Income Countries: Cross-Sectional Analysis Using World Health Organization Study of Global Ageing and Health." *Journal of the Royal Society of Medicine* 110 (9): 365–75. https://doi.org/https://doi.org/10.1177/0141076817724599.

Bennett, J. E., G. A. Stevens, C. D. Mathers, R. Bonita, J. Rehm, M. E. Kruk, L. M. Riley, et al. 2018. "NCD Countdown 2030: Worldwide Trends in Non-Communicable Disease Mortality and Progress towards Sustainable Development Goal Target 3.4." *The Lancet* 392 (10152): 1072–88. https://doi.org/10.1016/s0140-6736(18)31992-5.

Bitton, A., J. Fifield, H. Ratcliffe, A. Karlage, H. Wang, J. H. Veillard, D. Schwarz, and L. R. Hirschhorn. 2019. "Primary Healthcare System Performance in Low-Income and

Middle-Income Countries: A Scoping Review of the Evidence from 2010 to 2017." *BMJ Global Health* 4 (Suppl 8): e001551. https://doi.org/10.1136/bmjgh-2019 -001551.

Bloom, D. E., D. Chisholm, E. Jané-Llopis, K. Prettner, A. Stein, and A. Feigl. 2011. "From Burden to 'Best Buys': Reducing the Economic Impact of Non-Communicable Diseases." World Health Organization, Geneva. https://cdn.who.int/media/docs /default-source/medical-devices/health-technology-assessment/from-burden-to -best-buys-reducing-the-economic-impact-of-ncds-in-low-and-middle-income -countries.pdf.

Bodenheimer, T., and H. H. Pham. 2010. "Primary Care: Current Problems and Proposed Solutions." *Health Affairs* 29 (5): 799–805. https://doi.org/10.1377/hlthaff.2010.0026.

Botezat, A., and R. Ramos. 2020. "Physicians' Brain Drain—A Gravity Model of Migration Flows." *Global Health* 16 (1): 7. https://doi.org/10.1186/s12992-019 -0536-0.

Briggs, A. M., P. P. Valentijn, J. A. Thiyagarajan, and I. Araujo de Carvalho. 2018. "Elements of Integrated Care Approaches for Older People: A Review of Reviews." *BMJ Open* 8 (4): e021194. https://doi.org/10.1136/bmjopen-2017-021194.

Briggs, A. M., A. D. Woolf, K. Dreinhofer, N. Homb, D. G. Hoy, D. Kopansky-Giles, K. Akesson, and L. March. 2018. "Reducing the Global Burden of Musculoskeletal Conditions." *Bulletin of the World Health Organization* 96 (5): 366–68. https://doi .org/10.2471/BLT.17.204891.

Burton, M. J., J. Ramke, A. P. Marques, R. R. A. Bourne, N. Congdon, I. Jones, B. A. M. Ah Tong, et al. 2021. "The Lancet Global Health Commission on Global Eye Health: Vision beyond 2020." *The Lancet Global Health* 9 (4): e489–e551. https://doi .org/10.1016/S2214-109X(20)30488-5.

Chang, A. Y., V. F. Skirbekk, S. Tyrovolas, N. J. Kassebaum, and J. L. Dieleman. 2019. "Measuring Population Ageing: An Analysis of the Global Burden of Disease Study 2017." *The Lancet Public Health* 4 (3): e159–e167. https://doi.org/10.1016/S2468 -2667(19)30019-2.

Chiao, C. Y., H. S. Wu, and C. Y. Hsiao. 2015. "Caregiver Burden for Informal Caregivers of Patients with Dementia: A Systematic Review." *International Nursing Review* 62 (3): 340–50. https://doi.org/10.1111/inr.12194.

Clegg, A., J. Young, S. Iliffe, M. O. Rikkert, and K. Rockwood. 2013. "Frailty in Elderly People." *The Lancet* 381 (9868): 752–62. https://doi.org/10.1016/s0140-6736(12) 62167-9.

Davidson, P. M., and S. L. Szanton. 2020. "Nursing Homes and COVID-19: We Can and Should Do Better." *Journal of Clinical Nursing* 29 (15–16): 2758–59. https://doi. org/10.1111%2Fjocn.15297.

Donaldson, M.S., K. D. Yordy, K. N. Lohr, and N. A. Venselow, eds. 1996. *Primary Care: America's Health in a New Era*, edited by Institute of Medicine Committee on the Future of Primary Care. Washington, DC: National Academies Press.

Fleming, K. A., S. Horton, M. L. Wilson, R. Atun, K. DeStigter, J. Flanigan, S. Sayed, et al. 2021. "The Lancet Commission on Diagnostics: Transforming Access to Diagnostics." *The Lancet* 398 (10315): 1997–2050. https://doi.org/10.1016/S0140 -6736(21)00673-5.

Grant, J. S., and L. J. Graven. 2018. "Problems Experienced by Informal Caregivers of Individuals with Heart Failure: An Integrative Review." *International Journal of Nursing Studies* 80: 41–66. https://doi.org/10.1016/j.ijnurstu.2017.12.016.

Hagey, J. M., X. Li, J. Barr-Walker, J. Penner, J. Kadima, P. Oyaro, and C. R. Cohen. 2018. "Differentiated HIV Care in Sub-Saharan Africa: A Scoping Review to Inform Antiretroviral Therapy Provision for Stable HIV-Infected Individuals in Kenya." *AIDS Care* 30 (12): 1477–87. https://doi.org/10.1080/09540121.2018.1500995.

Haile, L. M., K. Kamenov, P. S. Briant, A. U. Orji, J. D. Steinmetz, A. Abdoli, M. Abdollahi, E. Abu-Gharbieh, A. Afshin, and H. Ahmed. 2021. "Hearing Loss Prevalence and Years Lived with Disability, 1990–2019: Findings from the Global Burden of Disease Study 2019." *The Lancet* 397 (10278): 996–1009. https://doi.org/https://doi.org/10.1016/s0140-6736(21)00516-x.

Keller, I., A. Makipaa, T. Kalenscher, and A. Kalache. 2002. "Global Survey on Geriatrics in the Medical Curriculum." World Health Organization, Geneva.

Kruk, M. E., A. Chukwuma, G. Mbaruku, and H. H. Leslie. 2017. "Variation in Quality of Primary-Care Services in Kenya, Malawi, Namibia, Rwanda, Senegal, Uganda and the United Republic of Tanzania." *Bulletin of the World Health Organization* 95 (6): 408–18. https://doi.org/10.2471/blt.16.175869.

Kruk, M. E., A. D. Gage, C. Arsenault, K. Jordan, H. H. Leslie, S. Roder-DeWan, O. Adeyi, et al. 2018. "High-Quality Health Systems in the Sustainable Development Goals Era: Time for a Revolution." *The Lancet Global Health* 6 (11): e1196–e1252. https://doi.org/10.1016/S2214-109X(18)30386-3.

Lawless, M. T., A. Marshall, M. M. Mittinty, and G. Harvey. 2020. "What Does Integrated Care Mean from an Older Person's Perspective? A Scoping Review." *BMJ Open* 10 (1): e035157. https://doi.org/10.1136/bmjopen-2019-035157.

Leutz, W. N. 1999. "Five Laws for Integrating Medical and Social Services: Lessons from the United States and the United Kingdom." *Milbank Quarterly* 77 (1): 77–110, iv–v. https://doi.org/10.1111/1468-0009.00125.

Lewis, T. P., S. Roder-DeWan, A. Malata, Y. Ndiaye, and M. E. Kruk. 2019. "Clinical Performance among Recent Graduates in Nine Low-and Middle-Income Countries." *Tropical Medicine and International Health* 24 (5): 620–35. https://doi.org/https://doi.org/10.1111/tmi.13224.

MacLeod, S., K. Schwebke, K. Hawkins, J. Ruiz, E. Hoo, and C. S. Yeh. 2018. "Need for Comprehensive Health Care Quality Measures for Older Adults." *Population Health Management* 21 (4): 296–302. https://doi.org/10.1089/pop.2017.0109.

Maher, R. L., J. Hanlon, and E. R. Hajjar. 2014. "Clinical Consequences of Polypharmacy in Elderly." *Expert Opinion on Drug Safety* 13 (1): 57–65. https://doi.org/10.1517/14740338.2013.827660.

Mathers, C. D., G. A. Stevens, T. Boerma, R. A. White, and M. I. Tobias. 2015. "Causes of International Increases in Older Age Life Expectancy." *The Lancet* 385 (9967): 540–48. https://doi.org/10.1016/S0140-6736(14)60569-9.

National Academies of Sciences, Engineering, and Medicine. 2021. *Implementing High-Quality Primary Care: Rebuilding the Foundation of Health Care.* Washington, DC: National Academies Press. https://doi.org/10.17226/25983.

Nichols, E., C. E. I. Szoeke, S. E. Vollset, N. Abbasi, F. Abd-Allah, J. Abdela, M. T. E. Aichour, et al. 2019. "Global, Regional, and National Burden of Alzheimer's Disease and Other Dementias, 1990–2016: A Systematic Analysis for the Global Burden of Disease Study 2016." *The Lancet Neurology* 18 (1): 88–106. https://doi.org/https://doi.org/10.1016/s1474-4422(18)30403-4.

O'Suilleabhain, P. S., S. Gallagher, and A. Steptoe. 2019. "Loneliness, Living Alone, and All-Cause Mortality: The Role of Emotional and Social Loneliness in the Elderly During 19 Years of Follow-Up." *Psychosomatic Medicine* 81 (6): 521–26. https://doi.org/10.1097/PSY.0000000000000710.

OECD (Organisation for Economic Co-operation and Development). 2021. *Health at a Glance 2021: OECD Indicators.* Paris: OECD Publishing.

OECD (Organisation for Economic Co-operation and Development) and European Union. 2013. *A Good Life in Old Age? Monitoring and Improving Quality in Long-term Care.* OECD Health Policy Studies. Paris: OECD Publishing.

Ouslander, J. G., and D. C. Grabowski. 2020. "COVID-19 in Nursing Homes: Calming the Perfect Storm." *Journal of the American Geriatrics Society* 68 (10): 2153–62.

Pew Research Center. 2020. "With Billions Confined to Their Homes Worldwide, Which Living Arrangements Are Most Common?" Pew Research Center, Washington, DC. https://www.pewresearch.org/fact-tank/2020/03/31/with-billions-confined-to -their-homes-worldwide-which-living-arrangements-are-most-common/.

Pham, H. H., D. Schrag, A. S. O'Malley, B. Wu, and P. B. Bach. 2007. "Care Patterns in Medicare and Their Implications for Pay for Performance." *New England Journal of Medicine* 356 (11): 1130–39. https://doi.org/https://doi.org/10.1056/nejmsa063979.

Pilleron, S., D. Sarfati, M. Janssen-Heijnen, J. Vignat, J. Ferlay, F. Bray, and I. Soerjomataram. 2019. "Global Cancer Incidence in Older Adults, 2012 and 2035: A Population-Based Study." *International Journal of Cancer* 144 (1): 49–58. https://doi .org/10.1002/ijc.31664.

Prince, M. J., F. Wu, Y. Guo, L. M. Gutierrez Robledo, M. O'Donnell, R. Sullivan, and S. Yusuf. 2015. "The Burden of Disease in Older People and Implications for Health Policy and Practice." *The Lancet* 385 (9967): 549–62. https://doi.org/10.1016/S0140 -6736(14)61347-7.

Reinhard, S., L. F. Feinberg, A. Houser, R. Choula, and M. Evans. 2019. "Valuing the Invaluable: 2019 Update Charting a Path Forward." AARP Public Policy Institute, Washington, DC. https://www.aarp.org/ppi/info-2015/valuing-the-invaluable-2015 -update.html.

Roy, M., C. B. Moore, I. Sikazwe, and C. B. Holmes. 2019. "A Review of Differentiated Service Delivery for HIV Treatment: Effectiveness, Mechanisms, Targeting, and Scale." *Current HIV/AIDS Reports* 16 (4): 324–34. https://doi.org/10.1007/s11904 -019-00454-5.

Saito, J., M. Haseda, A. Amemiya, D. Takagi, K. Kondo, and N. Kondo. 2019. "Community-Based Care for Healthy Ageing: Lessons from Japan." *Bulletin of the World Health Organization* 97 (8): 570–74. https://doi.org/10.2471/blt.18.223057.

Shortell, S. M. 2021. "Reflections on the Five Laws of Integrating Medical and Social Services—21 Years Later." *Milbank Quarterly* 99 (1): 91–98. https://doi.org/10.1111 /1468-0009.12495.

Starfield, B. 1992. *Primary Care: Concept, Evaluation, and Policy*. New York: Oxford University Press.

Suzman, R., J. R. Beard, T. Boerma, and S. Chatterji. 2015. "Health in an Ageing World— What Do We Know?" *The Lancet* 385 (9967): 484–86. https://doi.org/10.1016 /s0140-6736(14)61597-x.

Threapleton, D. E., R. Y. Chung, S. Y. S. Wong, E. Wong, P. Chau, J. Woo, V. C. H. Chung, and E. K. Yeoh. 2017. "Integrated Care for Older Populations and Its Implementation Facilitators and Barriers: A Rapid Scoping Review." *International Journal of Quality Health Care* 29 (3): 327–34. https://doi.org/10.1093/intqhc/mzx041.

Uijen, A. A., H. J. Schers, F. G. Schellevis, and W. J. van den Bosch. 2012. "How Unique Is Continuity of Care? A Review of Continuity and Related Concepts." *Family Practice* 29 (3): 264–71. https://doi.org/10.1093/fampra/cmr104.

UN DESA Population Division (United Nations Department of Economic and Social Affairs Population Division). 2019a. *World Population Prospects 2019: Highlights*. New York: UN DESA.

UN DESA Population Division (United Nations Department of Economic and Social Affairs Population Division). 2019b. "World Population Prospects 2019: Ten Key Findings." New York: UN DESA.

Valentijn, P. P., S. M. Schepman, W. Opheij, and M. A. Bruijnzeels. 2013. "Understanding Integrated Care: A Comprehensive Conceptual Framework Based on the Integrative Functions of Primary Care." *International Journal of Integrative Care* 13: e010. https:// doi.org/10.5334/ijic.886.

Veillard, J., K. Cowling, A. Bitton, H. Ratcliffe, M. Kimball, S. Barkley, L. Mercereau, et al. 2017. "Better Measurement for Performance Improvement in Low-and

Middle-Income Countries: The Primary Health Care Performance Initiative (PHCPI) Experience of Conceptual Framework Development and Indicator Selection." *Milbank Quarterly* 95 (4): 836–83. https://doi.org/10.1111/1468-0009.12301.

Walley, J., J. E. Lawn, A. Tinker, A. de Francisco, M. Chopra, I. Rudan, Z. A. Bhutta, R. E. Black, and *The Lancet* Alma-Ata Working Group. 2008. "Primary Health Care: Making Alma-Ata a Reality." *The Lancet* 372 (9642): 1001–7. https://doi.org/10.1016/S0140-6736(08)61409-9.

Wastesson, J. W., L. Morin, E. C. K. Tan, and K. Johnell. 2018. "An Update on the Clinical Consequences of Polypharmacy in Older Adults: A Narrative Review." *Expert Opinion on Drug Safety* 17 (12): 1185–96. https://doi.org/10.1080/14740338.2018.1546841.

WHO (World Health Organization). 1978. "Declaration of Alma-Ata. International Conference on Primary Health Care, Alma-Ata, USSR, 6–12 September 1978." World Health Organization (Alma-Ata, USSR). https://www.who.int/teams/social-determinants-of-health/declaration-of-alma-ata.

WHO (World Health Organization). 2015. *World Report on Ageing and Health.* Geneva: WHO. https://apps.who.int/iris/handle/10665/186463.

WHO (World Health Organization). 2016. "Framework on Integrated, People-Centred Health Services." WHO, Geneva. https://apps.who.int/iris/handle/10665/252698.

WHO (World Health Organization). 2017. *Integrated Care for Older People: Guidelines on Community-Level Interventions to Manage Declines in Intrinsic Capacity.* Geneva: WHO. https://www.who.int/publications/i/item/9789241550109.

WHO (World Health Organization). 2019. *Declaration of Astana: Global Conference on Primary Health Care: Astana, Kazakhstan, 25 and 26 October 2018.* Geneva: WHO. https://www.who.int/publications/i/item/WHO-HIS-SDS-2018.61.

Wilson, B. S., D. L. Tucci, G. M. O'Donoghue, M. H. Merson, and H. Frankish. 2019. "A Lancet Commission to Address the Global Burden of Hearing Loss." *The Lancet* 393 (10186): 2106–08. https://doi.org/10.1016/S0140-6736(19)30484-2.

Wimo, A., M. Guerchet, G. C. Ali, Y. T. Wu, A. M. Prina, B. Winblad, L. Jonsson, Z. Liu, and M. Prince. 2017. "The Worldwide Costs of Dementia 2015 and Comparisons with 2010." *Alzheimers and Dementia* 13 (1): 1–7. https://doi.org/10.1016/j.jalz.2016.07.150.

World Bank. 2021. *Walking the Talk: Reimagining Primary Health Care after COVID-19.* Washington, DC: World Bank. https://www.worldbank.org/en/topic/health/publication/walking-the-walk-reimagining-primary-health-care-after-covid-19-a-health-nutrition-and-population-global-practice-flagsh.

Zhou, B., R. M. Carrillo-Larco, G. Danaei, L. M. Riley, C. J. Paciorek, G. A. Stevens, E. W. Gregg, et al. 2021. "Worldwide Trends in Hypertension Prevalence and Progress in Treatment and Control from 1990 to 2019: A Pooled Analysis of 1,201 Population-Representative Studies with 104 Million Participants." *The Lancet* 398 (10304): 957–80. https://doi.org/https://doi.org/10.1016/s0140-6736(21)01330-1.

Zulman, D. M., S. B. Martins, Y. Liu, S. W. Tu, B. B. Hoffman, S. M. Asch, and M. K. Goldstein. 2015. "Using a Clinical Knowledge Base to Assess Comorbidity Interrelatedness among Patients with Multiple Chronic Conditions." *AMIA Annual Symposium Proceedings* 2015: 1381–89. https://www.ncbi.nlm.nih.gov/pmc/articles/PMC4765555/.

CHAPTER 2

Financing Primary Health Care for Older Adults: Framework and Applications

Victoria Y. Fan, Jigyasa Sharma, and Xiaohui Hou

Key Messages

- Population aging affects primary health care (PHC) through channels including increased demand for medical services, care coordination challenges related to rising multimorbidity and chronic disease burdens, and greater need for links between and referrals to specialist medical care and social services.

- Population aging has major impacts on macroeconomic and political resources.

- A life-course perspective on aging emphasizes how health earlier in life may affect one's health status at older ages, which has implications for health financing policy choices such as setting age cutoffs for certain health benefits versus adopting universal coverage.

- The financing framework presented in this chapter focuses on three key considerations: population eligibility criteria, benefits package design, and the means of financing.

- Applying the financing framework to country cases shows that countries can choose different paths to finance PHC services while considering population eligibility, benefits packages, and the means of financing.

Introduction

As a country's population ages, policy makers are increasingly called upon to address older people's health needs (Beard et al. 2016). In particular, access to PHC services for older adults requires health financing—the generation and allocation of resources for health—so that older adults can obtain high-quality PHC when needed without financial hardship (Bitton et al. 2017).

Public policy makers seeking to develop health financing options need to weigh at least three questions critical to achieving universal health coverage: First, who is or will be covered? Second, what are they covered for? Third, how are resources currently raised, how much is publicly financed, and how will resources be raised in the future (WHO 2015)? Put differently, health financing options must specify population eligibility, the benefits package, and revenue mobilization, among other things.

The objective of this chapter is to support policy makers' decision processes related to health financing, the first pillar of the financing, innovation, regulation, and evaluation (FIRE) model. The chapter is organized as follows. First, conceptual background on population aging relevant to PHC financing is introduced. Second, the chapter presents a financing framework that addresses PHC for older adults, which serves to clarify and organize policy options under the first domain of FIRE. Third, the framework is applied to seven countries spanning global regions and with disparate health financing systems. From these case studies, lessons are drawn that other countries may adapt as they seek to finance PHC for aging populations. The chapter concludes with recommendations for policy makers.

The analysis presented here focuses on financing for PHC. Approaches to long-term care (LTC) financing are not considered. LTC financing has been extensively analyzed in WHO (2021), and readers may refer to that important discussion. Later in this volume, issues pertinent to LTC financing are considered in the context of analyses of service delivery innovation (chapter 3) and governance (chapter 5) and in the case study of Japan's community-based integrated care system (chapter 7).

Conceptual Background

Understanding aging as a human phenomenon requires understanding it at both the individual level and the population level, that is, at the level of groups of individuals (Beard and Bloom 2015). People age differently over the course of their lives, but groups of people, whether at the community, society, or country level, also have different patterns of aging. This chapter refers to group or collective aging as *population aging* to describe how a given population's aging can be summarized and compared with that of other groups.

How Aging Affects Primary Health Care

Financing plays a critical role in shaping the system in which primary care functions. Well-designed financing can not only enhance the level of coordination across medical specialties, including mental health, but also enhance the links that older adults need for accessing social care and social services. Such services include transportation, housing, food, and ultimately LTC services, which are needed to meet a person's health *and* personal care needs.

At the individual level, the stages of human development over the life course—birth, growth, aging, and death—are universal (Kuruvilla et al. 2018). As one ages and the incidence of chronic diseases and morbidities rises

(GBD 2019 Diseases and Injuries Collaborators 2020), the complex interaction of these multiple comorbidities can require health care services spanning different medical specialties (Aggarwal, Woolford, and Patel 2020; Wittenberg 2015). Frailty and disability also increase with age, affecting one's ability to conduct activities of daily living such as bathing and eating (Apóstolo et al. 2018; Costenoble et al. 2021; Fried et al. 2004; Ofori-Asenso et al. 2019). A PHC provider[1] often serves as the linchpin in the coordination and integration of care across multiple morbidities while also providing person-centered care (Baxter et al. 2018; Peterson et al. 2019; Powell Davies et al. 2008; Wagner et al. 2014). PHC can therefore play a central role in the care of an older adult, which becomes especially critical when multiple comorbidities increase the complexity of care (Kogan, Wilber, and Mosqueda 2016; Mitchell, Tieman, and Shelby-James 2008; Smith et al. 2012).

In many high-income countries, the compartmentalization of health care into distinct specialties organized by biomedical disease can result in a lack of coordination and integration of person-centered care, which, in turn, can lead to fragmentation and low efficiency (for example, duplicate diagnostic tests) or low quality (for example, dangerous interactions of multiple prescribed medications, or polypharmacy, without coordination) (Monaco et al. 2020; Nothelle et al. 2022). Primary care can also improve health and help avert the use of costly inpatient services (Macinko, Starfield, and Erinosho 2009; Macinko, Starfield, and Shi 2003; Starfield, Shi, and Macinko 2005).

The importance of maintaining mental health also heightens as a person ages, in part because of the social isolation and decreased self-efficacy that can come with aging and reduced mobility and the debilitating, degenerative neurological conditions that disproportionately affect older adults, such as Alzheimer's and related dementias (Evans et al. 2019; Malcolm, Frost, and Cowie 2019). Beyond the coordination of care for physical illnesses, PHC can play an indispensable role in ensuring that the health care system engages each person *as a person* rather than an illness to be resolved. Such a holistic focus includes sensitivity toward the social determinants of health and therefore incorporates considerations of people's mental and social well-being as much as their physical condition (Davis et al. 2015; Mulvaney-Day et al. 2018; Teunissen et al. 2017). The effectiveness of primary care can thus be further enhanced when it is linked to social care and services, social determinants of health, and mental health services (Allen 2018; Allen et al. 2020; Hewner et al. 2017).

However, the success with which primary care can fulfill the care coordination function often depends on the particular configuration of two system-level features—first, the organizational architecture of the system or system architecture, that is, the relationships between the health payer or payers and the health provider organizations and, second, the robustness of the gatekeeping function of the primary care provider within that system (Roberts et al. 2008; Sripa et al. 2019). The configuration of the system architecture dictates the configuration of gatekeeping.

In some high-income countries such as the United Kingdom, and in some health maintenance organizations in the United States (such as

Kaiser Permanente), a patient first sees a primary care provider as the initial point of contact, or gatekeeper, who makes referrals to specialists as needed. The gatekeeping function has powerful benefits to health (through increased coordination of clinical services across specialties for a given patient) and the control of health care costs, a challenge for all countries (Espinosa-González et al. 2021; Rotar et al. 2018; Sripa et al. 2019). In the United States, in general, the low level of coordination of primary care stems in part from low consumer demand for gatekeeping in health plans (often argued as a reflection of con-sumer preference), compounded further by a fragmented system architecture (Gérvas, Pérez Fernández, and Starfield 1994).

The Importance of a Life-Course Perspective

Although the term "older adult" implies a certain age cutoff, the quality of aging depends not just on a person's chronological age but also on factors such as his or her access to PHC and ability to pay for health care costs, especially earlier in life. A life-course perspective on aging, rather than a narrow focus on adults older than a particular age, recognizes that the rate of aging, and therefore the quality of aging, depends on, and is influenced by, a wide range of sociohistorical events, personal and systemic experiences, life transitions, and environmental exposures that begin early in life—indeed some as early as gestation or birth—and continue throughout life (Chapko et al. 2018; Martínez-Mesa et al. 2013; McAdams and Olson 2010; Yaffe et al. 2021).

A life-course perspective on aging incorporates at least three key concepts—healthy aging, the compression of morbidity, and later health outcomes. The concept of "healthy aging" reflects the notion that even as one ages, one can continue to have good health, and that policies and programs support healthy aging. A corollary concept to healthy aging is that of "compression of morbidity," which occurs when morbidity is concentrated—and possibly reduced—toward the end of one's life (Fries 1980, 2005; Fries, Bruce, and Chakravarty 2011; Olshansky and Carnes 2019). Compression of morbidity may indicate that the amount of time a person spends in a state of poor health or disability is reduced. The opposite of compression, or the extension of morbidity, may also be true; some individuals may live longer but experience a longer period of disability.

However, there is no guarantee that healthy aging occurs universally; people may live longer without living in states of better health. How groups of people age differs across countries and populations. A person who is age 60 in India may be aging, on average, quite differently from a person who is age 60 in Japan.

Given the population differences in healthy aging and compression of morbidity, one key determinant may be experiences earlier in life. Research has found that one's health at an older age can be affected profoundly by one's health at a younger age, including as early as in utero (for example, flu or fam-ine exposure in utero), during childhood (for example, childhood obesity), or during young adulthood (Almond and Currie 2011; Rasmussen 2001). Early shocks to health, including from infectious or acute illness, can have long-term health consequences. As such, differences across populations in quality of aging are also expected. When comparing communities that differ in exposures to infectious disease, the quality of aging may diverge substantially decades later.

Population Aging Affects Macroeconomic and Political Resources

Population age structure and demographic transitions can create macroeconomic and political resources to drive reforms in health financing and policy change (Bloom et al. 2015).

The demographic transition theory is crucial to understanding population aging. This theory refers to how a population's age structure changes over decades, typically starting with a decline in mortality, followed by a decline in fertility (Bloom and Williamson 1998). That pattern leads to a population bulge—a growth in the number of people who are of working age and considered "economically productive" or in the prime years of life. Countries that take advantage of this demographic transition can also reap what is called the "demographic dividend," which can result in rapid economic growth, higher standards of living, and improvements to human capital and the economy (Bloom et al. 2009; Bloom, Canning, and Sevilla 2003).

This generational bulge in the population of the economically productive age group can lead to a boom in resources and economic expansion, creating more tax revenue and public resources for financing health care. Such large-scale resource shifts that accompany the changing structure of a nation's population age pyramid have important practical implications for national transfer accounts (D'Albis and Moosa 2015; Kuhn and Prettner 2018; Lee and Mason 2011). National transfer accounts offer a measure of the flow of economic resources from one age group to another. A clear understanding of intergenerational economic flows across age groups can help strategic planners and policy makers, including health care planners, make population-based spending and investment decisions—for example, whether Generation Xers can generate enough income to support the Social Security and health care needs of aging baby boomers in the United States. By shedding light on the current and future economic impact of changes in population age structure, national transfer accounts underscore the fact that, if managed well, the resources generated by one age group during its prime years could be used to support the health care and other consumption needs of a future generation, or of that generation itself as it ages.

The converse is also true: with inadequate resource planning, countries may be forced to face the reality that, despite the growing needs of an aging population, insufficient resources are available and countermeasures such as inbound immigration or increased fertility are inadequate in the short term to meet the gap.

Political and resource considerations also influence any policy change. The age of a country's leaders and of the most influential political constituencies can increase or diminish the priority that the country's political processes assign to the financing of PHC for older adults (Campbell 2002). In many countries, national leaders are, on average, older than the populations they govern. In democratic societies, older generations may also be more politically vocal, in part from wider reading and more time to participate in political processes (Quintelier 2007). A population boom for a given generation can thus be a significant political force in shaping public policy–making priorities. These political considerations are vital when weighing the viability of public reforms for universal health coverage (UHC) or reforms to address PHC financing for older adults.

Financing Framework for PHC of Older Adults

Financing is one of the key levers or tools available to policy makers with which to directly affect the accessibility, quality, and efficiency of health care services. From the perspective of a payer or government sponsor, financing for health care is the creation and allocation of resources. This book uses and integrates two key typologies to understand health financing; see figure 2.1.

The first typology is the concept of a universal health coverage cube developed by the World Health Organization (WHO), which examines health coverage along three key dimensions—population eligibility (who is covered), benefits packages (what is covered), and financial risk protection (how much is paid from pooled or public sources vs. out of pocket) (WHO 2015). These three dimensions are vital considerations for all health financing options—and each of them has political and economic ramifications.

The second typology, articulated by Roberts et al. (2008) and Hsiao (2003), emphasizes health financing in terms of the means of financing, including

FIGURE 2.1 Financing Framework for Population Eligibility, Benefits Package, and Means of Financing

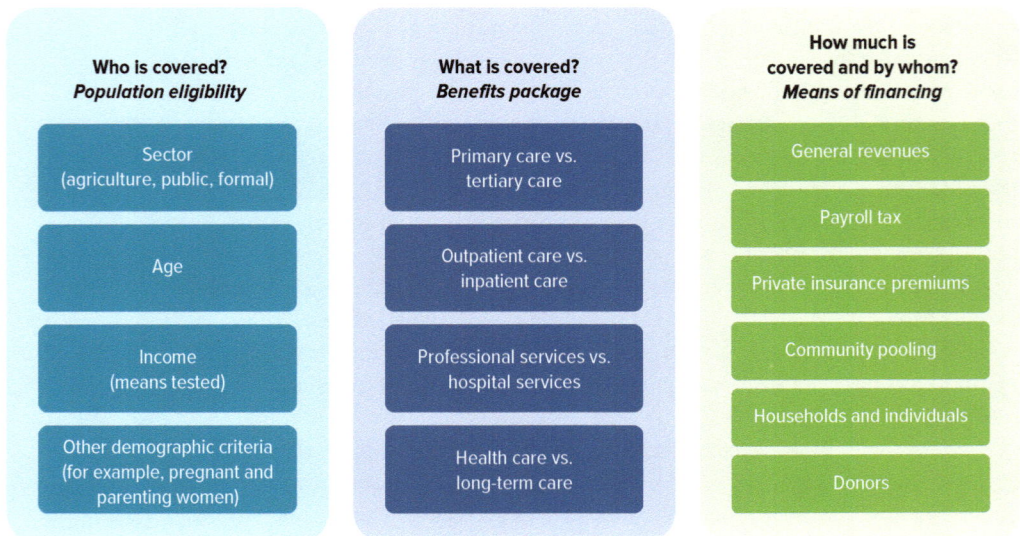

Source: Original figure for this publication.

public financing. This definition of financing encompasses general revenues, payroll taxes, private insurance premiums (with or without employer subsidies), community pooling, individual and household out-of-pocket expenses, and external sources, including donor funding.

Of these sources of financing, individual and household expenditures are the only source of "nonpooled" funding, that is, not pooled from an insurance risk perspective. The other sources represent, to some extent, pooled sources of financing. Although the out-of-pocket share is emphasized in the WHO (2015) framework, this chapter makes a novel contribution to integrate the out-of-pocket spending concept from WHO (2015) with the means of financing concept from Roberts et al. (2008) into a single framework; see figure 2.1. In addition, in some countries, the hospital serves as the payer of last resort, particularly in countries where there is a lack of UHC and where hospitals are prohibited from refusing care to any patient even if the patient lacks health insurance (Garthwaite, Gross, and Notowidigdo 2018). Hospitals that offer care to underserved populations in rural areas may also serve as payers whose financing comes from other sources. In that sense, financing either comes from the cross-subsidization of other sources of revenue that the hospital generates or otherwise is borne by the hospital itself.

The other tools identified by Roberts et al. (2008), such as payment, organization, regulation, and behavior change, are beyond the scope of this book. Financing is commonly viewed as similar to, or the same as, the policy tool of payment. Unlike financing, payment is the mechanism of paying health care providers to deliver a specific service (for example, fee for service or capitation), which can be decoupled to some extent from the way resources are financed or revenues are generated, often through public financing. But many health financing considerations cannot be separated from, and are closely integrated with, the design of payment policies and organizational policies and system architecture. The way a health system is financed depends crucially on how the system is organized and how the payers pay the providers, or what is called the organizational architecture of a health system, or system architecture, in this chapter.

It has been argued that financing is the most important lever or policy tool because it also shapes, and can greatly influence, payment policies and organizational and system architecture. The availability of new financing (which can occur through tax surplus, among other scenarios) or the absence of financing (which can occur in a recession) can sometimes drive new policies and reforms in light of new or limited resources available to the government.

The Critical Role of Public Financing

Both the WHO (2015) framework and the Roberts et al. (2008) framework implicitly emphasize the role of public payers in financing health care services as well as financial risk as a key goal of UHC (WHO 2015) or an outcome of a health system (Roberts et al. 2008). But work on the health financing transition makes an explicit link between how public financing reduces financial risk, which is typically measured by out-of-pocket spending in health care.

Thus, work on the health financing transition emphasizes the critical role of public financing as countries move toward the UHC goal of reducing financial risk arising from out-of-pocket spending (Fan and Savedoff 2014; Savedoff et al. 2012). As countries grow richer and age, public financing tends to increase as a share of total health care spending, but whether countries move toward greater financial risk protection depends on the use of public financing to reduce financial risk from out-of-pocket health spending. Put differently, financial risk protection and public financing are closely linked, with public financing serving as a critical driver of protection against the financial risks of ill health and health care costs, which present in the form of out-of-pocket spending. The extent to which health coverage protects an individual against the financial risks of illness and high health care costs depends greatly on the type of public financing mechanism.

Aging is a significant driver not only of increased health spending but also of the public financing of health care services and of out-of-pocket spending in particular (figure 2.2) (Fan and Savedoff 2014). As a population ages, a critical window of opportunity can open for increased public financing— either through a political opportunity created by greater vote share or through economic resources generated in part through the demographic dividend. Thus, as a country develops economically and its population ages, policy makers have the opportunity to use resources to increase the share of health spending that is pooled rather than out of pocket.

FIGURE 2.2 Out-of-Pocket Spending as a Percentage of Current Health Expenditure and Population Age 65 and Older as a Percentage of Total Population, 2019

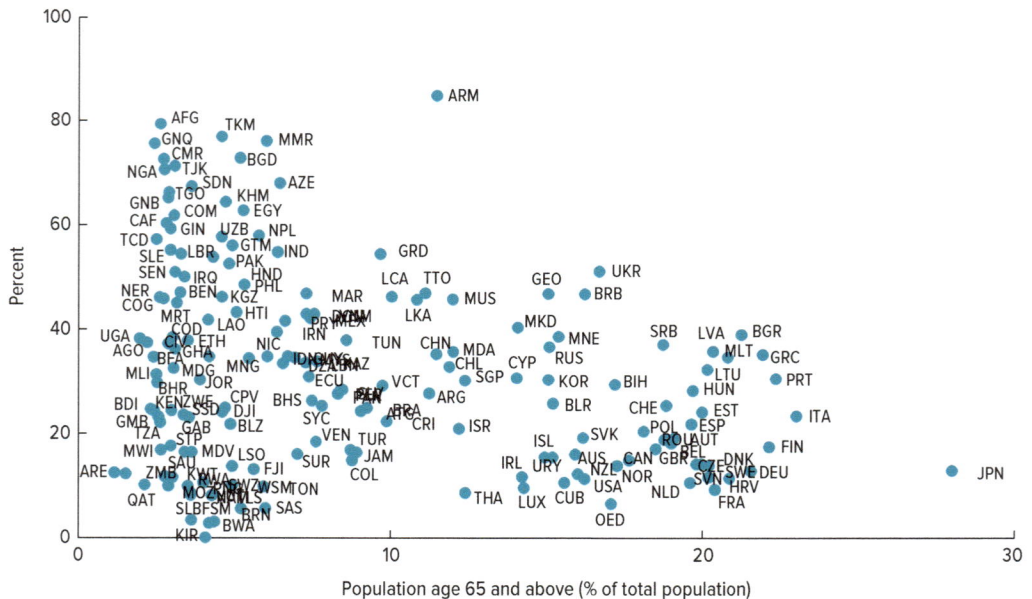

Sources: Data from WHO Global Health Expenditure Database and World Bank Open Data (accessed March 20, 2022).
Note: Country labels are International Standards Organization (ISO) 3-digit alphabetic codes.

The Importance of Pooling Across Population Strata

Public financing also requires an understanding of the importance of pooling resources across population strata or subgroups, which is, in turn, a form of insurance and cross-subsidization over the life course (that is, saving money before one gets old and sick) and over groups of people (that is, pooling resources between young and old people and between rich and poor people). Pooled financing allows funds from one strata to be shared with, and to insure, those in another strata, enabling the healthy to cross-subsidize the sick, or the rich to cross-subsidize the poor. Pooling funds across different population strata is necessary to help insure against the uncertain risks of ill health and helps create a buffer against unexpected shocks and losses from ill health.

Understanding the population age structure is crucial in intergenerational pooling, financing, and planning for PHC services across the generations, even when making plans for transfers and cross-subsidization across socioeconomic strata and classes. Planning for health financing and insurance, therefore, needs a qualified multidisciplinary planning workforce comprising demographers, statisticians, actuaries, analysts, and data scientists who can accurately analyze the population age structure alongside other financing and economic issues.

Many Roads to Expanding Coverage

Many roads lead to UHC. Each country may take a slightly different path to expanding coverage toward UHC, either incrementally or comprehensively, through the expansion of benefits by population eligibility or by benefits packages (figure 2.1). In the case of population eligibility, countries vary in the path they take to cover older adults, the disabled, specific sectors and occupations, or certain demographic groups. Policy makers inevitably face hard decisions about whom to cover and for which services and how to mobilize resources, given the economic and political situation of their country.

Further, population eligibility, the benefits package, and the means of financing have major implementation considerations. Earlier use in this chapter of terms such as "healthy" versus "sick," and "rich" versus "poor," were convenient but dichotomous and simplistic—used to convey the big picture outlook. In contrast, public policy has the difficult challenge of making these terms tractable, pragmatic, and implementable through specific definitions in the context of real policy and programmatic decisions and rules.

Making population eligibility a tractable and implementable concept is not a trivial task. For policy makers, simplicity of implementation can sometimes trump equity considerations. Bright-line concepts that are easily verifiable, such as chronological age, may be perceived as an easier category for population eligibility cutoff than a means-tested mechanism that might enable redistribution from rich to poor but would compound the political dynamics of population aging.

At the same time, policy makers must also weigh the challenge of expanding care toward universal population coverage within a given political window of opportunity for reform. The risk of using an age criterion for determining eligibility as a statutory cutoff for coverage can persist well after a law or policy is established. Future generations could receive a fragmented, age-based eligibility legacy system in an entrenched political and commercial environment that makes expansion of coverage challenging, if not infeasible. Interests become entrenched, and a stable but fragmented system emerges, even as the country faces significant need gaps in the segments of its population that are covered.

The classic case is that of the United States, which, since 1965, when the policy was first established, has continued to rely on a bright-line age criterion of 65 and older to define those who are "aged." Despite the occasional call to lower the threshold to 60 or 55 years old, reforms to expand Medicare have failed to gain any traction. Yet building in the elements of reform can be crucial to helping ensure that a system does not stay stagnant with a frozen criterion.

Similarly, implementation challenges persist in the face of mandating health benefits packages that are to be covered by public or private insurance programs. For example, it is not easy to compare benefits packages covered under public insurance programs internationally, given the lack of centralized resources or databases across countries, even in the presence of international health informatics standards that classify procedures and treatments. Additionally, the creation of benefits packages may be couched in existing classification and health informatics terminologies[2] that are complex and hard to implement, in part because they depend on information technology, or because they require low- and middle-income countries to adapt them before they can implement them.

Also, there are other issues of lack of uniformity across countries and regions. What one country means by "primary health care" may differ slightly from what another country means by it. In figure 2.1, the coverage for benefit packages outlines a variety of commonly used dichotomies, such as primary care vs. tertiary care, outpatient vs. inpatient care, professional services vs. hospital services, and health care vs. long-term care. These terms tend to reinforce dichotomies as mutually exclusive choices for policy makers, rather than emphasizing the role of primary care in integration across services, linkages to care, referrals, as gatekeeper, or care coordinator.

Thus, the extent to which countries or payers can deliberately design and implement a benefits package requires a specific conceptual framework that is tractable enough that it can be implemented even with a limited health informatics and information technology infrastructure. Typically, to determine what is covered in the benefits package, hundreds, if not thousands, of possible interventions that clinicians may provide to a patient need to be defined and classified. Whereas interventions in other sectors are well defined and arguably limited in scope (for example, education), the health care sector has a seemingly endless inventory of possible clinical and medical interventions, drugs, treatments, therapies, and procedures. Many reputable groups, including the United Kingdom's National Institute for Clinical Excellence, Thailand's Health Intervention and Technology Assessment Program, and others, have argued that health technology assessments are needed as an institutional mechanism to reduce the complexity of the vast array of interventions but also, and equally important, to ensure the cost-effectiveness, equity, and good value of national investments in a particular package of benefits. Thus, the creation of simplistic and dichotomous categories of care groupings are necessary for operations to reduce the complexity of health care, but their persistence also reinforces mutually exclusive approaches, such as primary care rather than tertiary care, as opposed to inclusive approaches, such as primary care with tertiary care. These simplistic categories are then, in turn, used for financing and payment design.

Despite the confusion and complexity of the benefits package, from a patient perspective, availability and access to the wide range of interventions that are typical in a hospital setting often make hospital care appear to be of "better" quality than that seen in a primary care setting, in part because of the availability of one-stop shop services for pharmacy and imaging, and greater specialization and availability of medical professionals. This chapter argues that the organization and delivery of the benefits package is just as important as the design of the benefits package contents. A primary care clinic that lacks a tertiary care referral site or adequate medicines may lack demand from patients. Thus, understanding patients' perspectives on the quality of primary care is important in designing the organization and delivery of the benefits package. Financing the package alone, including raising the resources to pay for expanded benefits and expanded population coverage, as important as it is, is not sufficient to implement a primary care policy.

Finally, the implementation challenges of the means of financing are also substantial, particularly because as countries develop their economies and industries change, so do their available resources. A country's ability to generate resources through general revenues or payroll taxes hinges on public sector capacity and implementation and enforcement mechanisms. A country's transition from rural to urban, from the informal to the formal sector, and from agriculture to manufacturing or other means of economic production, and the capacity of its public sector and taxing authorities, are all factors that policy makers must consider in determining the means of financing for health care coverage, including for older adults. Governments need to be able to tap into changing revenue sources and arrange financial systems to finance primary care.

A Review of Selected Country Cases

To illustrate how this financing framework applies to primary care in the form of a benefits package for older adults (a population eligibility criterion), financing systems across a range of selected countries and regions were reviewed. The selected countries are presented in figure 2.3 and table 2.1, revealing some variation in the percentage of out-of-pocket spending compared to the percentage of people age 65 and older. Information on the country cases was compared to glean lessons for financing PHC for older adults.

This literature review included the PubMed database and websites of the WHO, the World Bank, and national agencies. Resources from the WHO and the World Bank also provided key information about countries' health systems. Resources from the WHO Alliance for Health Policy and System Research

FIGURE 2.3 Selected Country Case Studies: Out-of-Pocket Spending as a Percentage of Current Health Expenditure and Population Age 65 Years and Older as a Percentage of the Total Population, 2019

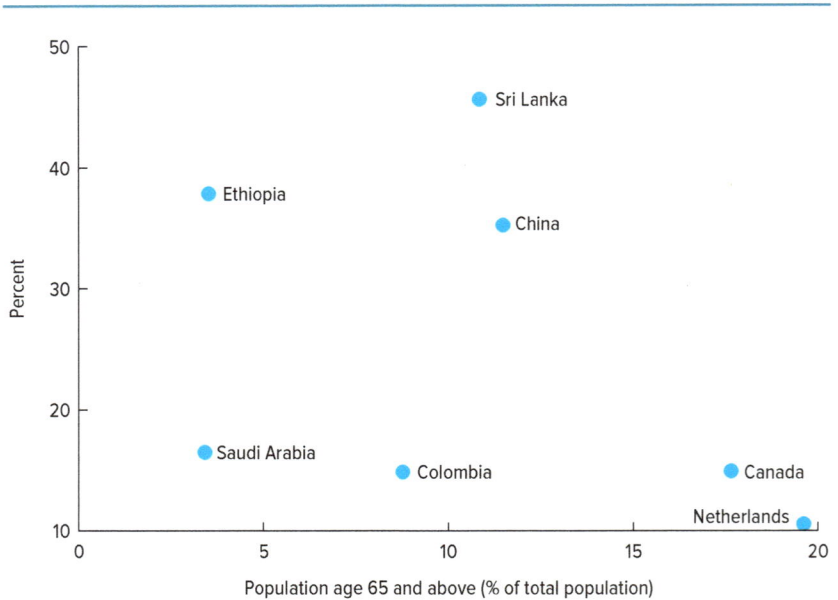

Sources: World Health Organization Global Health Expenditure Database for out-of-pocket spending; World Bank Open Data for population data (accessed March 20, 2022).

and the WHO Health Systems in Transition series, in partnership with the European Observatory (or North American Observatory, or the Asia Pacific Observatory) on Health Systems and Policies were also used. National ministry and government websites were also reviewed. The MEDLINE (PubMed) database was searched on March 20, 2022. Study abstracts were examined if there was discussion of PHC or LTC for older adults in the title or abstract of the article for a given country.[3]

The seven countries selected span the diversity of population size and health expenditure variables across the World Bank's regions and income groupings. Three high-income countries (Canada, the Netherlands, and Saudi Arabia), three middle-income countries (Colombia, China, and Sri Lanka), and one low-income country (Ethiopia) were selected. The country with the smallest population chosen was the Netherlands (17 million); the largest was China (1.4 billion). The Netherlands had the highest population 65 and older (19.6 percent), and Saudi Arabia had the lowest (3.4 percent). The Netherlands also had the highest annual per capita health expenditure (US$5,335) and the lowest percentage of out-of-pocket spending (10.6 percent). Sri Lanka had the highest percentage of out-of-pocket spending (45.6 percent). These country cases are summarized in tables 2.2 and 2.3.

TABLE 2.1 Summary of Countries Selected for Review

Country (model)	Population (thousands)	Population age 65 and older (% of total population)	Current health expenditure per capita (US$)	Current health expenditure as share of GDP (%)	Out-of-pocket expenditure as share of current health expenditure (%)	Primary health care expenditure as share of current health expenditure (%)
The Netherlands (Social Insurance)	17,282	19.6	5,335	10.1	10.6	31.9
Colombia (National Health Insurance)	50,339	8.8	495	7.7	14.9	—
Canada (National Health Insurance)	37,411	17.6	5,048	10.8	14.9	47.6
Saudi Arabia (Social Insurance; National Health Service)	34,269	3.4	1,316	5.7	16.5	—
China (Social Insurance)	1,433,784	11.5	535	5.4	35.2	20.1
Ethiopia (National Health Service)	112,079	3.5	27	3.2	37.9	77.2
Sri Lanka (National Health Service)	21,324	10.8	161	4.1	45.6	36.5

Sources: World Health Organization Global Health Expenditure Database for health care spending and total population; the World Bank Open Data for population data (accessed March 20, 2022).
Note: Countries are listed in order of out-of-pocket spending as a percentage of current health expenditure, indicating the level of pooled financing is higher as the percentage of out-of-pocket spending decreases. GDP = gross domestic product. — = not available.

TABLE 2.2 Eligibility Criteria, Premium, Cost Sharing, and Market Structure in Selected Countries

Country	Eligibility criteria, premium, cost sharing, and market structure
The Netherlands	Individuals are required to participate in the social health insurance and long-term care insurance model, with no explicit age criteria. Mixed public and private provision.
Colombia	Individuals must participate in the contributory or the subsidized insurance regime, and all individuals may benefit from the public health benefits plan, with no explicit age criteria. Mixed public and private provision.
Canada	Individuals are required to participate in the national health insurance program, with no explicit age criteria. Mixed public and private provision.
Saudi Arabia	Individuals are required to participate in a social health insurance model, with no explicit age criteria. All citizens and public sector employees are eligible to receive care in publicly provided facilities.
China	Eligibility is dependent on ability to pay and location of residence. More than 80 percent of the population are covered by basic medical insurance schemes, with variation in premium, premium subsidies, and cost sharing depending on local administration in urban or rural areas. No explicit age criteria. Mixed public and private provision. The voluntary private health insurance market is growing.
Ethiopia	Care is predominantly publicly provided with a sliding-scale fee schedule based on poverty level. A community-based health insurance program covers more than 80 percent of the population, and eligibility is dependent on program roll-out, with no explicit age criteria. Predominantly public provision.
Sri Lanka	All individuals of any age may use publicly provided services at no cost; no explicit age criteria. Individuals may opt out and pay out of pocket in the private market. Cost sharing in the private market is borne entirely by consumers unless purchasing voluntary health insurance (very limited) or participating in limited social insurance plans. No premium subsidies. Mixed public and private provision. The voluntary private health insurance market is growing.

Source: Original table for this publication.

TABLE 2.3 Role of Primary Care for Coordination, Gatekeeping, and Referrals to Long-Term Care

Country	Role of primary care for coordination and gatekeeping
The Netherlands	Gatekeeping is enforced for secondary care.
Colombia	Unclear role of gatekeeping, although plans functioning as managed care organizations may use selective contracting and alter provider network coverage and implement rules for referrals.
Canada	Gatekeeping is enforced for secondary care.
Saudi Arabia	Gatekeeping is likely enforced in the public system, but may not be enforced in the private system that is rapidly evolving with the introduction of mandatory insurance and changing provider networks.
China	Limited gatekeeping. Primary care is often bypassed by consumers in favor of higher levels of care. Limited referrals to secondary care.
Ethiopia	Hierarchically tiered system of care, further enhanced by health development armies. The health development armies build social networks and social capital within communities for health development, which serves in part as a mechanism for referrals.
Sri Lanka	The gatekeeping roles in both the public and the private system are unclear. No apparent role of coordination or referral system in the dual public-private market. Ad hoc referrals may be made in a predominantly private, long-term care system.

Source: Original table for this publication.

The Netherlands

The Netherlands requires residents to purchase health insurance from private insurers, and coverage is financed through premiums, tax revenues, and government grants (Kroneman et al. 2016; Wammes, Stadhouders, and Westert 2020). Coverage is universal for all individuals including older adults. All plans offer a standardized benefits package that includes hospitalization, physician care, home nursing, mental health care, and prescription drugs. The package includes care from a general practitioner (GP), some health promotion programs (for example, smoking cessation and weight management), and outpatient and inpatient mental health care. Most people supplement this with voluntary private insurance for dental care, vision, and alternative medicines and to reduce copayments for some medications.

Importantly, GPs serve a gatekeeping function; referrals from them are required for secondary care, including hospital and specialist care (Kroneman et al. 2016). GP group practices often employ salaried nurses and primary care psychologists. Payment to GPs is based on a capitated model for core primary care services. Additional payments are made to GPs based on a bundled payment model for multidisciplinary care for diabetes, asthma, chronic obstructive pulmonary disease, and cardiovascular health. A third form of payment to GPs is based on performance and innovation.

The Netherlands has a publicly financed LTC insurance model paid for by taxpayer contributions of 9.65 percent of taxable income. In addition, it has some policies to support informal caregivers, such as an allowance to the recipient and for paid and unpaid leave. The country relies heavily on personal budgets, that is, cash allowances for people entitled to LTC. In 2015, the Netherlands reformed the model to allow for reimbursement to vendors on behalf of the recipient who had purchased care (Mosca et al. 2017).

The Netherlands has a mixture of care provided in institutions, communities, and at home (Kroneman et al. 2016). Community-level LTC is the responsibility of municipalities (a decentralized function), but home nursing is covered to a limited extent under health plans, and residential LTC is covered by the LTC insurance model. Care assessments are not based on age but rather on functional domains (Joshua 2017). The Netherlands continues to experiment with different models and pilots, including efforts to integrate care for older adults living in their communities (Uittenbroek et al. 2018; Vestjens et al. 2019).

Colombia

Colombia's system is financed through multiple sources, but predominantly employee tax contributions and general revenues. Individuals are typically in one of two different insurance regimes: the contributory regime (funded by payroll taxes) or the subsidized regime (funded by general revenues). These programs have employment status as a criterion but do not have age as an explicit criterion.

Colombians choose their own insurers and providers within the insurer's network, with some variation in cost sharing and premium contributions and, to some extent, in the benefits package. The insurance plan determines the benefits package, in addition to the benefits of a public health intervention package, which is publicly provided. Coverage includes primary care, some inpatient care, and emergency care (Escobar et al. 2009). Plans function as managed care organizations receiving a capitated payment per enrollee to cover a benefits package (Vargas et al. 2013; Pinto and Hsiao 2007). Primary providers' provision of gatekeeping and referral to secondary or higher levels of care, including LTC, are likely to vary and be dependent on the provider networks and managed care rules implemented for a given health plan.

Canada

Canada's universal public national health insurance program, Medicare, is administered by its 13 provinces and territories (henceforth provinces). Care is free at the point of use, although benefits may vary across provinces beyond physician and hospital services. Medicare does not always cover outpatient prescription drugs and dental care, although some provinces may cover some population groups (Asada and Kephart 2007). Individuals may also opt to purchase private insurance for services that are excluded under Medicare (Allin, Marchildon, and Peckham 2020).

Importantly, GPs serve a gatekeeping function because referrals are required for secondary care, including hospital and specialist care (European Observatory on Health Systems and Policies et al. 2020). However, in most provinces, GPs continue to be paid on a fee-for-service basis.

Although outpatient prescription drugs are generally not covered, they are covered for those who are age 65 and older and for certain social assistance recipients (European Observatory on Health Systems and Policies et al. 2020). LTC policies, including for home and community care, vary greatly by province. Medicare coverage for institutional and home care depends on needs assessments and means testing. Provinces also vary in their coverage policies for informal caregivers, including paid leave for up to 26 weeks to care for a family member or other caregiver as part of employment insurance.

Saudi Arabia

Historically, Saudi Arabia has provided health care to all citizens and public sector employees primarily through government facilities, including outpatient and inpatient services (Walston, Al-Harbi, and Al-Omar 2008). Services were decentralized in 20 health directorates administering care in more than 3,300 health centers. These health centers functioned as gatekeepers for referrals to hospital services.

In 2002, Saudi Arabia began introducing mandatory health insurance and privatizing state-owned hospitals (Almalki, Fitzgerald, and Clark 2011). Across the world, with the introduction of health insurance came health maintenance organizations, preferred provider organizations, and provider network organizations—most commonly operating in the United States, a country not known for integrated care. Likewise, the changes in the broader financing system from a publicly provided system to a mandatory health insurance model in Saudi Arabia may have affected existing referral networks and expectations. For example, hospitals and physicians may be paid on a fee-for-service basis with varying levels of gatekeeping (AlRuthia et al. 2020). Similar to Colombia, the use of gatekeeping is likely to vary and be dependent on provider networks and managed care rules.

In November 2020, the Ministry of Human Resources and Social Development announced plans for care of older adults in collaboration with the private and nonprofit sectors, including the piloting of "social care homes" for citizens who meet certain eligibility criteria (Saudi Arabia, Ministry of Human Resources and Social Development 2022). There are likely to be minimal links between primary care and LTC.

China

The Chinese system of health care can be described as one of social insurance that is regionally tailored. Investments by the government have helped reduce out-of-pocket spending in recent years.

The three main social insurance plans available in China are the New Rural Cooperative Medical Scheme (NRCMS) (voluntary), Urban Employee Basic Medical Insurance (mandatory for urban workers), and Urban Resident Basic Medical Insurance (URBMI) (voluntary). These plans are financed by both government and individual contributions, covering outpatient and inpatient care, with significant variation between and within provinces. Each system has established distinct cost-sharing and premium rules. Coverage of outpatient services in NRCMS and URBMI vary by local government (for example, the county for NRCMS or the city for URBMI). Gatekeeping is not strictly required or enforced, and patients often demand care directly at secondary or tertiary levels of care rather than in primary care practices (Powell-Jackson, Yip, and Han 2015).

Beyond these three plans, there is some public provision, and two additional programs—Medical Financing Assistance and Insurance Program for Catastrophic Diseases—are intended to help cover catastrophic costs of medical services. Notably, age does not appear to be a criterion for specific assistance or insurance plans.

China has two dominant types of LTC—home and institutional. Family members primarily provide home LTC. Institutional LTC may be provided in hospitals, rehabilitation centers, and nursing homes. Community-based care remains less developed. The basic medical insurance plans do not cover LTC, and financing appears to rely primarily on pensions and savings. China has a strong record of using province-level social experiments to test and pilot different models of care, as was done for the various medical insurance plans. Thus, as expected, China is piloting LTC social insurance while also attempting to integrate health care and LTC services in selected settings across the country (Feng et al. 2020; Yang et al. 2016). The links between primary care and LTC may be limited except in the pilots.

Ethiopia

Ethiopia has broadened its PHC services through primary health care units that expanded health centers and health posts, with government serving as the main provider of care at the point of service free of charge for poor individuals. Care is structured through the standard three-tier system of services (primary, secondary, and tertiary) while also relying on health development armies comprising health development teams—up to 30 households residing in the same neighborhood—that complement the three-tier system. The network of health development armies enhances community mobilization and participatory learning and empowers community members, which likely improves social capital and health communications through existing social networks.

This public system is largely funded by external sources, followed by household spending and domestic government resources. Crucially, the "one budget" approach led by the Ethiopian government creates pooled resources from multiple donors and payers into a single delivery platform.

In parallel, the government has been implementing a community-based health insurance program, currently covering 83 percent of the population, which covers primary, secondary, and tertiary services. However, private premium contributions to the insurance program appear to be limited. The success of the gatekeeping role of the primary health care units is unclear and potentially in flux with the introduction of community-based health insurance.

LTC in Ethiopia is also very limited, although the presence of health development armies and the social network approach may, to some extent, help mitigate the care needs of older individuals in their community. The health development army and health development team may function with some limited referrals to informal care for older adults, and the role of volunteers to enhance social capital and create links to care may offer lessons for other countries, including high-income countries.

Sri Lanka

Sri Lanka's health care system is a mix of government and private providers, with government playing a significant role in inpatient care. The system is financed largely by general government revenues, with out-of-pocket spending playing an increasingly large share, as shown in table 2.1. In practice, there is little pooling outside of government revenues, and the voluntary private health insurance market catering to wealthier Sri Lankans is limited. Because public providers do not charge at the point of service, the increase in out-of-pocket spending, noted in table 2.1, may be due to a greater number of wealthier people seeking private provision, although more in-depth research is needed to understand the observed growth of out-of-pocket spending in Sri Lanka.

Historically, Sri Lanka's health care system was shaped by the British Medical Service (now the National Health Service in the United Kingdom), in which public provision is a central hallmark, along with medical officers dispatched to local and provincial regions for both preventive and curative functions. As in many countries with large public provision, the public budget for the hospital sector continued to grow compared with the nonhospital sector. In recent years, the central government assumed a larger share of health financing compared with provinces and local governments (Rajapaksa et al. 2021).

The public system is free at the point of charge, although there may be longer wait times than in the private system. There may also be more opting out from wealthier population segments to the private health provider market. Out-of-pocket spending is limited for inpatient care because of the availability of government hospitals. The growth in out-of-pocket spending for nonhospital services stems from the growing market for private provision, particularly for outpatient care, including PHC services. In short, in Sri Lanka, long-standing public provision of services now faces increasing competition from private provision as consumer demand for health care services grows with a rise in incomes.

There is no referral system in place, even in the existing public tiered system. A referral system could be established through the financing mechanism, including through expansion of social insurance or national health insurance. There is currently no significant social health insurance or national health insurance in the country, with only a few small insurance programs, including Agrahara for government employees and Suraksha for people ages 5 to 19 years. The discussion of a social health insurance or national health insurance scheme as a means of health care reform, however, has not advanced.

Despite a rapidly aging society, LTC in the country is limited, with nursing homes largely only in the private sector. There are a few limited public initiatives for home-care services and preventive services. The links from primary care to LTC are likely minimal.

Policy Recommendations

This section offers a few policy recommendations for financing by summarizing the conceptual background, financing framework, and selected case studies.

Use Financing to Ensure Gatekeeping and Care Coordination

The integration and coordination of PHC services for referrals to secondary care and LTC needs to be examined, as does the role of gatekeeping as a key requirement to ensure integration and coordination. Of the country case studies, only the Netherlands and Canada have clearly enforced gatekeeping as part of their health insurance programs. GPs and primary care providers may play a key gatekeeping role in referrals for secondary and long-term care. In countries where public provision played a historically important role, such as China, Colombia, Saudi Arabia, and Sri Lanka, there is a growing presence of privately provided care in competition with the public sector. In China, Colombia, and Saudi Arabia, which have growing health insurance models, insurance can help equalize access and benefits and design incentives for care coordination and referrals in a provider network.

Design Benefits Packages with Referrals in Mind

In the absence of a national benefits package, benefits packages often vary by insurance plan under a social insurance regime. Comparison of benefits packages within a country across plans is quite challenging for patients, let alone policy makers. Further, comparison of benefits packages across countries is also challenging and remains a major gap for those working to set priorities and design health benefits packages. Nevertheless, the quality of primary care and its role in care coordination as a key benefit may depend on the overall coverage and availability of benefits for secondary care and LTC in a jurisdiction.

Use Universal Coverage Rather Than Age Cutoffs to Help Older Adults

One key lesson drawn from this book is that policy makers concerned about older adults should not use age cutoffs for determining coverage. A life-course perspective on primary health services emphasizes that health at older ages depends on one's health at younger ages. Of the seven country case studies, no country uses an explicit age cutoff; they all offer universal mandatory coverage regardless of age (for example, Canada, Colombia, the Netherlands, and Saudi Arabia), voluntary coverage (for example, China and Ethiopia), and no state health insurance programs in Sri Lanka. In contrast, the United States has an older adult health insurance coverage plan with an age cutoff of 65 years, which has persisted since 1965 without any change to lower or alter eligibility criteria. Avoiding the use of an age cutoff can help all older adults regardless of their specific age.

Consider System Architecture and Organization When Designing the Means of Financing

Although financing through general revenues or payroll taxes may be a central focus of policy reform, it is just as important to consider the system architecture—how the system is designed and organized, including the publicly provided tier or referral system and the regulations governing provider networks in a system with insurance. Regulations governing insurance and financing can enable and require gatekeeping and thereby increase care coordination by primary care providers. Countries where public provision is dominant need to be cautious as private sector care expands and should design and plan a system for the eventual growth of a private sector insurance model that is regulated and managed. Public financing at scale can take one of two approaches—either (1) a national health insurance model in which all individuals of a given jurisdiction are covered under a unitary benefits package or (2) a social insurance model in which there are multiple plans and multiple benefits packages. The risk of the latter is potential variation in provider networks and referral rules that can affect the quality of care, especially PHC services.

Use the Reform Window Based on Population Aging and Macroeconomic and Political Resources

Population aging, far from being a burden, can be a crucial part of a country's economic development, as demonstrated by extensive work on the demographic dividend. As the pyramid structure of a population changes as a result of reductions in mortality followed by reductions in fertility, windows of opportunity for policy reform can emerge to help policy makers implement programs for universal coverage for health insurance and even LTC insurance. The Netherlands is the only one of the seven countries reviewed with mandatory LTC insurance. The uncertain availability of economic resources implies that the window of opportunity is short for countries to make health policy reforms to cover more people and offer more benefits.

Consider the Role of Nonprofit Organizations and Volunteers to Enhance Links to Care

The case study from Ethiopia demonstrates the value and importance of health development teams, which comprise volunteers within a neighborhood who care for and offer important services to other community members, including helping members to navigate care. In other countries, nonprofit organizations or other contracted entities, such as in the pilot models in China, can be used to enhance overall quality of care and referrals to care. The ways in which volunteers and voluntary organizations can help older adults to navigate referral services from primary care to long-term care, for example, were not explicitly examined in this chapter, but represent a key feature of system architecture. Government planners may see benefits from the broad inclusion of civil society to achieve the policy goals of enhancing efficiency and quality of care.

Notes

1. Also called a primary care practitioner or primary care provider.
2. These include the Healthcare Common Procedure Coding System, produced by the US Centers for Medicare and Medicaid Services; Current Procedural Terminology, owned by the American Medical Association; and International Classification of Diseases, Tenth Revision, Clinical Modification (ICD-10-CM), maintained by the US Centers for Disease Control and Prevention's National Center for Health Statistics under authorization from the World Health Organization.
3. Search strategy for literature review:
    Search 1 (912 results): "primary care"[tiab] or "primary health care"[tiab] or "primary care practitioner*"[tiab] or "primary care provider*"[tiab] AND (Netherlands[tiab] OR Colombia[tiab] OR Canada[tiab] OR "Saudi Arabia"[tiab] OR China[tiab] OR Ethiopia[tiab] OR "Sri Lanka"[tiab]) AND (elderly[tiab] OR older[tiab] OR seniors[tiab])
    Search 2 (827 results): ("long-term care" OR "long-term care financing") AND (Netherlands[tiab] OR Colombia[tiab] OR Canada[tiab] OR "Saudi Arabia"[tiab] OR China[tiab] OR Ethiopia[tiab] OR "Sri Lanka"[tiab]) AND (elderly[tiab] OR older[tiab] OR seniors[tiab])

References

Aggarwal, Pritti, Stephen J. Woolford, and Harnish P. Patel. 2020. "Multi-Morbidity and Polypharmacy in Older People: Challenges and Opportunities for Clinical Practice." *Geriatrics* 5 (4): E85. https://doi.org/10.3390/geriatrics5040085.

Allen, Luke N. 2018. "Leveraging Primary Care to Address Social Determinants." *The Lancet. Public Health* 3 (10): e466. https://doi.org/10.1016/S2468-2667(18)30186-5.

Allen, Luke N., Robert W. Smith, Fiona Simmons-Jones, Nia Roberts, Rory Honney, and Jonny Currie. 2020. "Addressing Social Determinants of Noncommunicable Diseases in Primary Care: A Systematic Review." *Bulletin of the World Health Organization* 98 (11): 754–65B. https://doi.org/10.2471/BLT.19.248278.

Allin, Sara, Greg Marchildon, and Allie Peckham. 2020. "Canada." Commonwealth Fund International Health Care System Profiles. https://www.commonwealthfund .org/international-health-policy-center/countries/canada.

Almalki, M., G. Fitzgerald, and M. Clark. 2011. "Health Care System in Saudi Arabia: An Overview." *Eastern Mediterranean Health Journal* 17 (10): 784–93. https://doi .org/10.26719/2011.17.10.784.

Almond, Douglas, and Janet Currie. 2011. "Killing Me Softly: The Fetal Origins Hypothesis." *Journal of Economic Perspectives* 25 (3): 153–72. https://doi.org/10.1257 /jep.25.3.153.000000000000000.

AlRuthia, Yazed, Norah Abdulaziz Bin Aydan, Nora Sulaiman Alorf, and Yousif Asiri. 2020. "How Can Saudi Arabia Reform Its Public Hospital Payment Models? A Narrative Review." *Saudi Pharmaceutical Journal* 28 (12): 1520–25. https://doi .org/10.1016/j.jsps.2020.09.020.

Apóstolo, João, Richard Cooke, Elzbieta Bobrowicz-Campos, Silvina Santana, Maura Marcucci, Antonio Cano, Miriam Vollenbroek-Hutten, et al. 2018. "Effectiveness of Interventions to Prevent Pre-Frailty and Frailty Progression in Older Adults: A Systematic Review." *JBI Database of Systematic Reviews and Implementation Reports* 16 (1): 140–232. https://doi.org/10.11124/JBISRIR-2017-003382.

Asada, Yukiko, and George Kephart. 2007. "Equity in Health Services Use and Intensity of Use in Canada." *BMC Health Services Research* 7 (1): 1–12. https://doi.org/10.1186 /1472-6963-7-41.

Baxter, Susan, Maxine Johnson, Duncan Chambers, Anthea Sutton, Elizabeth Goyder, and Andrew Booth. 2018. "The Effects of Integrated Care: A Systematic Review of UK and International Evidence." *BMC Health Services Research* 18 (1): 350. https:// doi.org/10.1186/s12913-018-3161-3.

Beard, John R., and David E. Bloom. 2015. "Towards a Comprehensive Public Health Response to Population Ageing." *The Lancet* 385 (9968): 658–61. https://doi .org/10.1016/S0140-6736(14)61461-6.

Beard, John R., Alana Officer, Islene Araujo de Carvalho, Ritu Sadana, Anne Margriet Pot, Jean-Pierre Michel, Peter Lloyd-Sherlock, et al. 2016. "The World Report on Ageing and Health: A Policy Framework for Healthy Ageing." *The Lancet* 387 (10033): 2145–54. https://doi.org/10.1016/S0140-6736(15)00516-4.

Bitton, Asaf, Hannah L. Ratcliffe, Jeremy H. Veillard, Daniel H. Kress, Shannon Barkley, Meredith Kimball, Federica Secci, et al. 2017. "Primary Health Care as a Foundation for Strengthening Health Systems in Low- and Middle-Income Countries." *Journal of General Internal Medicine* 32 (5): 566–71. https://doi.org/10.1007/s11606 -016-3898-5.

Bloom, David E., David Canning, Günther Fink, and Jocelyn E. Finlay. 2009. "Fertility, Female Labor Force Participation, and the Demographic Dividend." *Journal of Economic Growth* 14 (2): 79–101. https://doi.org/10.1007/s10887-009-9039-9.

Bloom, David E., David Canning, and Jaypee Sevilla. 2003. "The Demographic Dividend: A New Perspective on the Economic Consequences of Population Change." Rand Corporation, Santa Monica, CA.

Bloom, David E., Somnath Chatterji, Paul Kowal, Peter Lloyd-Sherlock, Martin McKee, Bernd Rechel, Larry Rosenberg, and James P. Smith. 2015. "Macroeconomic Implications of Population Ageing and Selected Policy Responses." *The Lancet* 385 (9968): 649–57. https://doi.org/10.1016/S0140-6736(14)61464-1.

Bloom, David E., and Jeffrey G. Williamson. 1998. "Demographic Transitions and Economic Miracles in Emerging Asia." *World Bank Economic Review* 12 (3): 419–55. https://doi.org/10.1093/wber/12.3.419.

Campbell, Andrea Louise. 2002. "Self-Interest, Social Security, and the Distinctive Participation Patterns of Senior Citizens." *American Political Science Review* 96 (3): 565–74. https://doi.org/10.1017/S0003055402000333.

Chapko, Dorota, Roisin McCormack, Corri Black, Roger Staff, and Alison Murray. 2018. "Life-Course Determinants of Cognitive Reserve (CR) in Cognitive Aging and Dementia—A Systematic Literature Review." *Aging and Mental Health* 22 (8): 915–26. https://doi.org/10.1080/13607863.2017.1348471.

Costenoble, Axelle, Veerle Knoop, Sofie Vermeiren, Roberta Azzopardi Vella, Aziz Debain, Gina Rossi, Ivan Bautmans, Dominique Verté, Ellen Gorus, and Patricia De Vriendt. 2021. "A Comprehensive Overview of Activities of Daily Living in Existing Frailty Instruments: A Systematic Literature Search." *Gerontologist* 61 (3): e12–e22. https://doi.org/10.1093/geront/gnz147.

D'Albis, Hippolyte, and Dalal Moosa. 2015. "Generational Economics and the National Transfer Accounts." *Journal of Demographic Economics* 81 (4): 409–41. https://doi.org/10.1017/dem.2015.14.

Davis, Tamara S., Joe Guada, Rebecca Reno, Adriane Peck, Shannon Evans, Laura Moskow Sigal, and Staci Swenson. 2015. "Integrated and Culturally Relevant Care: A Model to Prepare Social Workers for Primary Care Behavioral Health Practice." *Social Work in Health Care* 54 (10): 909–38. https://doi.org/10.1080/00981389.2015.1062456.

Escobar, María-Luisa, Ursula Giedion, Antonio Giuffrida, and Amanda L. Glassman. 2009. "Colombia: After a Decade of Health System Reform." In *From Few to Many: Ten Years of Health Insurance Expansion in Colombia*, edited by Amanda L. Glassman, María-Luisa Escobar, Antonio Giuffrida, and Ursula Giedion, 1–14. Washington, DC: Inter-American Development Bank.

Espinosa-González, Ana Belén, Brendan C. Delaney, Joachim Marti, and Ara Darzi. 2021. "The Role of the State in Financing and Regulating Primary Care in Europe: A Taxonomy." *Health Policy* 125 (2): 168–76. https://doi.org/10.1016/j.healthpol.2020.11.008.

European Observatory on Health Systems and Policies, Gregory P. Marchildon, Sara Allin, and Sherry Merkur. 2020. "Canada: Health System Review." *Health Systems in Transition* 22 (3). https://apps.who.int/iris/handle/10665/336311.

Evans, Isobel E. M., Anthony Martyr, Rachel Collins, Carol Brayne, and Linda Clare. 2019. "Social Isolation and Cognitive Function in Later Life: A Systematic Review and Meta-Analysis." *Journal of Alzheimer's Disease* 70 (s1): S119–44. https://doi.org/10.3233/JAD-180501.

Fan, Victoria Y., and William D. Savedoff. 2014. "The Health Financing Transition: A Conceptual Framework and Empirical Evidence." *Social Science and Medicine* 105: 112–21.

Feng, Zhanlian, Elena Glinskaya, Hongtu Chen, Sen Gong, Yue Qiu, Jianming Xu, and Winnie Yip. 2020. "Long-Term Care System for Older Adults in China: Policy Landscape, Challenges, and Future Prospects." *The Lancet* 396 (10259): 1362–72. https://doi.org/10.1016/S0140-6736(20)32136-X.

Fried, Linda P., Luigi Ferrucci, Jonathan Darer, Jeff D. Williamson, and Gerard Anderson. 2004. "Untangling the Concepts of Disability, Frailty, and Comorbidity: Implications for Improved Targeting and Care." *Journals of Gerontology: Series A* 59 (3): M255–63. https://doi.org/10.1093/gerona/59.3.M255.

Fries, James F. 1980. "Aging, Natural Death, and the Compression of Morbidity." *New England Journal of Medicine* 303 (3): 130–35. https://doi.org/10.1056/NEJM198007173030304.

Fries, James F. 2005. "The Compression of Morbidity." *Milbank Quarterly* 83 (4): 801–23. https://doi.org/10.1111/j.1468-0009.2005.00401.x.

Fries, James F., Bonnie Bruce, and Eliza Chakravarty. 2011. "Compression of Morbidity 1980–2011: A Focused Review of Paradigms and Progress." *Journal of Aging Research* 2011: 261702. https://doi.org/10.4061/2011/261702.

Garthwaite, Craig, Tal Gross, and Matthew J. Notowidigdo. 2018. "Hospitals as Insurers of Last Resort." *American Economic Journal: Applied Economics* 10 (1): 1–39. https://doi.org/10.1257/app.20150581.

GBD 2019 Diseases and Injuries Collaborators. 2020. "Global Burden of 369 Diseases and Injuries in 204 Countries and Territories, 1990–2019: A Systematic Analysis for the Global Burden of Disease Study 2019." *The Lancet* 396 (10258): 1204–22. https://doi.org/10.1016/S0140-6736(20)30925-9.

Gérvas, Juan, Mercedes Pérez Fernández, and Barbara Starfield. 1994. "Primary Care, Financing and Gatekeeping in Western Europe." *Family Practice* 11 (3): 307–17. https://doi.org/10.1093/fampra/11.3.307.

Hewner, Sharon, Sabrina Casucci, Suzanne Sullivan, Francine Mistretta, Yuqing Xue, Barbara Johnson, Rebekah Pratt, Li Lin, and Chester Fox. 2017. "Integrating Social Determinants of Health into Primary Care Clinical and Informational Workflow during Care Transitions." *eGEMs: The Journal of Electronic Health Data and Methods* 5 (2): 2. https://doi.org/10.13063/2327-9214.1282.

Hsiao, William C. 2003. "What Is a Health System? Why Should We Care?" Working Paper 33, Harvard School of Public Health, Cambridge, MA.

Joshua, Laurie. 2017. "Aging and Long Term Care Systems: A Review of Finance and Governance Arrangements in Europe, North America and Asia-Pacific." Social Protection and Labor Discussion Paper 1705, World Bank, Washington, DC. https://doi.org/10.1596/28952.

Kogan, Alexis Coulourides, Kathleen Wilber, and Laura Mosqueda. 2016. "Person-Centered Care for Older Adults with Chronic Conditions and Functional Impairment: A Systematic Literature Review." *Journal of the American Geriatrics Society* 64 (1): e1–7. https://doi.org/10.1111/jgs.13873.

Kroneman, M., W. Boerma, M. van den Berg, P. Groenewegen, J. de Jong, and E. van Ginneken. 2016. "The Netherlands: Health System Review." *Health Systems in Transition* 18 (2): 1–239. https://apps.who.int/iris/handle/10665/330244.

Kuhn, Michael, and Klaus Prettner. 2018. "Population Age Structure and Consumption Growth: Evidence from National Transfer Accounts." *Journal of Population Economics* 31 (1): 135–53. https://doi.org/10.1007/s00148-017-0654-z.

Kuruvilla, Shyama, Ritu Sadana, Eugenio Villar Montesinos, John Beard, Jennifer Franz Vasdeki, Islene Araujo de Carvalho, Rebekah Bosco Thomas, et al. 2018. "A Life-Course Approach to Health: Synergy with Sustainable Development Goals." *Bulletin of the World Health Organization* 96 (1): 42–50. https://doi.org/10.2471/BLT.17.198358.

Lee, Ronald, and Andrew Mason. 2011. *Population Aging and the Generational Economy.* Cheltenham, UK: Edward Elgar Publishing Ltd.

Macinko, James, Barbara Starfield, and Temitope Erinosho. 2009. "The Impact of Primary Healthcare on Population Health in Low- and Middle-Income Countries." *Journal of Ambulatory Care Management* 32 (2): 150–71. https://doi.org/10.1097/JAC.0b013e3181994221.

Macinko, J., B. Starfield, and L. Shi. 2003. "The Contribution of Primary Care Systems to Health Outcomes within Organization for Economic Cooperation and Development (OECD) Countries, 1970–1998." *Health Services Research* 38 (3): 831–65. https://doi.org/10.1111/1475-6773.00149.

Malcolm, Martin, Helen Frost, and Julie Cowie. 2019. "Loneliness and Social Isolation Causal Association with Health-Related Lifestyle Risk in Older Adults: A Systematic Review and Meta-Analysis Protocol." *Systematic Reviews* 8 (1): 48. https://doi .org/10.1186/s13643-019-0968-x.

Martínez-Mesa, J., M. C. Restrepo-Méndez, D. A. González, F. C. Wehrmeister, B. L. Horta, M. R. Domingues, and A. M. B. Menezes. 2013. "Life-Course Evidence of Birth Weight Effects on Bone Mass: Systematic Review and Meta-Analysis." *Osteoporosis International* 24 (1): 7–18. https://doi.org/10.1007/s00198-012-2114-7.

McAdams, Dan P., and Bradley D. Olson. 2010. "Personality Development: Continuity and Change over the Life Course." *Annual Review of Psychology* 61: 517–42. https:// doi.org/10.1146/annurev.psych.093008.100507.

Mitchell, Geoffrey K., Jennifer J. Tieman, and Tania M. Shelby-James. 2008. "Multidisciplinary Care Planning and Teamwork in Primary Care." *Medical Journal of Australia* 188 (S8): S61–64. https://doi.org/10.5694/j.1326-5377.2008.tb01747.x.

Monaco, Alessandro, Katie Palmer, Alessandra Marengoni, Stefania Maggi, Tarek A. Hassan, and Shaantanu Donde. 2020. "Integrated Care for the Management of Ageing-Related Non-Communicable Diseases: Current Gaps and Future Directions." *Aging Clinical and Experimental Research* 32 (7): 1353–58. https://doi.org/10.1007 /s40520-020-01533-z.

Mosca, Ilaria, Philip J. van der Wees, Esther S. Mot, Joost J. G. Wammes, and Patrick P. T. Jeurissen. 2017. "Sustainability of Long-Term Care: Puzzling Tasks ahead for Policy-Makers." *International Journal of Health Policy and Management* 6 (4): 195–205. https://doi.org/10.15171/ijhpm.2016.109.

Mulvaney-Day, Norah, Tina Marshall, Kathryn Downey Piscopo, Neil Korsen, Sean Lynch, Lucy H. Karnell, Garrett E. Moran, Allen S. Daniels, and Sushmita Shoma Ghose. 2018. "Screening for Behavioral Health Conditions in Primary Care Settings: A Systematic Review of the Literature." *Journal of General Internal Medicine* 33 (3): 335–46. https://doi.org/10.1007/s11606-017-4181-0.

Nothelle, Stephanie, Amy S. Kelley, Talan Zhang, David L. Roth, Jennifer L. Wolff, and Cynthia Boyd. 2022. "Fragmentation of Care in the Last Year of Life: Does Dementia Status Matter?" *Journal of the American Geriatrics Society* 70 (8): 2320–29. https://doi .org/10.1111/jgs.17827.

Ofori-Asenso, Richard, Ken L. Chin, Mohsen Mazidi, Ella Zomer, Jenni Ilomaki, Andrew R. Zullo, Danijela Gasevic, et al. 2019. "Global Incidence of Frailty and Prefrailty among Community-Dwelling Older Adults: A Systematic Review and Meta-Analysis." *JAMA Network Open* 2 (8): e198398. https://doi.org/10.1001 /jamanetworkopen.2019.8398.

Olshansky, S. Jay, and Bruce A. Carnes. 2019. "Inconvenient Truths about Human Longevity." *Journals of Gerontology. Series A, Biological Sciences and Medical Sciences* 74 (Suppl_1): S7–12. https://doi.org/10.1093/gerona/glz098.

Peterson, Kim, Johanna Anderson, Donald Bourne, Martin P. Charns, Sherri Sheinfeld Gorin, Denise M. Hynes, Kathryn M. McDonald, Sara J. Singer, and Elizabeth M. Yano. 2019. "Health Care Coordination Theoretical Frameworks: A Systematic Scoping Review to Increase Their Understanding and Use in Practice." *Journal of General Internal Medicine* 34 (Suppl 1): 90–98. https://doi.org/10.1007/s11606 -019-04966-z.

Pinto, Diana, and William C. Hsiao. 2007. "Colombia: Social Health Insurance with Managed Competition to Improve Health Care Delivery." In *Social Health Insurance for Developing Nations*, edited by W. C. Hsiao and R. P. Shaw, 105–32. Washington, DC: World Bank.

Powell Davies, Gawaine, Anna M. Williams, Karen Larsen, David Perkins, Martin Roland, and Mark F. Harris. 2008. "Coordinating Primary Health Care: An Analysis of the Outcomes of a Systematic Review." *Medical Journal of Australia* 188 (S8): S65–68. https://doi.org/10.5694/j.1326-5377.2008.tb01748.x.

Powell-Jackson, Timothy, Winnie Chi-Man Yip, and Wei Han. 2015. "Realigning Demand and Supply Side Incentives to Improve Primary Health Care Seeking in Rural China." *Health Economics* 24 (6): 755–72. https://doi.org/10.1002/hec.3060.

Quintelier, Ellen. 2007. "Differences in Political Participation between Young and Old People." *Contemporary Politics* 13 (2): 165–80. https://doi.org/10.1080/13569770701562658.

Rajapaksa, Lalini, Padmal De Silva, Palitha Abeykoon, Lakshmi Somatunga, Sridharan Sathasivam, Susie Perera, Eshani Fernando, et al. 2021. "Sri Lanka Health System Review." *Health Systems in Transition* 10 (1). World Health Organization. Regional Office for South-East Asia. https://apps.who.int/iris/handle/10665/342323.

Rasmussen, Kathleen Maher. 2001. "The 'Fetal Origins' Hypothesis: Challenges and Opportunities for Maternal and Child Nutrition." *Annual Review of Nutrition* 21 (1): 73–95. https://doi.org/10.1146/annurev.nutr.21.1.73.

Roberts, Marc, William Hsiao, Peter Berman, and Michael Reich. 2008. *Getting Health Reform Right: A Guide to Improving Performance and Equity*. New York: Oxford University Press.

Rotar, Alexandru M., Michael J. Van Den Berg, Willemijn Schäfer, Dionne S. Kringos, and Niek S. Klazinga. 2018. "Shared Decision Making between Patient and GP about Referrals from Primary Care: Does Gatekeeping Make a Difference?" *PLOS ONE* 13 (6): e0198729. https://doi.org/10.1371/journal.pone.0198729.

Saudi Arabia, Ministry of Human Resources and Social Development. 2022. "Care for the Elderly in the Kingdom of Saudi Arabia." https://www.my.gov.sa/wps/portal/snp/careaboutyou/elderly/!ut/p/z0/04_Sj9CPykssy0xPLMnMz0vMAfIjo8zijQx93d0NDYz8LYIMLA0CQ4xCTZwN_Ay8Qgz1g1Pz9AuyHRUB-ivojg!!/.

Savedoff, William D., David de Ferranti, Amy L. Smith, and Victoria Fan. 2012. "Political and Economic Aspects of the Transition to Universal Health Coverage." *The Lancet* 380 (9845): 924–32.

Smith, Susan M., Hassan Soubhi, Martin Fortin, Catherine Hudon, and Tom O'Dowd. 2012. "Managing Patients with Multimorbidity: Systematic Review of Interventions in Primary Care and Community Settings." *BMJ (Clinical Research Ed.)* 345 (September): e5205. https://doi.org/10.1136/bmj.e5205.

Sripa, Poompong, Benedict Hayhoe, Priya Garg, Azeem Majeed, and Geva Greenfield. 2019. "Impact of GP Gatekeeping on Quality of Care, and Health Outcomes, Use, and Expenditure: A Systematic Review." *British Journal of General Practice: The Journal of the Royal College of General Practitioners* 69 (682): e294–303. https://doi.org/10.3399/bjgp19X702209.

Starfield, Barbara, Leiyu Shi, and James Macinko. 2005. "Contribution of Primary Care to Health Systems and Health." *Milbank Quarterly* 83 (3): 457–502. https://doi.org/10.1111/j.1468-0009.2005.00409.x.

Teunissen, E., K. Gravenhorst, C. Dowrick, E. Van Weel-Baumgarten, F. Van den Driessen Mareeuw, T. de Brún, N. Burns, et al. 2017. "Implementing Guidelines and Training Initiatives to Improve Cross-Cultural Communication in Primary Care Consultations: A Qualitative Participatory European Study." *International Journal for Equity in Health* 16 (1): 32. https://doi.org/10.1186/s12939-017-0525-y.

Uittenbroek, Ronald J., Antoinette D. I. van Asselt, Sophie L. W. Spoorenberg, Hubertus P. H. Kremer, Klaske Wynia, and Sijmen A. Reijneveld. 2018. "Integrated and Person-Centered Care for Community-Living Older Adults: A Cost-Effectiveness Study." *Health Services Research* 53 (5): 3471–94. https://doi.org/10.1111/1475-6773.12853.

Vargas, Ingrid, Jean-Pierre Unger, Amparo Susana Mogollón-Pérez, and M. Luisa Vázquez. 2013. "Effects of Managed Care Mechanisms on Access to Healthcare: Results from a Qualitative Study in Colombia." *International Journal of Health Planning and Management* 28 (1): e13–33. https://doi.org/10.1002/hpm.2129.

Vestjens, Lotte, Jane M. Cramm, Erwin Birnie, and Anna P. Nieboer. 2019. "Cost-Effectiveness of a Proactive, Integrated Primary Care Approach for Community-Dwelling Frail Older Persons." *Cost Effectiveness and Resource Allocation* 17: 14. https://doi.org/10.1186/s12962-019-0181-8.

Wagner, Edward H., Nirmala Sandhu, Katie Coleman, Kathryn E. Phillips, and Jonathan R. Sugarman. 2014. "Improving Care Coordination in Primary Care." *Medical Care* 52 (11 Suppl 4): S33–38. https://doi.org/10.1097/MLR.0000000000000197.

Walston, Stephen, Yousef Al-Harbi, and Badran Al-Omar. 2008. "The Changing Face of Healthcare in Saudi Arabia." *Annals of Saudi Medicine* 28 (4): 243–50. https://doi.org/10.5144/0256-4947.2008.243.

Wammes, Joost J. G., Niek Stadhouders, and Gert Westert. 2020. "Netherlands." Commonwealth Fund International Health Care System Profiles. https://www.commonwealthfund.org/international-health-policy-center/countries/netherlands.

Wittenberg, Raphael. 2015. "The Challenge of Measuring Multi-Morbidity and Its Costs." *Israel Journal of Health Policy Research* 4: 1. https://doi.org/10.1186/2045-4015-4-1.

WHO (World Health Organization). 2015. *Tracking Universal Health Coverage: First Global Monitoring Report.* Geneva: WHO.

WHO (World Health Organization). 2021. *Framework for Countries to Achieve an Integrated Continuum of Long-Term Care.* Geneva: WHO.

Yaffe, Kristine, Eric Vittinghoff, Tina Hoang, Karen Matthews, Sherita H. Golden, and Adina Zeki Al Hazzouri. 2021. "Cardiovascular Risk Factors across the Life Course and Cognitive Decline: A Pooled Cohort Study." *Neurology* 96 (17): e2212–19. https://doi.org/10.1212/WNL.0000000000011747.

Yang, Wei, Alex Jingwei He, Lijie Fang, and Elias Mossialos. 2016. "Financing Institutional Long-Term Care for the Elderly in China: A Policy Evaluation of New Models." *Health Policy and Planning* 31 (10): 1391–401. https://doi.org/10.1093/heapol/czw081.

CHAPTER 3

Innovations in Models of Care for an Aging Population

Xiaohui Hou, Zhanlian Feng, Sana Haider,
and Guadalupe Suarez

Key Messages

- This chapter surveys the global care landscape for older adults and highlights emerging innovations in care delivery for older people, focusing on long-term care (LTC).

- Across low- and middle-income countries (LMICs), familial or informal care remains the dominant care model of LTC. Publicly financed LTC is limited, and paid care is largely funded out of pocket. Demand for quality, affordable LTC is growing rapidly.

- Some, mostly high-income, countries have leveraged innovative delivery models to advance person-centered, integrated care systems that encompass a full range of routine, acute, postacute, and LTC services in a continuum, anchored in primary health care (PHC).

- Innovative integrated service provision models remain rare in LMICs, but some are testing such approaches and adapting them to local contexts and cultural preferences.

- Aided by cross-country learning and a growing knowledge base from international health care and LTC research, more countries can grasp opportunities to "leapfrog" stages of LTC development by adapting international best practices.

Introduction

Population aging—an increase in the proportion of older persons within the age composition of a population—is occurring in virtually all countries across the world. Population aging is occurring more rapidly in LMICs than in high-income countries (HICs).

Across LMICs, familial (or informal) care remains the primary form of care provided for older persons. However, a number of long-term factors—chief among them industrialization, urbanization, changes in family structure such as nuclearization and shrinking family size, and an increase in women's labor force participation—are rendering this form of care increasingly unsustainable (Feng 2019; Holmes 2021). As life expectancy also steadily increases across LMICs, the burden of noncommunicable diseases (NCDs) and age-related disabilities is also on the rise (Kazibwe, Tran, and Annerstedt 2021).

The decline of the physical and functional capacities of aging populations, compounded by the demographic, social, and economic trends mentioned above and the existing gaps between demand for and supply of care, are causing greater attention to be focused on the need to provide better health services for older adults, including in LMICs. Although many LMICs are in the early stages of developing formal care for older adults and LTC delivery systems, some have begun exploring and applying innovative care provision and delivery models to meet their unique population needs and implementing tailored models from other countries, including HICs.

Many innovative models have emerged in HICs because wealthier countries are also experiencing population aging that outpaces the supply of LTC. Given countries' diversity, there is no single best care model for older adults in all countries. The optimal form of a national LTC system reflects the interaction of numerous factors in each country, including political and economic contexts, social and cultural factors, and existing health and social welfare system structures. Nevertheless, researchers and policy makers in LMICs can learn much from the LTC systems in HICs.

This and the following chapter address the innovation domain of the financing, innovation, regulation, and evaluation (FIRE) framework. This chapter starts with a synthesis of the findings from a literature review on the current care landscape for older adults in select LMICs in five world regions: Central and South America, Asia, the Middle East and North Africa, Sub-Saharan Africa, and Eastern and Southern Europe. It then describes a number of leading innovative LTC models, mostly from HICs, organizing the analysis by five themes—population, governance, platforms, workforce, and the use of information and other tools to innovate in-service delivery. The chapter then presents several innovative LTC models implemented in LMICs that may provide examples for adaptation in lower-resource settings. The concluding discussion explores policy options and offers recommendations for practical approaches to integrating innovative LTC models in LMICs.

This chapter focuses on LTC. It does not address the vast topic of care delivery innovations for older adults in PHC. Integrated, person-centered PHC delivery as a distinct topic is explored in chapter 1 of this volume and has been extensively analyzed in recent publications, notably Baris et al. (2021); National Academies of Sciences, Engineering, and Medicine (2021); and OECD (2020). At the same time, many of the promising LTC models analyzed in this chapter, from both HICs and LMICs, have been selected because they integrate social, personal, and medical care, including PHC. Such examples are beginning to show how PHC systems and LTC delivery may work together in practice, improving outcomes for older adults.

The Current Landscape of LTC Services in LMICs: An Overview[1]

This section reviews and summarizes the existing evidence on the availability of formal LTC services and delivery systems in LMICs, organized by region. In most LMICs, publicly financed LTC is limited, and paid care is funded out of pocket primarily by older persons and their families. Availability of, or access to, formal home-care services, community-based services such as community care and adult day-care centers, or institutional services such as nursing and residential care facilities, is generally limited.

Central and South America

In Central and South America, comprehensive LTC policies and systems are essentially nonexistent. Public funding or direct provision of LTC services is scarce. A private market for senior care is emerging in some countries, but access is limited by the ability to pay.

In Central America, Mexico does not have an LTC system organized at the federal level and leaves the responsibility for service development to the states (OCED 2011). No publicly funded LTC system currently exists, and health care for the older population is provided by the Mexican Health System, which also covers all other age groups (Gutiérrez Robledo, López Ortega, and Arango Lopera 2012). The few government services for older adults are extensions of poverty reduction or other social service programs (Gutiérrez Robledo, López Ortega, and Arango Lopera 2012). There are few private (for-profit and not-for-profit) institutions offering services such as adult day care and institutional LTC for non-self-sufficient older people without family (OCED 2011).

In Costa Rica, efforts have been made in recent years to formalize a national LTC system (Matus-Lopez and Chaverri-Carvajal 2022). The government has focused on facilitating access to services, such as long-term residential services, day centers, and home care visits, using subsidies to families or nonprofit service providers (Medellín 2020). In 2010, Costa Rica's National Council for Older People established the Progressive Attention Network for Integral Elder Care, aimed at establishing community-based LTC networks nationwide to conduct activities such as training retired teachers to act as unpaid community volunteer pensioners (Lloyd-Sherlock et al. 2017). Private services are increasing but mostly limited to consumers with higher incomes (Medellín 2020).

Brazil does not provide federally mandated coverage for its older populations who need LTC. Through a means-tested system, the country provides some public LTC services focused on sheltering economically deprived people (Giacomin et al. 2021). LTC homes are scarce, public LTC expenditure per older adult is minimal, and it is estimated that at least 600,000 formal LTC workers are needed to fill the gap (Giacomin et al. 2021).

Argentina does not have a public LTC system. Although the government covers a range of public care services, these services are fragmented and uncoordinated because of the indistinct overlapping of functions and services provided by national, provincial, and municipal agencies (Oliveri 2020). Private schemes are estimated to cover no more than 8 percent of older people with higher incomes (Dyer, Valeri, et al. 2019). The services offered by private and civil society organizations include LTC facilities, home-care units, day centers, rehabilitation centers, and home-care services (Dyer, Valeri, et al. 2019).

Similarly, in Chile, a range of public LTC services, including residential care facilities, day centers, and home-care services, are offered, but an organized nationwide LTC system does not exist (Aranco 2020). Private services include those provided in residential care settings, home-care and support services, day centers, and telecare services, with the nonprofit sector, particularly religious organizations, playing a strong role in service provision (Aranco 2020).

Asia

In Vietnam, although the government has issued many policies to support older persons, and offers subsidies and health insurance to those age 80 and older and to vulnerable older adults, there is no comprehensive LTC-based model or national integration of LTC service provision. The Ministry of Health provides health care for older adults in health care facilities and communities, but LTC service provision largely supports family care with home-based services. Nongovernmental organizations and the private sector also provide LTC, and paid home care is emerging for older people who lack the means to pay for private care (Van, Tuan, and Oanh 2021). Residential care, including care centers, is not widely available. In 2015–16, of residential care centers, 36 percent were public, 36 percent were run by nongovernmental organizations or religious providers, and 27 percent were private, of which 82 percent were licensed (Dyer, Valeri, et al. 2019). Nursing homes are mostly located in urban areas and are affordable mainly by the wealthy (Van, Tuan, and Oanh 2021). The government provides social assistance payments to older, poorer persons without close family or retirement pensions, but the number of beneficiaries is limited (Dyer, Valeri, et al. 2019).

In Indonesia, the government is responsible for LTC coordination and delivery, including home- and community-based care (ADB 2021). In 2016, the government launched the National Strategic Plan, which stated that government-mandated community health centers were responsible for providing older people with PHC and LTC, including free health checkups and the organization of social activities (Dyer, Valeri, et al. 2019). However, LTC is not yet being provided in an integrated and coordinated way; the minimum requirements for care provision are not being met at many state-funded community health centers; and low levels of local political commitment and resource availability have limited LTC delivery (ADB 2021). There are approximately 277 residential homes for older people, with a total capacity of 18,100 beds. Of these, 3 are run by the central government, 71 by local governments, and 189 are private (ADB 2021). Only a few private organizations offer institutional LTC. Some private companies supply day-care and equipment services, estimated to support no more than a few thousand older people, mainly in urban areas (ADB 2021).

The LTC system in Thailand prioritizes aging in place and home- and community-based care. The government, alongside local authorities, has implemented an integrated home- and community-based care model (further described later in this chapter). Residential LTC is available for those who have complex care needs and insufficient caregiving support at home. Services for dependent older persons are available at private nursing homes, private hospitals, government residential homes, and homes set up for poor older persons supported by charitable organizations (ADB 2020). In 2016, there were 442 private facilities offering residential LTC services (ADB 2020).

Middle East and North Africa

In the Middle East and North Africa region, there is growing evidence of increased demand for a formal LTC market and the emergence of aged-care economies that are still relatively unregulated. (Hussein 2022).

In Turkey, as in most of the rest of the region, care for older people is primarily provided informally by the family and community (Ismail and Hussein 2021). However, sociodemographic trends such as changes in family structure, migration, and rising numbers of women in formal employment are placing pressure on the availability of such care. LTC is provided at home by informally employed domestic and migrant live-in care workers and funded either through cash-for-care schemes or out of pocket. Home care is viewed as a culturally appropriate option whereas residential care is stigmatized. In recent years, the Ministry of Family and Social Policies has piloted some new older adult care interventions such as shared living and care centers, organized by the state for groups of older people to live together with support workers attending to their needs during the day. Since 2010, the Ministry of Health has implemented a national community-based palliative care program in line with the National Turkish palliative care policy, making Turkey the only country in the Middle East and North Africa region other than Israel to have such a policy (Ismail and Hussein 2021).

The social welfare systems in the Arab region are characterized by heavy reliance on family or community-based social support, especially for social care, which has long been neglected in the region (Hussein and Ismail 2017). Policies directed toward meeting LTC needs are scant, given deeply rooted cultural norms emphasizing the role of the family (particularly women) in providing care and support for older adults. However, although informal LTC continues to dominate, evidence suggests that the use of formal care by older people is rising, including care homes or home-care services, which are mostly initiated and covered by civil society and religious organizations, and sometimes subsidized by public funds (Hussein and Ismail 2017).

Sub-Saharan Africa

In Sub-Saharan Africa, most organized care is provided in urban areas, and the two most common models for LTC delivery are through charitable organizations (faith-based civil society or public welfare bodies) or private services for higher-income populations, provided mainly in residential homes (WHO 2017). Institutional care is relatively new and often not available. In Kenya, there were approximately 16 LTC facilities in 2017, mainly provided by religious organizations (Dyer, Valeri, et al. 2019). Some limited publicly funded LTC is available in South Africa. Residential care is provided mainly by nongovernmental organizations or religious organizations; only 2 percent of existing residential care homes are run by the government (Dyer, Valeri, et al. 2019).

Eastern and Southern Europe

In Bulgaria, LTC health services and social services are managed and regulated by separate authorities. LTC health services, including long-term treatment, rehabilitation and physical therapy, and palliative care, are regulated by the Medical Treatment Facilities Act and are provided through such institutions as hospitals and hospices (European Commission 2021). LTC social services, including home- and community-based services, are decentralized and managed by municipalities, with some services offered by private providers. Bulgaria is currently undergoing a fundamental shift from residential care to home and community services. The country has launched a series of LTC reforms in recent years. The first wave, planned for 2018–21, focused on developing integrated services, implementing quality standards, strengthening prevention, and launching outreach initiatives. The second wave (planned for 2022–27) will center on the deinstitutionalization of care for people with disabilities and older people (European Commission 2021). However, the actual implementation of these reform measures remains to be seen and evaluated (European Commission 2021).

In Serbia, family law requires that adult children care for and financially support their parents. Older adults are also provided a cash benefit for LTC by both the contributory social insurance system and the noncontributory social welfare system (Hirose and Czepulis-Rutkowska 2016). Local governments are responsible for home- and community-based services, including home-care and day centers, but these services are not expansive and are minimally accessible. Residential care is available both in public institutions (financed by the state or user payments, or both) and in private institutions. Serbia has experienced a dramatic increase in the number of private providers offering residential care, yet costs still remain much higher than for public institutions. In 2011, there were 99 registered, private institutions for the care of older adults; in 2014 there were 40 public institutions providing such care (Hirose and Czepulis-Rutkowska 2016).

Innovations in LTC in HICs

This section samples some innovations in LTC service delivery systems, mostly in HICs. The innovations discussed here encompass multiple aspects of service delivery. For clarity of presentation and to facilitate policy applications, the discussion is organized according to the foundational system components set out in chapter 1 and adapted from Kruk et al. (2018): population, governance, platforms, workforce, and information and tools. As discussed in the overview, this approach makes it possible to clarify and prioritize specific policy options for country decision-makers under the broad functional headings of the FIRE (financing, innovation, regulation, evaluation) model.

Population

Individual autonomy and the meeting of population needs are vital goals in the health care process. When designing innovative service delivery models, directly focusing on and addressing the needs and preferences of the populations they aim to serve is important; the *who* is as important as the *what*. There should be active efforts to bridge the gaps between the needs of older populations and the design of care delivery. Ultimately, a people-centered approach is required for any innovative model for care delivery. This could mean both of the following:

- Respecting older adults' autonomy in their health care experience
- Taking active steps to bridge the communication gap between the older population and care delivery.

Respecting older adults' autonomy in their health care experience. Inclusive and people-centered strategies, such as granting older adults autonomy in their health care experiences, can help improve their quality of life. In geriatric residences in Israel, this simple strategy led to changes in daily routines and to increases in the satisfaction of older people and increases in social activity (Barkay and Tabak 2002). Health care recipients, especially those who have lived a long time and developed a deep sense of their values and identity, are experts on their own values, goals, and preferences. Their physicians, on the other hand, are experts on the medical means for effecting the person's aims and aspirations (Billings and Krakauer 2011). Ideally, a unified team is in place, at the center of which is the older adult who makes care decisions with support from providers and caregivers.[2]

Taking active steps to bridge the communication gap between the older population and care delivery. Some countries are developing collaborations to break down communication barriers between local authorities and older adults. In the Roskilde Municipality in Denmark, this effort has led to new visitation procedures, cost savings, and organizational changes (Verleye and Gemmel 2009). In the Marstal Municipality, "future workshops" engaged senior citizens to discuss innovative initiatives, which eventually led to improved service for older adults, whether at home or in care centers (Verleye and Gemmel 2011). When the older person is directly involved in the process of developing and implementing innovations, the strategy is more likely to achieve its goal.

Ultimately, a people-centered approach is required for any successful model of care delivery. This is particularly important for older people with multimorbidity. Care elements centered on the older person, such as shared involvement in goal setting, decision-making, and individualized care plans should be integrated into innovative care approaches.

Governance

Governance begins with effective health system leadership at national, subnational, and facility levels. It includes the effective regulation of providers in the public and private sectors, accountability mechanisms, and financing to promote appropriate access and limit financial hardship through fund pooling, insurance, contracting, and payment. Good governance of LTC systems is realized by strategies such as the following:

- Introducing a global capitation payment for greater integration of care for older adults
- Shifting certain services away from or out of hospitals to achieve better coordination among facilities, greater synergies in the use of resources, and provision of care in the most appropriate settings
- Using strategic planning and legislation to enhance the preparation and implementation of care for older adults.

Introducing a global capitation payment for greater integration of care for older adults. In the United States, more than 30 states have implemented the Program of All-Inclusive Care for the Elderly (PACE). The program targets adults age 55 and older living in a PACE service area who would otherwise qualify for nursing-home placement. One innovative feature is that the program contracts with a wide range of health care professionals to form a PACE interdisciplinary team, which provides a comprehensive array of preventive, primary, acute, and long-term care services in a community-based center and participants' homes. Another innovative feature is the global capitation payment—the program is paid for under a capitated rate to provide total care for frail older adults.

The impact of PACE can be quite significant. First, the programs are better tailored to older adults' needs because PACE provides customized care to everyone—the interdisciplinary team meets regularly with each participant and his or her caregivers to assess the participant's needs and establish a plan of care. Second, the global capitation payment system, by shifting more financial risk to providers, encourages them to give more useful and preventive care to enrollees. Last, the integrated care model reduces some fragmentation in care delivery (Mui 2001).

The Wisconsin Partnership Program, a variation of the PACE model, was designed to offer additional flexibility by allowing frail clients who are dual-eligible for both Medicare and Medicaid to use their regular primary care physicians rather than relying on the physician hired by PACE. Case management is provided by a team that includes a nurse, a social worker, and a nurse practitioner who communicates with the client's primary physician. Although the impact of the Wisconsin Partnership Program is currently limited, there is some evidence that families feel they are receiving better coordinated care (Kane et al. 2002).

Shifting certain services away from or out of hospitals to achieve better coordination among facilities, greater synergies in the use of resources, and provision of care in the most appropriate settings. The US Veterans Health Administration is an example of shifting certain medical services that are traditionally provided in hospital settings. Resources received from the federal government are allocated to 21 regional integrated services networks, facilitating integration and accountability. Robust measurement and reporting mechanisms were also established to improve accountability and enhance performance. The Veterans Health Administration organizes care processes around the individual's needs and enables self-management through supportive information technology. This innovation has made gains in effectiveness and efficiency through better coordination among facilities and shifting from more expensive hospital care services to specialist and primary outpatient care (Satylganova 2016).

Using strategic planning and legislation to enhance the preparation and implementation of care for older adults. Nordic countries have a history of developing national policies for the care of older people to prioritize independent living and restructure publicly provided care for older adults. In Sweden, the Ädel reform (1992) demedicalized institutions for the care of the older population and increased the focus on home care to reduce costs and promote more accessible health services (Verleye and Gemmel 2011). Local governments were encouraged to implement interorganizational networks and standardize guidelines for administrative activities, and information technology systems and chains of care were developed (Verleye and Gemmel 2011). In Denmark, older people with limited physical or cognitive skills have a right to receive in-home support. The result is that 20 percent of older people receive professional home care (Verleye and Gemmel 2011). The number of older people in long-stay hospital care settings (Djellal and Gallouj 2006) has also been reduced by a policy to provide sheltered housing[3] supported by professional services. In Finland, municipal-level networking and cooperation among institutions for the care of older people has led to better results (Verleye and Gemmel 2011). For example, institutional care can be provided in nursing homes and inpatient departments of health care centers (Johansson 2010). These policies demonstrate that a culture of support for older populations can indeed be developed from the top down, trickling down to all levels of care and types of institutions.

Platforms

Care platforms, or the place from which care is provided, should reflect the specific needs of the various groups that comprise the older population—from independent, healthy adults to more dependent older people with multiple health problems. Platforms that reflect specific needs could include the following attributes:

- Offering community-based care, with local agencies responsible for the full range and coordination of community and institutional (acute and long-term) health and social services
- Enhancing the role of care coordinators to organize care
- Providing both diversified and comprehensive, and convenient and accessible, service delivery through referral management and continuity-of-care arrangements
- Encouraging healthy aging in place
- Establishing a more patient-friendly environment for older adults with dementia.

Offering community-based care, with local agencies responsible for the full range and coordination of community and institutional (acute and long-term) health and social services. Canada's Program of Research to Integrate the Services for the Maintenance of Autonomy (PRISMA), created in 1999 in Quebec, in a region south of Montreal called Eastern Townships or Estrie, serves as a single entry point to the health system and coordinates care across a network of providers. A joint governing board of health and social care professionals defines the strategy, allocates resources to the network, and manages provider groups. Key tools used by PRISMA include case management, coordination among decision-makers, a single entry point, individualized service plans, assessment instruments, and computerized clinical charts for communication (Hébert et al. 2003). The evaluation study (Hébert et al. 2010) finds that this coordinated integrated service delivery system has resulted in a decrease in prevalence and incidence of functional decline, emergency room visits, and hospitalizations, together with an improvement in participants' satisfaction with services and empowerment. It also shows that the cost of implementing the integrated network was compensated for by the overall improved efficiency of services utilization.

Because of the PRISMA model's overall ability to improve care for aging populations, in 2005 the Quebec Ministry of Health and Social Services scaled up PRISMA to RSIPA (Réseau de Services Intégrés aux Personnes Âgées), a provincewide initiative that has become the standard system of care for Quebec's older population (MacAdam 2015). Although there have been some ongoing challenges, such as case manager recruitment and training, closing the unmet need gap for home services, and providing incentives for physician participation, RSIPA has become one of the few integrated care models that policy makers have adopted at the system level (MacAdam 2015).

Providing diversified and comprehensive, and convenient and accessible, service delivery through referral management and continuity-of-care arrangements. Qatar has developed a unified approach to managing complex patient needs through greater utilization of available resources. A centralized referral management system and a specialized on-site team deliver comprehensive care based on daily assessments. The services are complemented with geriatric telephone guidance and telemedicine and telepharmacy. Specialized care centers adopt a person-centered, care-based approach, focusing on compassionate patient-provider interactions, access to information, and family and patient involvement. Community-based residential care services help older people make the transition from long-stay acute care to the home environment. The goal is to provide person-centered care in a home setting, nationally coordinated integrated home care, and mobile health care services (WHO 2021a).

Enhancing the role of care coordinators to organize care. Singapore's SingHealth Community Hospitals (SCH)—made up of Bright Vision Hospital, Sengkang Community Hospital, and Outram Community Hospital—serves patients who require subacute care, rehabilitation, and palliative care. The multidisciplinary SCH team includes nurses, doctors, allied health staff, and community relations and engagement administrators. They establish partnerships with community services and their health teams. Well-being coordinators design personalized plans and offer community services and social recommendations based on the patient's interests. The coordinators work with patients during their community hospital stay, following up to monitor progress. When older patients are discharged, SCH's Complementary Integrated Primary Care Program for At-Risk Elders reconnects them back to medical practitioners in their neighborhood, ensuring postdischarge continuity of care at the neighborhood level (WHO 2021b).

Encouraging healthy aging in place. Singapore's Kampung Admiralty is its first public housing innovation that integrates housing and care for seniors. The 11-story "vertical village" includes older people–friendly studio apartments, dining and shopping facilities, a community plaza, a park, and a garden. Health care services are also convenient and accessible, with a nurse on site, referrals to specialized care, and a medical center with outpatient services. The active-aging hub offers aging programs, such as life skills courses, and preventive health programs, such as health checks and fall-risk screenings. With a wide range of amenities and programs, this housing innovation encourages seniors to age in place and to pursue active, healthy lifestyles while bonding with others (Heng and Chua 2014).

Establishing a more patient-friendly environment for older adults with dementia. Korongee Dementia Village, in Australia, is a good example of a patient-friendly platform. The village comprises 12 houses, each situated on one of four quiet cul-de-sacs. It includes a community center, gardens, hair salon, general store, cafe, and wellness center. The village uses dementia design principles, such as enhanced visual cues for directions. The people-centered approach uses a questionnaire to match individuals to an appropriate household based on their expressed values. The small-house model and tailored matching process leads to increased social engagement opportunities and enhanced well-being, which can have an impact on happiness, health, and self-fulfillment.[4]

The Hogeweyk Dementia Village, in the Netherlands, shares a similar design (Harris, Topfer, and Ford 2019). The villages have houses where people live together based on similar lifestyles, and staff and volunteers support quality of life. The neighborhood includes a full range of amenities and entertainment, while retaining links to the broader society.

These innovative models in Singapore, Australia, and the Netherlands support unique needs, lifestyles, and personal preferences for nursing-home living, care, and well-being for people living with severe dementia.

Workforce

The health workforce includes health workers and managers with the preparation, professionalism, and motivation to tailor health and social care services to the needs of the older population. Some innovations include the following:

• Shifting roles among health care professionals or expanding roles to include new tasks

• Creating a team of professionals from multiple disciplines to improve efficiency

• Introducing training and quality-assurance mechanisms at the national level.

Shifting roles among health care professionals or expanding roles to include new tasks. Very few health professionals are trained in geriatrics and fewer than 5 percent are licensed for geriatrics care (Flaherty and Bartels 2019). As a result, caring for older patients requires the development of new care infrastructure, teams, and professionals that facilitate the delivery of integrated care. In Spain's Basque Country, integrated care is offered through the coordination of care processes between primary and secondary care—merging hospital and primary care structures to create integrated health care organizations. Within continuity of care units are designated referral internists responsible for admitting and stabilizing chronically ill patients. Liaison nurses support patients' discharge and transition, and general practitioners follow up with patients. The general practitioners then work with the referral internists in care planning outside the acute episodes. These health care professionals have their own preexisting responsibilities but expand their tasks to offer efficient care to aging populations (Satylganova 2016).

Creating a team of professionals from multiple disciplines to improve efficiency. Canada is exploring and adapting collaborative care models especially for patients experiencing co-occurring mental and physical health conditions (Shulman et al. 2021). This model uses care managers to provide initial and follow-up assessments with standardized monitoring and psychotherapy for self-management. The care managers work with geriatricians and geriatric psychiatrists and communicate recommendations to the primary care providers. The evaluation shows that the program is feasible and effective given that it was well received by patients and patient outcomes improved. Despite these positive outcomes, financing such a program can prove to be difficult in public fee-for-service health care systems (Shulman et al. 2021).

The Coordination of Professional Care model in France targets high-risk groups (very weak, older people living in a particular service area) and coordinates treatment at two levels—within primary care, and between primary care and specialized care. The multidisciplinary primary care team, including case managers, works with the primary care physician to assess and provide care. Primary care and specialist care are integrated, with geriatricians visiting homes, and primary care physicians directing hospitalizations (Kalantari et al. 2021). This model balances available services with older patients' needs, reduces excessive use, and improves convenience with home visits and accessible specialist care.

Introducing training and quality-assurance mechanisms at the national level. To address the geriatrics workforce shortage in the United States, the US Health Resources and Services Administration developed the Geriatrics Workforce Enhancement Program as a comprehensive, three-year initiative to train and increase the number of doctors, nurses, social workers, and other health care professionals who work with older adults. The program funds 44 organizations in 29 states to create educational and training environments to address the needs of the aging population and to upgrade the professional skills needed to improve their health outcomes and quality of care (Flaherty and Bartels 2019). The interprofessional education and training curriculum addresses interprofessional collaboration—specifically, providing older adult– and family-centered care, managing environmental risks, providing disease management coaching, identifying ethical issues, providing effective care transition, and communicating effectively with older adults and their families (Flaherty and Bartels 2019).

Disease management programs in Germany foster evidence-based treatment, service delivery across levels of care, patient self-management, and the introduction of new quality-assurance mechanisms. General practitioners serve as care coordinators. This standardizes nationwide programs for individuals with chronic conditions, based on a regulatory, top-down framework (Satylganova 2016).

Information and Tools

A key component in the foundation for creating innovations in models of care for older adults is the information and tools used to design integrated and robust solutions. They include the following:

- Using comprehensive geriatric assessment instruments to assess needs and allocate limited resources
- Enhancing the sharing of medical records among providers to enable more integrated care.

Using comprehensive geriatric assessment instruments to assess needs and allocate limited resources. In Italy, each patient under the integrated home-care program is assessed using the Minimum Data Set for Home Care (MDS-HC), a comprehensive geriatric assessment instrument. Subsequently, a case manager and a multidisciplinary team deliver social and health care services. In the Silver Network Project in Italy, the Community Geriatric Evaluation Unit plays a key role in allocating LTC for older adults (Kalantari et al. 2021). Case managers use the MDS-HC assessment tool to determine eligibility for home care and deliver health and social services. Such an integrated home-care program, based on a comprehensive geriatric assessment instrument guided by a case manager, has a significant impact on hospitalization rates (reductions in hospitalizations and hospital days) and is cost-effective (29 percent cost reduction, with an estimated savings of US$1,260 per patient per year) (Landi et al. 2001).

In Poland, the Camberwell Assessment of Need for the Elderly is often used for older adults living in the community or in LTC residences. One advantage of this tool over other instruments is that it interprets a need as a remediable deficit and is able to separate "met needs" from "unmet needs." It assesses need in 24 areas of life that cover a broad range of socioeconomic, psychological, and health domains and provides a strong foundation for a holistic approach to care (Tobis et al. 2018).

Enhancing the sharing of medical records among providers to enable more integrated care. Spain's Basque Country developed a new health information system in collaboration with users and has facilitated coordination among providers. This information system and strategies for its use also enable older adults to manage their diseases. Performance indicators such as hospital admissions and readmissions for conditions related to ambulatory care present evidence of improvements in patient outcomes and savings (Satylganova 2016).

Innovations in LTC in LMICs

LTC is complex because it combines clinical and personal care. The care delivery model—the way in which services are provided—can therefore vary depending on the context. With increasing demand for such care, some LMICs have introduced a variety of innovative and emerging LTC provision and delivery models. This section summarizes these innovative models, with examples grouped by key characteristics, which may serve as useful templates for other countries looking to develop and integrate feasible care models for older adults.

People-Centered Comprehensive Innovations

Individualized care assessments and care planning as the foundation of efficient and effective home- and community-based service delivery. Home- and community-based services allow people with significant physical and cognitive limitations to remain integrated in the community by living at home or in a home-like setting. This model seems to be increasingly welcomed by older adults and their family members, particularly in the post-COVID-19 (coronavirus) era. In Tanzania, from 2014 to 2017, HelpAge International implemented the Better Health for Older People in Africa program, funded by the UK's Foreign, Commonwealth and Development Office, to improve access to home-based services for poorer older people. The program, which supported approximately 4,500 older people, was delivered by 425 trained volunteers selected in consultation with the local community and supervised by registered nurses and clinical officers (Petsoulas 2019). Under this program, care plans were developed to assist with activities of daily living. It also offered social support programs, for example, to aid in socialization with other older people, and volunteer-led workshops to learn about topics such as nutrition (Petsoulas 2019).

Engaging multidisciplinary teams to deliver LTC that is unique to the individual. In Kenya, a private nursing agency provides individualized in-home care to those who can afford to pay for it or whose medical insurance covers home-based care (Petsoulas 2019). Services include personal care, specialized home-health care, nutritional advice, psychosocial support, and disease management services. Teams of health professionals and patient participants come together to create personalized care plans for delivering care. Although this type of private sector–driven model is growing in popularity, gaps in access exist for older individuals without insurance.

Utilizing care management to optimize service delivery. In Thailand, an LTC pilot program established in 2016 and managed by the National Health Security Office and local authorities operates through a care-management system and provides two to eight hours of home-based care support a week, depending on need. The caregivers, who each receive 70 hours of training, are supervised by a care manager (ADB 2020). Social services such as assistance with housework, activities of daily living, and obtaining assistive devices are provided to older persons who meet the eligibility criteria. Medical services, including preventive services and physiotherapy, are also available through the program and the Thailand universal health coverage package (ADB 2020).

Community Empowerment Innovations

Delivering care in a way that is not only culturally acceptable but also culturally appropriate. In Ghana, the Care for Aged Foundation provides individualized care plans developed in collaboration with the older people they serve and their families along with in-home care visits and assistance with personal care errands (Petsoulas 2019). Training on how to provide these home-care services and medical supplies is funded by donors through cash or in-kind donations. Young volunteer workers receive free health care in exchange for their service (Petsoulas 2019). This model acknowledges and incorporates the existing structure of care in which the young assist older adults and therefore home-care services are provided in a manner that is not only culturally acceptable but culturally comfortable. It is, however, important to note that because volunteers are unpaid, it may be difficult for this type of model to be scaled up, retain workers, or be sustainable in the long run.

Drawing on older people's knowledge, skills, and support to establish a community-based model of LTC provision and delivery. In Cambodia, China, India, Indonesia, Myanmar, Nepal, the Philippines, Sri Lanka, and Vietnam, Older People's Associations (OPAs)—membership organizations led or managed by older people—often facilitate activities and deliver services for older people. By partnering with government service providers, OPAs provide an added layer of support for older persons' well-being that complements existing medical service delivery mechanisms with social and community engagement (HelpAge International 2020). OPAs have been involved in organizing medical checkups, conducting home visits, and providing older people with health education. Additionally, OPAs play an important role in campaigning for and promoting older people's interests to policy makers (Petsoulas 2019).

Promoting care integration through community participation. In Indonesia, the government has implemented the *posyandu lansia* program in the form of integrated community health service posts at which health activities for older people are carried out. Posts are managed and run by the community and include teams of volunteers and health providers. Health services commonly available include checkups, consultations, and free treatments. The posts also provide opportunities for older adults to socialize (Permata 2020). However, it has been shown that issues such as insufficient staff training and resource shortages can endanger the viability of these types of community programs (Permata 2020).

Financial Sustainability Innovations

Providing retirement accommodations and LTC to older people who can afford it while generating a source of income to be used to assist other older people in need, thereby serving a dual function. Rand Aid, a nonprofit organization in Johannesburg, South Africa, provides a range of upscale retirement residential accommodations, effectively giving older people who pay a purchase price the right to live in that unit for the remainder of their lives. This "life right" is not the same as ownership of the property; the housing unit remains the property of the Rand Aid Welfare Development Trust. When the occupant no longer lives there, 80 percent of the original purchase price is refunded to the occupant or his or her estate.[5] The accommodations offer services such as security, nursing care, domestic services, and physiotherapy.

In addition to the residential properties, there is also the opportunity to reside in two separate LTC facilities that focus on providing people-centered care through care planning (Petsoulas 2019). In one of these facilities, residents pay board and lodging in full if they are financially able. There is an additional LTC facility that provides 24-hour nursing care on the same property; this one is funded in part by a small government subsidy and in part through a portion of the 20 percent of the life rights residential accommodation purchase price (Petsoulas 2019).

Discussion and Policy Considerations

The rapid growth of aging populations and the concomitant increase in the number of older people with disabilities and complex care needs present both challenges and opportunities for strengthening the health and long-term care delivery systems to meet such needs in all countries. A wide variety of innovative care delivery models have emerged. Not surprisingly, most of these models are found in HICs, with very few in LMIC settings.

This chapter describes a sample of innovations in health and LTC provision and service delivery models. The brief descriptions of these models are organized around five conceptual domains—population, governance, platforms, workforce, and information and tools—while recognizing the overlap in key themes, parameters, and components that cut across virtually all the innovations. Many of the innovation examples share key features of person-centered integrated care approaches tailored to the unique needs of older adults. Chief among them are the deployment of multidisciplinary (or inter-disciplinary) teams, care coordination among providers across different care settings, care planning, case management based on individualized comprehensive geriatric assessment, and effective communication and sharing of medical records among providers.

Systematic reviews find that the most common key elements of integrated care approaches are multidisciplinary teams, comprehensive assessment, and case management (Briggs et al. 2018; Kirst et al. 2017). A review of what works in implementation of integrated care programs for older adults with complex needs highlights the importance of trusting multidisciplinary team relationships for effective collaboration, communication, and knowledge sharing (Kirst et al. 2017). The review also identifies contextual factors—such as strong leadership that sets clear goals, an organizational culture that embraces innovation, and joint governance structures—that are conducive to team collaboration and successful program implementation. In addition, the review finds provider commitment to, and understanding of, the integrated care program; clear governance; time to build an infrastructure to implement; and flexibility in implementation to be key processes that are instrumental to program success (Kirst et al. 2017).

Relatively few of the many innovative care models or programs for older adults identified in the research literature have been subjected to rigorous evaluation of their performance and cost-effectiveness, as also pointed out by other reviewers (Dyer, van den Berg, et al. 2019; Kirst et al. 2017). Some types of integrated care models have been known for achieving desired outcomes, supported by solid research evidence. Even so, scalability for widespread application may still be a challenge. The PACE program in the United States is a good example. Multidisciplinary professional teams, case management, individualized care planning and care coordination, housing, transportation, community-based day programs, and functional information technology systems are hallmark features of the PACE program that allow participating older adults to age in place. A growing body of evidence from credible evaluations shows that the PACE program has reduced hospitalizations and nursing home utilization, increased use of ambulatory services, and improved perceived health status and quality of life relative to the comparison group of individuals with similar care needs (Kirst et al. 2017). However, despite PACE's favorable outcomes and popularity and the program's long existence since the 1970s and presence in 31 US states, total PACE enrollment is a mere 53,000 participants nationwide (National PACE Association 2020), which is a very small portion of all community-living older adults with nursing-home level of care needs. Among other factors, high upfront capital investment and operating costs are significant constraints on further expansion of the program.

In LMICs, creating and scaling up effective integrated care programs such as PACE will be even more challenging, given limited resources and the lack of health care and LTC service infrastructure. In particular, the shortage of a professional workforce with which to build multidisciplinary teams—an essential ingredient of successful integrated care programs—remains a major barrier. Policy makers in these countries should consider substantially increasing investment in education and training programs, not only to upgrade the skills of current and prospective LTC workers but also to produce a cadre of multidisciplinary professionals, including geriatricians, pharmacists, therapists, dietitians, nurses, social workers, case managers, and LTC facility administrators. These staff are crucial for integrating health care and LTC services (Feng et al. 2020).

Furthermore, as noted in this book and by other reviewers (Dyer, van den Berg, et al. 2019; Kalantari et al. 2021), nearly all innovative care models for older adults identified in the literature, including those sampled here, are local in scope. Perhaps this should not be a surprise, given that health care and LTC for older people are local by nature. This also means scalability can be a challenge and some adaptation may be necessary for an innovative care model to take root in another local context. Diffusion of innovative care models across different countries, especially from HICs to LMICs, requires even greater scrutiny and more thorough review and evaluation by experts and policy makers.

Conclusion

In most countries, health care and LTC delivery systems for older people remain siloed across different providers and care settings. Much of the care is provided in hospitals and other institutional settings, which is a facility- or provider-centric model rather than person-centered. However, this review identifies a relatively recent shift, albeit primarily in HICs, toward establishing person-centered, PHC-driven, integrated delivery systems that encompass the full continuum of acute, postacute, and long-term care services and palliative and end-of-life care. Person-centeredness entails the delivery of care and services at or near the place where older people live, either in their homes or the community, consistent with their preference for aging in place. Regardless of the setting the person considers home, "treating in place," rather than navigating the complicated care delivery system and moving across multiple providers and care settings, may also be preferred by many seniors. The appeal and benefit of this approach has been aptly underscored during challenging times such as the ongoing COVID-19 pandemic.

Many of the innovative care models reviewed in this chapter hold promise for achieving the desired goals of person-centered integrated care for older adults. Yet in most LMICs, these innovative service provision and delivery models largely remain a concept. However, this gap should not prevent policy makers and practitioners in LMICs from "aiming high" toward building their own delivery systems that reflect as many desirable system features as are feasible. Aided by cross-country learning and a growing knowledge base from international health care and LTC research, leapfrogging to that stage by adopting and adapting international best practices can be achievable.

Notes

1. The material included in this section draws from Glinskaya, Feng, and Suarez 2022.
2. SCAN Foundation, "Person-Centered Care." Accessed June 6, 2022, https://www .thescanfoundation.org/initiatives/person-centered-care.
3. Sheltered housing facilities, or residential care or service homes, are a block of small, independent dwellings with optional group-level services, such as catering and health centers (Djellal and Gallouj 2006; Johansson 2010).
4. "Korongee Dementia Village," accessed June 1, 2022 (https://glenview.org.au /korongee).
5. Rand Aid Association, "Rand Aid Association—Retirement Villages," https:// www.seniorservice.co.za/property/johannesburg/rand-aid-retirement-villages.

References

Aranco, Natalia. 2020. "Panorama of Aging and Long-Term Care: Chile." Inter-American Development Bank, Washington, DC. http://dx.doi.org/10.18235/0002770.

ADB (Asian Development Bank). 2020. *Country Diagnostic Study on Long-Term Care in Thailand*. Manila: Asian Development Bank. doi:http://dx.doi.org/10.22617 /TCS200373-2.

ADB (Asian Development Bank). 2021. *Country Diagnostic Study on Long-Term Care in Indonesia*. Manila: Asian Development Bank. doi:http://dx.doi.org/10.22617 /TCS210416-2.

Baris, Enis, Rachel Silverman, Huihui Wang, Feng Zhao, and Muhammad Ali Pate. 2021. *Walking the Talk: Reimagining Primary Health Care after COVID-19*. Washington, DC: World Bank.

Barkay, Aliza, and Nili Tabak. 2002. "Elderly Residents' Participation and Autonomy within a Geriatric Ward in a Public Institution." *International Journal of Nursing Practice* 8 (4): 198–209. https://doi.org/10.1046/j.1440-172X.2002.00363.x.

Billings, J. Andrew, and Eric L. Krakauer. 2011. "On Patient Autonomy and Physician Responsibility in End-of-Life Care." *Archives of Internal Medicine* 171 (9): 849–53. https://doi.org/10.1001/archinternmed.2011.180.

Briggs, Andrew M., Pim P. Valentijn, Jotheeswaran A. Thiyagarajan, and Islene Araujo de Carvalho. 2018. "Elements of Integrated Care Approaches for Older People: A Review of Reviews." *BMJ Open* 8 (4): e021194. https://doi.org/10.1136/bmjopen -2017-021194.

Djellal, Faridah, and Faïz Gallouj. 2006. "Innovation in Care Services for the Elderly." *Service Industries Journal* 26 (April): 303–27. https://doi.org/10.1080/02642060600 570943.

Dyer, Suzanne, Madeleine Valeri, Nimita Arora, Tyler Ross, Megan Winsall, Dominic Tilden, and Maria Crotty. 2019. *Review of International Systems for Long-Term Care of Older People*. Adelaide, Australia: Flinders University.

Dyer, Suzanne, Maayken E. L. van den Berg, Kate Barnett, Alex Brown, Georgina Johnstone, Kate E. Laver, Judy Lowthian, et al. 2019. *Review of Innovative Models of Aged Care*. Adelaide, Australia: Flinders University.

European Commission. 2021. *Long-Term Care Report: Trends, Challenges and Opportunities in an Ageing Society. Volume II, Country Profiles*. European Commission, Directorate-General for Employment, Social Affairs and Inclusion. Luxembourg: Publications Office. doi:https://data.europa.eu/doi/10.2767/183997.

Feng, Zhanlian. 2019. "Global Convergence: Aging and Long-Term Care Policy Challenges in the Developing World." *Journal of Aging and Social Policy* 31 (4): 291–97. doi:10.1080/08959420.2019.1626205.

Feng, Zhanlian, Elena Glinskaya, Hongtu Chen, Sen Gong, Yue Qiu, Jianming Xu, and Winnie Yip. 2020. "Long-Term Care System for Older Adults in China: Policy Landscape, Challenges, and Future Prospects." *The Lancet* 396 (10259): 1362–72.

Flaherty, Ellen, and Stephen J. Bartels. 2019. "Addressing the Community-Based Geriatric Healthcare Workforce Shortage by Leveraging the Potential of Interprofessional Teams." *Journal of the American Geriatrics Society* 67 (S2): S400–8. https://doi.org/10.1111/jgs.15924.

Giacomin, Karla Cristina, Paulo José Fortes Villas Boas, Marisa Accioly Rodrigues da Costa Domingues, and Patrick Alexander Wachholz. 2021. "Caring throughout Life: Peculiarities of Long-Term Care for Public Policies without Ageism." *Geriatrics, Gerontology and Aging* 15: e0210009. doi:https://doi.org/10.5327/Z2447-21232021 EDITESP.

Glinskaya, E., Z. Feng, and G. Suarez. 2022. "Understanding the "State of Play" of Long-Term Care Provision in Low- and Middle-Income Countries." *International Social Security Review* 75 (3–4): 71–101. doi:https://doi.org/10.1111/issr.12308.

Gutiérrez Robledo, Luis Miguel, Mariana López Ortega, and Victoria Eugenia Arango Lopera. 2012. "The State of Elder Care in Mexico." *Current Geriatrics Reports* 1 (4): 183–89. doi:10.1007/s13670-012-0028-z.

Harris, Jonathan, Leigh-Ann Topfer, and Caitlyn Ford. 2019. "Dementia Villages: Innovative Residential Care for People with Dementia." *CADTH Issues in Emerging Health Technologies* 178 (October): 28.

Hébert, Réjean, Pierre J. Durand, Nicole Dubuc, and André Tourigny. 2003. "PRISMA: A New Model of Integrated Service Delivery for the Frail Older People in Canada." *International Journal of Integrated Care* 3 (March): e08. https://doi.org/10.5334/ijic.73.

Hébert, Réjean, Michel Raîche, Marie-France Dubois, N'Deye R. Gueye, Nicole Dubuc, Michel Tousignant, and The PRISMA Group. 2010. "Impact of PRISMA, a Coordination-Type Integrated Service Delivery System for Frail Older People in Quebec (Canada): A Quasi-Experimental Study." *Journals of Gerontology. Series B* 65B (1): 107–18. https://doi.org/10.1093/geronb/gbp027.

HelpAge International. 2020. "Older People's Associations in Asia: Strengths and Key Factors for Sustainability and Replication." HelpAge International, Chiang Mai, Thailand.

Heng, Janice, and Grace Chua. 2014. "'Modern Kampung' to Launch in July BTO." *Straits Times*, April 27, 2014. https://www.straitstimes.com /singapore/housing/modern-kampung-to-launch-in-july-bto.

Hirose, Kenichi, and Zofia Czepulis-Rutkowska. 2016. *Challenges in Long-Term Care of the Elderly in Central and Eastern Europe.* Budapest: International Labour Organization, ILO DWT and Country Office for Central and Eastern Europe.

Holmes, Wendy. 2021. "Projecting the Need for and Cost of Long-Term Care for Older Persons." Sustainable Development Working Paper Series 74, Asian Development Bank, Manila. doi:http://dx.doi.org/10.22617/WPS210072-2.

Hussein, Shereen. 2022. "Ageing Demographics in the Middle East and North Africa: Policy Opportunities and Challenges." Report prepared for the World Bank, Washington, DC.

Hussein, Shereen, and Mohamed Ismail. 2017. "Ageing and Elderly Care in the Arab Region: Policy Challenges and Opportunities." *Ageing International* 42 (3): 274–89. doi:10.1007/s12126-016-9244-8.

Ismail, Mohamed, and Shereen Hussein. 2021. "An Evidence Review of Ageing, Long-Term Care Provision and Funding Mechanisms in Turkey: Using Existing Evidence to Estimate Long-Term Care Cost." *Sustainability* 13 (11): 6306.

Johansson, Edvard. 2010. "The Long-Term Care System for the Elderly in Finland." Research Report 76, European Network of Economic Policy Research Institutes, Brussels.

Kalantari, Ali Reza, Mohammad Hossein Mehrolhassani, Mohsen Shati, and Reza Dehnavieh. 2021. "Health Service Delivery Models for Elderly People: A Systematic Review." *Medical Journal of the Islamic Republic of Iran* 35: 21. https://doi.org/10.47176/mjiri.35.21.

Kane, Robert L., Patricia Homyak, Boris Bershadsky, and Yat-Sang Lum. 2002. "Consumer Responses to the Wisconsin Partnership Program for Elderly Persons: A Variation on the PACE Model." *Journals of Gerontology. Series A, Biological Sciences and Medical Sciences* 57 (4): M250–58. https://doi.org/10.1093/gerona/57.4.m250.

Kazibwe, Joseph, Phuong Bich Tran, and Kristi Sidney Annerstedt. 2021. "The Household Financial Burden of Non-Communicable Diseases in Low- and Middle-Income Countries: A Systematic Review." *Health Research Policy and Systems* 19 (1): 96. doi:10.1186/s12961-021-00732-y.

Kirst, Maritt, Jennifer Im, Tim Burns, G. Ross Baker, Jodeme Goldhar, Patricia O'Campo, Anne Wojtak, and Walter P. Wodchis. 2017. "What Works in Implementation of Integrated Care Programs for Older Adults with Complex Needs? A Realist Review." *International Journal for Quality in Health Care* 29 (5): 612–24. doi:10.1093/intqhc/mzx095.

Kruk, Margaret E., Anna D. Gage, Catherine Arsenault, Keely Jordan, Hannah H. Leslie, Sanam Roder-DeWan, Olusoji Adeyi, et al. 2018. "High-Quality Health Systems in the Sustainable Development Goals Era: Time for a Revolution." *The Lancet Global Health* 6 (11): e1196–e1252. https://doi.org/10.1016/S2214-109X(18)30386-3.

Landi, Francesco, Graziano Onder, Andrea Russo, Sandro Tabaccanti, Rodolfo Rollo, Stefano Federici, Ennio Tua, Matteo Cesari, and Roberto Bernabei. 2001. "A New Model of Integrated Home Care for the Elderly: Impact on Hospital Use." *Journal of Clinical Epidemiology* 54 (9): 968–70. https://doi.org/10.1016/S0895-4356(01)00366-3.

Lloyd-Sherlock, Peter, Anne Margriet Pot, Siriphan Sasat, and Fernando Morales-Martinez. 2017. "Volunteer Provision of Long-Term Care for Older People in Thailand and Costa Rica." *Bulletin of the World Health Organization* 95 (11): 774–78. doi:10.2471/BLT.16.187526.

MacAdam, Margaret. 2015. "PRISMA: Program of Research to Integrate the Services for the Maintenance of Autonomy. A System-Level Integration Model in Quebec." *International Journal of Integrated Care* 15 (September): e018. https://doi.org/10.5334/ijic.2246.

Matus-López, Mauricio, and Alexander Chaverri-Carvajal. 2022. "Progress toward Long-Term Care Protection in Latin America: A National Long-Term Care System in Costa Rica." *Journal of the American Medical Directors Association* 23 (2): 266–71. doi:10.1016/j.jamda.2021.06.021.

Medellín, Nadin. 2020. *Panorama of Aging and Long-term Care: Summary Costa Rica.* Washington, DC: Inter-American Development Bank. https://policycommons.net/artifacts/812798/panorama-of-aging-and-long-term-care/1686190.

Mui, Ada Chan. 2001. "The Program of All-Inclusive Care for the Elderly (PACE): An Innovative Long-Term Care Model in the United States." *Journal of Aging and Social Policy* 13 (2–3): 53–67. https://doi.org/10.1300/j031v13n02_05.

National Academies of Sciences, Engineering, and Medicine. 2021. *Implementing High-Quality Primary Care: Rebuilding the Foundation of Health Care.* Washington, DC: National Academies Press.

National PACE Association. 2020. "PACE by the Numbers." https://www.npaonline.org/sites/default/files/images/NPA%20infographic%203%2020%20%281%29.pdf.

OECD (Organisation for Economic Co-operation and Development). 2011. "Mexico: Long-Term Care." OECD, Geneva. https://fliphtml5.com/ulmf/aovi.

OECD (Organisation for Economic Co-operation and Development). 2020. *Realising the Potential of Primary Health Care*. OECD Health Policy Studies. Paris: OECD.

Oliveri, María Laura. 2020. *Panorama of Aging and Long-Term Care: Summary Argentina*. Washington, DC: Inter-American Development Bank. doi:http://dx.doi.org/10.18235/0002929.

Permata, Sri Putri. 2020. "Improving the Quality of Life of the Elderly through Participation in the Activities of Posyandu Lansia (Integrated Community Health Service of Elderly)." The 2nd International Conference on Social Work, University of Muhammadiyah Jakarta, Jakarta, Indonesia, February 29–March 1, 2020.

Petsoulas, Christina. 2019. "Thinking about Long-term Care in a Global Context—A Literature Review." Green Templeton College, Oxford University, Oxford, U.K.

Satylganova, Altynai. 2016. *Integrated Care Models: An Overview*. Copenhagen: WHO Regional Office for Europe.

Shulman, Richard, Reenu Arora, Rose Geist, Amna Ali, Julia Ma, Elizabeth Mansfield, Sara Martel, Jane Sandercock, and Judith Versloot. 2021. "Integrated Community Collaborative Care for Seniors with Depression/Anxiety and Any Physical Illness." *Canadian Geriatrics Journal* 24 (July): 251–57. https://doi.org/10.5770/cgj.24.473.

Tobis, Sławomir, Katarzyna Wieczorowska-Tobis, Dorota Talarska, Mariola Pawlaczyk, and Aleksandra Suwalska. 2018. "Needs of Older Adults Living in Long-Term Care Institutions: An Observational Study Using Camberwell Assessment of Need for the Elderly." *Clinical Interventions in Aging* 13: 2389–95. https://doi.org/10.2147/CIA.S145937.

Van, Phan Hong, Khuong Anh Tuan, and Tran Thi Mai Oanh. 2021. "Older Persons and Long-Term Care in Viet Nam." In *Coping with Rapid Population Ageing in Asia*, edited by Osuke Komazawa and Yasuhiko Saito. Jakarta: Economic Research Institute for ASEAN and East Asia (ERIA).

Verleye, Katrien, and Paul Gemmel. 2009. "Innovation in the Elderly Care Sector—At the Edge of Chaos." Vlerick Business School, Belgium. https://repository.vlerick.com/handle/20.500.12127/3366.

Verleye, Katrien, and Paul Gemmel. 2011. "Innovation in the Elderly Care Sector—At the Edge of Chaos." *Journal of Management and Marketing in Healthcare* 4 (2): 122–28. https://doi.org/10.1179/1753304X11Y.0000000002.

WHO (World Health Organization). 2017. *Towards Long-Term Care Systems in Sub-Saharan Africa*. Geneva: WHO. https://www.who.int/publications/i/item/9789241513388.

WHO (World Health Organization). 2021a. *Framework for Countries to Achieve an Integrated Continuum of Long-Term Care*. Geneva: WHO. https://apps.who.int/iris/handle/10665/349911.

WHO (World Health Organization). 2021b. "Promoting Healthy Ageing in Singapore." June 14, 2021. https://www.who.int/news-room/feature-stories/detail/promoting-healthy-ageing-in-singapore.

CHAPTER 4

How Digital Health Technology Is Transforming Health Care for Older Adults

Gabriel Catan Burlac and Xiaohui Hou

Key Messages

- Digital health can transform care for older populations, but many older adults face access gaps.

- Digital technologies support older people's health through clinical applications, information integration, and case management applications and by enabling healthier lifestyles.

- Key digital health access barriers for older people reflect technology design, affordability, and ease of use. A senior-centric design approach can optimize digital technologies for older adult care.

- Assessing older adults' preferences, capabilities, and challenges with digital health technology is a first step for effective policy.

- To promote older people's use of digital health, governments and partners can enlist families and caregivers as key allies.

- Countries are leveraging new business models for digital health in older populations, including public-private partnerships. Financial incentives and an enabling ecosystem can foster local start-ups and expand this promising market.

Delivering Health to Older Adults in a Digital World

Introduction

From wearable sensors to mobile health apps, from electronic health records to personalized medicine, from predictive diagnostics to first-aid instructions delivered in a soothing voice by cute little robotic devices, the rapid advance of digital and virtual technologies is transforming the way health care is delivered. The advancement of technology and the exponential growth of data[1] are providing countries with an unprecedented opportunity to leapfrog intermediate development stages in their health systems. Thanks to digital solutions, growing numbers of countries are poised to improve the quality and efficiency of their health care by strengthening evidence-based decision-making, reducing disease burdens and associated costs, optimizing resource management and utilization, harnessing new clinical decision-support tools, and expanding care access and quality for the poor and vulnerable.

In the digital era, many health systems are also encountering a growing awareness of, and demand for, person-centered health care—the provision, coordination, and integration of services in a holistic way that empowers patients and puts them at the center of care processes. Enhanced by technology, person-centered care can enable high levels of patient self-efficacy and a greater emphasis on prevention.

Concurrently, most countries are seeing a trend toward the consumerization of health care to accommodate patients' and families' personal preferences so that the care they receive is better tailored to their unique needs. As part of this process, people are integrating technology, coaching programs, self-education, and social networks to achieve a healthy life. According to Kent (2021), consumers can access more than 350,000 digital health apps globally through different platforms.

Digital health can be defined as the use of information and communications technology—including artificial intelligence, big data analytics, and mobile, wireless, and computer technologies—to promote health and support health-related fields such as health care services, health surveillance, health literature, and health education, knowledge, and research (WHO 2019). Digital health has the potential to solve pernicious health care challenges and can help transform and strengthen primary health care (McKinsey & Company 2021).

Digital health can influence the way health services are provided to older adults. Understanding how technology is currently being used while anticipating future opportunities and challenges can guide policy makers in realizing new long-term care patient pathways that maximize digital health. The aim is to incorporate age-responsive digital tools and strategies in a way that is beneficial for both older users and the care system itself.

This chapter extends the exploration of the innovation component of the financing, innovation, regulation, and evaluation (FIRE) framework. The chapter focuses on the interaction between older adults and digital health technology, examining current digital health technology use by older adults and how digital technology innovations could increasingly transform health services, care outcomes, and living conditions for older people. The chapter begins by reviewing how technology is already transforming service delivery for older adults in many settings. It then explains challenges and barriers for expanded implementation, with attention to digital divides between and within countries. It ends with policy recommendations for the integration of digital health in care for older adults. Like the preceding chapter, this one organizes its policy recommendations under the foundational health system components identified by Kruk et al. (2018) and discussed in chapter 1. These components—population, governance, platforms, workforce, information and tools—bring policy entry points and options in the innovation domain of FIRE into clearer view.[2]

This chapter casts a wide net in analyzing digital health challenges and solutions, incorporating tools and approaches that can enhance primary health care delivery and others that are relevant to long-term care. The analysis takes account of existing digital divides and barriers to uptake among older adults and considers how they can be addressed.

Digital Health Utilization by Older Adults

The internet and other digital health technologies have brought profound changes to many people's lives, but these experiences vary across countries, socioeconomic contexts, and age groups. Because of their extensive use of social media and other online technology, many younger people worldwide share common experiences as members of a globalized culture. But among older adults, the use of the internet and other digital tools varies significantly. For example, in the United Kingdom from 2011 to 2019, internet use among people age 65 to 74 rose from 52 percent to 83 percent (ITU 2020a). Meanwhile, in the United States, between 2016 and 2021 the number of adults age 65 and older who say they use the internet rose by approximately 20 percent to 75 percent (Pew Research Center 2021). In Canada, approximately 71 percent of older adults reported access to the internet in 2018 (Statistics Canada 2019). Yet an International Telecommunication Union report indicates that roughly 3.7 billion people, mostly concentrated in developing countries and rural areas, are still unconnected (ITU 2021).[3]

Even in developed countries, where older adults generally have greater access to digital tools, the use of digital health technology is hampered because many health insurance schemes and other third-party payers do not cover health-related digital services. A 2018 survey shows that, although interest among US seniors in virtual health and artificial intelligence– (AI-) enabled technology is high, there are unmet needs because many payers are slow to offer or support these services, seemingly unaware of the huge business opportunity within their grasp (Accenture 2018).[4] Most survey respondents expressed interest in receiving appointment and prescription reminders (72 percent), engaging in telemedicine visits (71 percent), and receiving follow-up support on health management (63 percent) by digital means.[5] Similar preferences were found in Australia and the United Kingdom.[6]

COVID-19 (coronavirus) highlighted the critical need for all countries to strengthen their health systems and provide equitable and timely access to health care backed by reliable information systems. During the pandemic, digital health grew exponentially in many settings, signaling the power and potential of these new forms of technology. Movement restrictions and social distancing measures increased the use of telemedicine services, prompting new populations to embrace them. In the United States, for example, telemedicine services for the older adult population expanded by 300 percent during the pandemic.[7] Research shows that Americans 50 and older spent more during the pandemic than before the pandemic on technology, video services, smartphones, and wearable devices (Kakulla 2021).

Although these developments and changes are occurring primarily in high-income countries, awareness about the significance of digital health is also increasing in low- and middle-income countries (LMICs). However, the same awareness is not always true among older adults, who may be less comfortable using newer technologies because of physical limitations, lack of knowledge, lower levels of habituation, or simply a lack of trust (Evangelista, Steinhubl, and Topol 2019).

Transforming Service Delivery for Older Populations

Digital health technologies for older adults can be viewed as a class of assistive technology, which can be defined as equipment, smart devices, or software apps that people can use to enhance or maintain their functional capabilities so that they can learn, communicate, and function better in everyday life or get things done that might otherwise be difficult or impossible (Marasinghe, Lapitan, and Ross 2015). Technologies and software that support older adults have been termed "gerontechnology" (WHO 2022).

Digital health can support various clinical interventions to tackle ongoing or newly diagnosed conditions. It can also support lifestyle changes and health monitoring in situations in which diagnosis and medical intervention may be less effective (Joe and Demiris 2013). The internet can also mitigate loneliness by increasing social connectivity, which is a factor in older persons' health and well-being. These interactions can also support disease management by providing connections with peers who have similar conditions (Sun et al. 2020).

Telemedicine and telecare technologies, including monitoring technology that tracks health and vital signs, can overcome physical distance, architectural barriers, time, and other obstacles that often complicate older people's access to services. Digital health devices with sensors (for example, pill reminders and voice-assisted technologies) can support older patients and transmit information to medical staff for remote monitoring. Resulting data not only facilitate health care but also enable advanced algorithms to predict future outcomes and recommend preventive care (Sardis 2019). Some examples are shown in box 4.1.

For simplicity, digital health technologies and their applications can be divided into three categories:

- *Clinical applications.* The clinical uses of digital health technology are multi-faceted and expanding. Applications range from assisted diagnostics and image reading to more advanced robotics-assisted surgeries. Specifically related to older adults are advances in remote monitoring technology that permit the collection of patients' health information as they go about their daily lives. Encompassing vital signs, other basic health indicators, and user signals, such data can inform patients, caregivers, and medical staff without the need for repeated clinic visits (Elgazzar, Yoong, and Finkelstein 2020).

BOX 4.1 Examples of Digital Health Technology Use

Japan: Robot helpers for fragile older adults

An aging population and a dearth of human resources to assist older patients have motivated Japan to invest in developing robots for use in nursing homes. Assistive humanoids are supporting patients with dementia by providing information, engaging them through games and activities, and functioning as companions through stimulating interactions. Robotic exoskeletons help patients get in and out of their beds without the need of a nurse or other health care worker, reducing staff workloads (Lufkin 2020).

The Russian Federation: Telemedicine services for older adults

The SberHealth program is providing telemedicine consultations through primary care doctors and specialists to older people with chronic diseases in 11 regions in Russia. The patients need to regularly update a health diary through a web portal to inform their provider; they can also provide updates by using voice-recognition software.

Additionally, in 2020, because of social distancing requirements linked to COVID-19 (coronavirus), Russia introduced a teleconsultation program in six constituent territories as part of mandatory health insurance and is expected to expand this program (Salakhutdinova et al. 2021).

Singapore: SHINESeniors smart homes initiative

Singapore has a rapidly aging population. A joint venture between the Singapore Management University and Tata Consultancy Services has developed several kinds of assistive-technology sensors that are being installed in homes for older adults to help them live more independently. Currently present in about 100 Housing and Development Board apartments, the sensors use data analytics and Internet of Things technology to capture and transmit information about falls, prolonged inactivity, food consumption patterns, mobility, and social interactions. Different from many other initiatives, the sensors used in the SHINESeniors pilot project intervene nonintrusively, that is, only when they detect a significant deviation from a normal pattern, which avoids unnecessary actions while reducing excessive data flows and system fatigue. By using a community-based system of caregivers, rather than Singapore's health care system, to provide last-mile human assistance, the SHINESeniors project has lowered the costs of this technology substantially (Bai et al. 2015; Bajaj 2020).

United States: Virtual and augmented reality tools reduce isolation in nursing homes

Several companies in the United States have developed glasses with virtual and augmented reality capabilities to provide older people with entertainment and immersive experiences, such as memories, hikes, and travel through nature and to places they would like to go. The goal is to reduce patients' feelings of isolation and help them develop or maintain their cognitive capabilities. This may be especially important for patients with neurological disorders (Rogers 2019).

Receiving information in real time can help caregivers and clinicians better understand patients' behavior, personalize treatment, and intervene quickly when required. One challenge is to help patients understand the importance of using the applications in a way that minimizes irrelevant information or potential biases, avoiding adverse effects on clinical decision-making.

- *Information integration and case management applications.* Clinical applications can be integrated with supportive technologies for living. The combination promises the holistic delivery of long-term care, integrating case management in a flow of real-time data. Digital health services can be combined with more traditional support services, such as physical therapy, and with virtual (non-health-related) platforms to provide a broad spectrum of social services.

• *Convenience or "better living" applications.* Digital health applications can help older adults manage their lifestyles more autonomously. Healthy aging entails not just overall good health and health-promoting behaviors but also the opportunity to lead an independent life. Relevant tools and strategies include virtual coaches, "nudge" applications, and game-playing simulations or playful competitions that encourage positive behavior change. Such tools can help seniors lead active and healthy lives and improve their cognitive skills without the inconvenience of frequent clinic visits. Smart-home technologies and the Internet of Things can provide health information that is immediately useful to the patient and also share data with caregivers and medical providers. For example, fall-detection technology can inform emergency services without the need for the constant presence of a human caregiver (Akinola 2021). Remote monitoring options also encompass wearable devices and activity sensors that include emergency buttons, along with Global Positioning System (GPS) reminders and sensors that detect patients' movements or other small behavioral changes. These features connect to apps that can give caregivers and family ongoing access, enabling rapid response in case of emergency. Video can be incorporated so that families or caregivers can monitor older patients visually. Using AI-powered algorithms, sensors can monitor and collect information to help prevent future adverse events (for example, a stroke or heart attack) by detecting abnormal patterns in vital signs (Lanzito 2020).

Robotic companions can engage older people in conversation, offer recommendations such as music streaming and physical exercise, connect patients with family, and remind them about medications and check-ins. These technologies are often interactive and may reinforce older people's social connectedness and cognitive function (Corbyn 2021).

These technologies must be user-friendly—designed so that a user with relatively modest digital skills can understand, interpret, and act on the information provided. There is some risk that isolation and loneliness could be exacerbated if technology supplants human interaction, but this effect can be counterbalanced by virtual support networks and online peer groups (Elgazzar, Yoong, and Finkelstein 2020).

Challenges and Barriers to Implementation

For older adults, the three main barriers to accessing digital health solutions concern the design of technologies, their affordability, and their ease of use, including available support (Elgazzar, Yoong, and Finkelstein 2020). The first barrier involves design processes and the thinking that underlies them. Too often, digital health applications for older adults are designed based on assumptions that are not evidence based but shaped by ageist biases (WHO 2022).[8]

Technology for older persons should be designed with their active participation. Failure to consider the user's needs and preferences will reduce uptake and use (Knox and Tenenbaum 2021).

Second, even the most user-friendly technology will not be used if it is not affordable. Although health-promotive technology can in the long run reduce the costs of expensive clinical and personal care, it can itself be prohibitively expensive. Finally, even superbly designed and affordable technology will not be used very often, or sustainably, without the necessary support. For each application, every process step—from registration, to updates, to on-demand support—needs to be easy, understandable, and accessible.

A senior-centric design approach concerns how products look and "feel" to users and how well they actually work. Although some digital technologies may be simple and helpful, others may look particularly sophisticated (and expensive), which can limit their market penetration (Soja 2017). This means that, while in principle digital health technologies can resolve some health service delivery bottlenecks, in practice, ill-suited technologies may increase access barriers and inequalities from cost and the digital literacy needed to use them, creating some potential challenges in the promotion of digital health solutions for older adults. A senior-centric design approach helps avoid this trap by engaging older adults' participation at all stages—design, production, and implementation—never assuming that users already have the required digital expertise (WSIS Forum 2020). A successful approach can include universally proven design features such as large font sizes, simple interfaces, and fewer procedural steps (Elgazzar, Yoong, and Finkelstein 2020). The result is likely to be enhanced compliance.

Stark inequalities mark the availability and use of digital health technologies among older adults. There is already a clear digital divide between developed and developing countries for internet and mobile phone coverage, use, access, capability, outcomes, and digital skills (Elgazzar, Yoong, and Finkelstein 2020). This divide widens to a veritable gulf when the gap is measured between older adult populations in the Global North and South.[9] Even in middle- and high-income countries, older adults' uptake of digital health tools can be hampered by inappropriate design, physical and cognitive capacity challenges, mistrust among potential users, and lack of time (Sun et al. 2020), which reinforce digital exclusion (Yee 2020). At present, therefore, the risk is that expanded implementation of digital health for older adults will benefit only a part of the world, exacerbating existing health inequities rather than helping overcome them (Soja 2017).

Beyond age, the use of digital technology is correlated with a complex nexus of intertwined social factors. Sociodemographic characteristics such as income, education, and gender—and physical and functional health-related problems—are correlated with internet use, for example (Rogers and Mitzner 2017; Sun et al. 2020). Studies have shown lower use of technology in general—and digital health in particular—in lower-income and lower-education settings and among certain ethnic groups (Tappen et al. 2021).[10]

Awareness of, and comfort with, technology among today's older adults will be exceeded by those in the generations set to enter the "silver age" in the next 30, 40, or 50 years. It is also important to keep in mind that the experience of using today's technology may barely resemble the options and experiences that future technologies will provide (Hall 2020; Rogers and Mitzner 2017).

Policy Recommendations

Based on the challenges and opportunities described above, the use of digital health for older adults needs to be reframed in a way that can benefit people inclusively, taking cultural, knowledge, and access barriers into account. Digital health can provide foundations for improving care processes and outcomes but it is a means, not an end. It serves the goal of better health and well-being for older adults and the population as a whole. The following policy recommendations can inform country action in the FIRE innovation domain. The recommendations are structured under the foundational health system components of population, governance, platforms, workforce, information and tools, with platforms and tools combined into one subheading (see chapter 1).

Population—First, Understand the Context

Understanding the context and needs of older adult populations is a necessary condition for smart investment in digital health technologies. Digital health solutions for older adults should be prioritized, created, and adopted in collaboration with older people themselves and with a continual focus on the end user—the patient, caregiver, or provider (Danielsson et al. 2017). Action to bring digital health tools to older adults faces four main hurdles (WSIS Forum 2020):

- Incorrect assumptions about who older persons are and what they want
- Exclusion of older people from product research and design processes
- Need to nurture acceptance of technologies and the skills to use them in target populations
- Lack of access caused by cultural differences, language barriers, limited infrastructure, and high cost.

Decision-makers can get the best results by prioritizing digital health interventions for older adults based on people's preferences. Structured grass-roots consultations can ensure that older adults' voices are heard and clarify their preferences, capabilities, and challenges with digital health. Based on the findings of such consultative processes, a comprehensive program can be devised to upgrade digital skills among older people and care providers.[11] Road maps for implementation should be drawn up early, including ensuring that a robust regulatory framework for digital health technologies and services is in place. These steps should always accommodate the ability and willingness of older adults to use digital health tools (Elgazzar, Yoong, and Finkelstein 2020).

Communication and messaging are essential to increasing uptake of digital health among older adults (Danielsson et al. 2017). The right kind of communication strategy can build trust and interest in digital health technologies among target groups (Soja 2017). This communication includes nurturing a community environment that supports older people's social participation; devising educational activities to increase technology awareness, such as trainings and workshops; and building a pool of culturally competent digital health instructors, both young and old (the latter serving as role models). Activities to build digital skills should not only be directed to patients, but also to physicians, nurses, and other providers and caregivers who need to feel comfortable delivering person-centered services by digital means.

Governance

Regulation and Privacy

Robust regulatory frameworks foster digital health innovation while protecting users. A strong regulatory framework is needed to ensure older adults' privacy and data security, promote equity of access, and tackle digital divides. Balanced regulation can also facilitate a country's digital health ecosystem and uptake of senior-focused technologies. Committed participation by the ministry of health is essential to achieving a balanced regulatory framework. Comprehensive regulations encompass legal measures; the privacy and security of data; evidence-based assessments of medical devices, technologies, and algorithms; medical liability; compliance to secure value-based care; and partnerships and collaboration between the supply side (for example, technology companies and start-ups) and the demand side (for example, ministries, patients, and providers) (Bresnick 2019). The sensitivity of personal health data that is collected, shared, and analyzed means that digital health solutions need to be rigorously assessed for compliance with cybersecurity and privacy requirements. Clear operational rules are needed to guide technology suppliers, including rules on data protection and sharing, guidance on collecting only the minimum amount of data necessary, and explicit delimitation of permissible uses and prohibited abuses of data (Elgazzar, Yoong, and Finkelstein 2020).

Intercountry regulations and harmonization between international and local rules are needed, together with multistakeholder coordination. Remote monitoring may involve connecting patients with providers across local or provincial boundaries or even national borders, making regulatory harmonization and coordination at all these levels important. Similarly, the use of multistakeholder frameworks in decision-making processes can enhance coordination and collaboration with other sectors that may facilitate digital health advances (for example, the communications and infrastructure sectors) or benefit from them (for example, social service systems and new kinds of consumers).

Financing and Incentives

Policy choices for financing digital health will help shape the innovation landscape. With the increased uptake of telemedicine and remote monitoring, especially during the pandemic, new questions have arisen in many jurisdictions about payment schemes and the financing of digital health services. Should the full cost of digital health tools and services be borne by the patient, or should digital health services be covered by universal health coverage programs?

The decisions that policy makers make on these issues will substantively shape incentives for technology companies and providers to develop tools for older adults.

New business models, including public-private partnerships, hold promise for fostering digital health innovation for older adults. These options merit exploration in all countries, though enabling conditions may take time and sustained investment to achieve. Coordination with the private sector is essential because the bulk of relevant innovation comes from this sector. In recent years, big tech companies such as Amazon, Apple, Google, Meta, and Microsoft have together invested more than US$6.8 billion in health care–related deals, financing many innovations in the areas of social networking and data management (Thomason 2021). Partnerships with governments and global actors helped digital developers in several LMICs take innovations swiftly to scale in response to COVID-19. In Nigeria, for example, the Surveillance Outbreak Response Management and Analysis System, an open-source, mobile e-health platform, emerged from a sustained collaboration between the Nigeria Centre for Disease Control and the Helmholtz Centre for Infection Research in Germany. The partners drew on Nigeria's prior experiences with Ebola and monkeypox, allowing the program to grow from its initial concept as a process-management tool to a full health-surveillance platform that accelerated Nigeria's COVID-19 response (McKinsey & Company 2021).

Financial incentives for companies can spur the creation of local start-ups, nurture innovation ecosystems, and expand markets. Reimbursement policies may increase the affordability and uptake of digital health tools. For example, Apple has been in conversation with multiple US commercial health payers to subsidize the adoption of its Apple Watch by at-risk and vulnerable older adults through Medicare Advantage plans.[12] The watch has multiple applications for tracking health markers, including an FDA-approved electrocardiogram function, which can help prevent strokes (Bresnick 2019). Creative financing solutions are also emerging in some lower-income settings. In Rwanda, the telemedicine start-up Babylon (Babyl) has incorporated multiple revenue streams, including subscription-based and pay-as-you-go services, and centralized funding, such as the government's community-based health insurance program (McKinsey & Company 2021).

Workforce: The Digital Ecosystem and the Role of Caregivers

Caregivers can be pivotal players in the development and use of digital health tools. Governments, payers, care organizations, and technology companies seeking to develop and promote digital health products for older adults can gain leverage by engaging caregivers. Many caregivers are family members and key sources of support for older patients. If caregivers are engaged as technology users—and especially if they are given the chance to participate in product development—the result will be increased awareness, adoption, and compliance, in short, better outcomes. Caregivers may also serve as trainers and sources of formal or informal technical support for older adults in their care. "Train-the-trainer" programs could be designed to build caregivers' proficiency with digital applications.[13] This approach could also be relevant in nursing homes, where workers are not necessarily proficient with new technologies and with the collection and analysis of data to improve care quality (Akinola 2021).

In some settings, burgeoning interest in digitally enabled technology for older adults has fueled a rising number of start-ups and increased funding for home health solutions and old-age care.[14] This is part of the emerging "silver economy." The pattern is seen in areas such as in-home services (for example, telemedicine, home testing, and self-examination), loneliness alleviation (for example, social networks), and support to caregivers. This trend is more prominent in middle- and high-income countries, where regulations and incentives are often already in place to enable the emergence of such an ecosystem. In LMICs, technology hubs and other supportive structures can nurture innovation and attract investment. Successful solutions can increase value by digitizing and standardizing processes. For example, health software developer Medic and the nongovernmental organization Living Goods are collaborating to automate and standardize task and decision-support lists for community health workers in low-income settings, shifting their workflows from reactive to proactive or predictive outreach, which could save costs and improve results over time (McKinsey & Company 2021).

Platforms and Tools

Quality Assurance

Common-sense strategies can help ensure the quality of user-provided health data. The operation and results of digital health applications depend on data that are passively or actively generated by the user. Data quality is crucial given that data shape health-related decision-making. This raises important questions. For example, how can we be sure that sensors are sending reliable information? And how can clinicians be confident that it is the patient herself who is using the sensors? Two preliminary practical answers are (1) provide incentives for proper usage and (2) do not overwhelm the user. In other words, technology should not be complicated and invasive for users, but should be simple and interfere as little as possible with everyday life. Full acceptance, adherence, and compliance by older adults using the applications is the best guarantee of the security and quality of the system's inputs and outputs (Joe and Demiris 2013).

"Pilotitis"—Chronic Affliction of E-Health Projects?

To fulfill the promise of digital health technology for older people, digital health needs to move beyond research and evaluation studies toward full-scale commercial rollout of proven tools. Most current digital health interventions are in the form of relatively small early-stage pilots, which therefore cannot easily and reliably be generalized; hence, the health sector's frustration with "pilotitis"—the criticism that today's digital health interventions tend to be carefully controlled pilot projects implemented among small, well-chosen populations of patients. In many instances, the criticism is deserved. Despite success stories colorfully told by enthusiastic advocates, there is a relative lack of solid evidence and proven assessments of digital health technologies for older people—at least of the kind that can generate the momentum needed to integrate them into national health systems and induce populationwide acceptance and adoption (Lenca et al. 2021). A given technology may be sophisticated and impressively innovative, but if the outcomes cannot successfully be scaled into full commercial rollout, then further investments cannot be sustained (Joe and Demiris 2013).

Economic evaluation tools such as measures of cost-effectiveness could help prioritize interventions and offer a clearer picture of their comparative commercial feasibility. Detailed development plans and incentives will be necessary to facilitate the agile development and scale-up of the most promising solutions. It is also possible that the current, arguably hyperbolic, wave of fascination with digital health solutions will subside or at least settle, as more moderate hybrid models eventually emerge. These might combine well-designed, simple-to-use, supportive or assistive digital health solutions, powered by AI, with the necessary human interaction to provide last-mile health service delivery for older adults that is securely anchored in the participation of professionals, caregivers, and family members.

Conclusion

Demographic changes, longer lives, and a higher prevalence of chronic diseases—plus exogenous events such as the COVID-19 pandemic—warrant thinking in new ways about how health care services are delivered, especially for older adults. Digital health interventions can provide one set of solutions, increasing access while supporting healthy aging and independent living. However, significant barriers to uptake have thus far tended to discourage the investment needed for a genuinely transformative deployment of digital health technologies in old-age care. Principal among these barriers are affordability; older people's relative lack of digital literacy and skills, particularly among the most at-risk and low-income populations; and product or software designs that do not yet have the level of user-friendly features that would catalyze widespread adoption.

These problems are often aggravated by a perception of digital health algorithms and their associated protocols as a dehumanizing or even conspiratorial intrusion into personal space and lives. This perception feeds into a genuine risk that the increasing reliance on digital health technology could intensify isolation among older people if new technologies are introduced clumsily, hurriedly, or with insufficient human backup.

To enable the development and uptake of relevant, helpful digital health technology, transformations are needed on three levels (WSIS Forum 2020). On the macro level, the creation of a set of well-sorted-out, long-term policies, strategies, and regulations will enable the ecosystem to flourish, protect ordinary citizens, provide economic incentives to encourage pilot projects to mature into full-scale initiatives, and support the broader transformation of service delivery. On the micro level, technology companies and start-ups should more extensively include end-user feedback in the development of solutions, explore partnerships with service providers to increase the likelihood of uptake, and make their solutions more affordable. On the societal level, collaborative efforts linking multiple stakeholders are needed to build digital skills among older people, health care workers, and care providers. This will involve combating ageism, engaging with cultural patterns and mindsets that might be unreceptive or hostile toward technology, and ensuring that the digital divide between different populations does not widen.

Notes

1. Thomason (2021) estimates that 30 percent of all data generated around the world can be attributed to the health care sector.
2. In this chapter, platforms and tools are combined into one topic given that both refer to the technological component.
3. Connectivity gaps in rural areas are particularly pronounced in least-developed countries, where 17 percent of the rural population live in areas with no mobile coverage at all, and 19 percent of the rural population is covered by only a 2G network (ITU 2020b).
4. In the health care industry, payers are typically organizations, such as insurance companies, that set service rates, collect payments, and then process and pay claims on behalf of patients who have subscribed to that insurance plan.
5. Somewhat fewer people (but still a significant number) were interested in discussing specific health concerns virtually (48 percent), having a virtual examination (41 percent), or using AI doctors to handle information, navigate health care services, or obtain emergency advice (Accenture 2018).
6. In Australia, almost 30 percent of older adults may prefer robot-assisted surgery, and 51 percent would very likely use AI-assisted technology for emergency advice (Accenture 2019). In the United Kingdom, remote monitoring and video examinations are reportedly the preferred telecare tools for 50 percent of patients over age 55 (Health Europa 2021). Data on preferences for digital health tools among older adults in low- and middle-income countries would be similarly useful (and perhaps surprising).
7. The Medical Futurist, "How Seniors Got Lost In The Digital Health Revolution." February 11, 2021, https://medicalfuturist.com/senior-health-2021.
8. Ageism refers to stereotypical depictions, attitudes of prejudice, and discriminatory behaviors directed toward others or sometimes toward ourselves (internalized ageism), on the basis of advanced age (WHO 2022).
9. According to the WHO, in many LMICs, only 5 to 15 percent of people who require assistive technology can access it. This share might be even lower if digital health technologies were included as part of assistive technology. With the population of LMICs expected to undergo even more rapid aging shifts than those seen in higher-income countries (Marasinghe, Lapitan, and Ross 2015), the 5 to 15 percent figure could well drop lower unless it is combatted by countertrends.
10. Data from the US National Health and Aging Trends Study also point to socioeconomic disparities: higher income and educational levels were associated with greater use of digital health technology. Those who were older, in poor health, divorced, Black, or Latino reported lower usage. Widely differing levels of internet access and usage are likewise found in smaller, more focused samples, reflecting differences across socioeconomic and ethnic groups (Tappen et al. 2021).
11. Digital skills are crucial, and this is more of a challenge for older persons than for younger people. The pandemic has underlined how important it is to have the digital skillset to navigate social platforms and websites to stay connected, remain

informed, and combat isolation. An example would be the difficulties many older persons experienced in seeking to secure COVID-19 vaccine appointments (ITU 2021).

12. The Apple Watch costs approximately US$400, which is beyond the reach of many older people, especially those on a low income or pension.

13. Some applications allow caregivers to gain access so that they can manage various services on behalf of their dependents.

14. In 2018, venture and seed funding for elder care and home health care globally reached approximately US$490 million (Hall 2020).

References

Accenture. 2018. "Baby Boomers Demand Digital Medicare Now." Accessed June 1, 2021. https://www.accenture.com/_acnmedia/PDF-86/Accenture-Health-Baby-Boomers -Demand-Digital-Medicare-Now.pdf.

Accenture. 2019. "Australian Seniors Ride Digital Care Wave." Accessed June 1, 2021. https://www.accenture.com/_acnmedia/PDF-97/Accenture-Health-Australian -Silver-Surfer-Wave.pdf.

Akinola, Sofiat. 2021. "What Is the Biggest Benefit Technology Will Have on Ageing and Longevity?" *World Economic Forum* (blog), March 30, 2021. https://www.weforum .org/agenda/2021/03/what-is-the-biggest-benefit-technology-ageing-longevity -global-future-council-tech-for-good.

Bai, Liming, Alex I. Gavino, Wei Qi Lee, Jungyoon Kim, Na Liu, Hwee-Pink Tan, Lee Buay Tan, et al. 2015. "SHINESeniors: Personalized Services for Active Ageing-in-Place." Conference proceedings. 2015 IEEE First International Smart Cities Conference ISC2, Guadalajara, Mexico, October 25–28, 2015. doi:http://doi .org/10.1109/ISC2.2015.7366181; https://ink.library.smu.edu.sg/sis_research/2948.

Bajaj, Amit. 2020. "This Tiny Nation Is Showing the World How Technology Can Make a Huge Difference to the Elderly." World Economic Forum Annual Meeting, January 17, 2020. https://www.weforum.org/agenda/2020/01/ageing-demographic-elderly -technology-singapore.

Bresnick, Jennifer. 2019. "Apple Floats Idea of Subsidizing Watches for Medicare Advantage." *HealthPayerIntelligence Private Payers News*, January 17, 2019. https:// healthpayerintelligence.com/news/apple-floats-idea-of-subsidizing-watches -for-medicare-advantage.

Corbyn, Zoë. 2021. "ElliQ Is 93-year-old Juanita's Friend. She's also a Robot." *The Guardian*, August 13, 2021. https://www.theguardian.com/us-news/2021/aug/13 /elliq-robot-companion-seniors.

Danielsson, Karin, Helena Lindgren, Maurice Mulvenna, Ingeborg Nilsson, and John Waterworth. 2017. "Digital Technology in Healthcare and Elderly Care." In *Proceedings of the European Conference on Cognitive Ergonomics 2017*, 188–90. doi:https://doi.org/10.1145/3121283.3121425.

Elgazzar, Sarah, Joanne Yoong, and Eric Finkelstein. 2020. "Digital Health as an Enabler of Healthy Aging in Southeast Asia." Duke-NUS Medical School Centre of Regulatory Excellence, Singapore. https://www.duke-nus.edu.sg/core/think-tank /news/publications/digital-health-as-an-enabler-of-healthy-aging-in-southeast-asia.

Evangelista, Lorraine, Steven R. Steinhubl, and Eric J. Topol. 2019. "Digital Health Care for Older Adults." *The Lancet* 393 (10180): 1493. doi:https://doi.org/10.1016 /S0140-6736(19)30800-1.

Hall, Christine. 2020. "Living Their Best Life at Home: Senior-Focused Startups and VCs Reevaluate Elder Care." Crunchbase News, October 13, 2020. https://news .crunchbase.com/news/living-their-best-life-at-home-senior-focused-startups -vcs-reevaluate-elder-care.

Health Europa. 2021. "Senior Patients Prefer Digital Health Tools to In-Person Consultations." Health Europa Research & Innovation News, January 22, 2021. https://www.healtheuropa.eu/senior-patients-prefer-digital-health-tools-to-in-person-consultations/105172.

ITU (International Telecommunication Union). 2020a. "Coronavirus: How Can We Help Our Elderly Embrace Technology?" ITU News, October 1, 2020. https://www.itu.int/en/myitu/News/2020/10/01/09/30/Coronavirus-elderly-embrace-technology.

ITU (International Telecommunication Union). 2020b. "Estimates on Internet Access in Small Island Developing States and Landlocked Developing Countries Available for the First Time." Press Release, ITU News, November 30, 2020. https://www.itu.int/en/mediacentre/Pages/pr27-2020-facts-figures-urban-areas-higher-internet-access-than-rural.aspx.

ITU (International Telecommunication Union). 2021. "Technology and Older Persons: Ageing in the Digital Era." ITU News, February 8, 2021. https://www.itu.int/en/myitu/News/2021/02/08/17/18/Technology-older-persons-ageing-digital-era-Malcolm-Johnson.

Joe, Jonathan, and George Demiris. 2013. "Older Adults and Mobile Phones for Health: A Review." *Journal of Biomedical Information* 46 (5): 947–54. doi:https://doi.org/10.1016/j.jbi.2013.06.008.

Kakulla, Brittne. 2021. "Personal Tech and the Pandemic: Older Adults Are Upgrading for a Better Online Experience." AARP, September 2021. https://www.aarp.org/research/topics/technology/info-2021/2021-technology-trends-older-americans.html-CMP=RDRCT-PRI-TECH-040721/?cmp=RDRCT-907b618d-20210416.

Kent, Chloe. 2021. "Digital Health App Market Booming, Finds IQVIA Report." Medical Device Network, August 5, 2021. https://www.medicaldevice-network.com/news/digital-health-apps.

Knox, Ryan, and Cara Tenenbaum. 2021. "Regulating Digital Health Apps Needs User-Centered Reform." STAT, August 3, 2021. https://www.statnews.com/2021/08/03/refor-regulatory-landscape-digital-health-applications.

Kruk, M. E., A. D. Gage, C. Arsenault, K. Jordan, H. H. Leslie, S. Roder-DeWan, O. Adeyi, et al. 2018. "High-Quality Health Systems in the Sustainable Development Goals Era: Time for a Revolution." *Lancet Global Health* 6 (11): e1196–e1252. https://doi.org/10.1016/S2214-109X(18)30386-3.

Lanzito, Christina. 2020. "Remote Monitoring Systems Can Give Caregivers Peace of Mind." AARP *Care at Home* (blog), January 10, 2020. https://www.aarp.org/caregiving/home-care/info-2020/ces-caregiving-products.html.

Lenca, Marcello, Christophe Schneble, Reto W. Kressig, and Tenzin Wangmo. 2021. "Digital Health Interventions for Healthy Ageing: A Qualitative User Evaluation and Ethical Assessment." *BMC Geriatrics* 21 (412). doi:https://doi.org/10.1186/s12877-021-02338-z.

Lufkin, Bryan. 2020. "What the World Can Learn from Japan's Robots." BBC *Japan 2020* (blog), February 6, 2020. https://www.bbc.com/worklife/article/20200205-what-the-world-can-learn-from-japans-robots.

Marasinghe, Keshini Madara, Jostacio Moreno Lapitan, and Alex Ross. 2015. "Assistive Technologies for Ageing Populations in Six Low-Income and Middle-Income Countries: A Systematic Review." *BMJ Innovations* 1 (4): 182–95. doi:http://dx.doi.org/10.1136/bmjinnov-2015-000065.

McKinsey & Company. 2021. "Unlocking Digital Healthcare in Lower- and Middle-Income Countries." November 10, 2021. https://www.mckinsey.com/industries/healthcare-systems-and-services/our-insights/unlocking-digital-healthcare-in-lower-and-middle-income-countries.

Pew Research Center. 2021. "Internet/Broadband Fact Sheet." https://www.pewresearch.org/internet/fact-sheet/internet-broadband.

Rogers, Sol. 2019. "Five Companies Using Virtual Reality to Improve the Lives of Senior Citizens." Forbes, August 21, 2019. https://www.forbes.com/sites/solrogers/2019/08/21 /five-companies-using-virtual-reality-to-improve-the-lives-of-senior-citizens/?sh =6b10d6a74279.

Rogers, Wendy A., and Tracy L. Mitzner. 2017. "Envisioning the Future for Older Adults: Autonomy, Health, Well-being, and Social Connectedness with Technology Support." *Futures* 87 (March): 133–39. doi:https://doi.org/10.1016/j.futures.2016.07.002.

Salakhutdinova, Sevil Kamalovna, Jake Spitz, Oxana Sinyavskaya, Elena Selezneva, and Elizaveta Gorvat. 2021. "Improving Service Delivery for the Elderly in the Russian Federation through Integration, Innovation, and Empowerment." World Bank, Washington, DC. http://documents.worldbank.org/curated/en/654961625746062755 /Improving-Service-Delivery-for-the-Elderly-in-the-Russian-Federation-through -Integration-Innovation-and-Empowerment.

Sardis, Barry. 2019. "What Is Digital Health?" December 13, 2019. *An Introduction to Digital Healthcare Technology for Seniors.* TechForAging website. https://techforaging .com/digital-health-elderly.

Soja, Ewa. 2017. "Information and Communication Technology in Active and Healthy Ageing: Exploring Risks from Multi-Generation Perspective." *Information Systems Management* 34 (4): 320–32. doi:https://doi.org/10.1080/10580530.2017.1366217.

Statistics Canada. 2019. "Canadian Internet Use Survey." Press Release, October 29, 2019. https://www150.statcan.gc.ca/n1/daily-quotidien/191029/dq191029a-eng.htm.

Sun, Xinran, Wenxin Yan, Hao Zhou, Zhaoqing Wang, Xueying Zhang, Shuang Huang, and Li Li. 2020. "Internet Use and Need for Digital Health Technology among the Elderly: A Cross-Sectional Survey in China." *BMC Public Health* 20 (September): 1386. doi:https://doi.org/10.1186/s12889-020-09448-0.

Tappen, Ruth M., Mary E. Cooley, Roger Luckmann, and Somi Panday. 2021. "Digital Health Information Disparities in Older Adults: A Mixed Methods Study." *Journal of Racial and Ethnic Health Disparities* 9: 82–92. https://doi.org/10.1007/s40615 -020-00931-3.

Thomason, Jane. 2021. "Big Tech, Big Data and the New World of Digital Health." *Global Health Journal* 5 (4): 165–68. https://doi.org/10.1016/j.glohj.2021.11.003.

WHO (World Health Organization). 2019. *Recommendations on Digital Interventions for Health System Strengthening.* WHO Guideline. Geneva: WHO. https://www.who.int/ publications/i/item/9789241550505.

WHO (World Health Organization). 2022. *The Global Report on Ageism.* Geneva: WHO. https://www.who.int/publications/i/item/9789240016866.

WSIS Forum. 2020. "Digital Inclusion of Older Persons." Thematic Workshop, Session 285. United Nations Department of Economic and Social Affairs. https://www.itu .int/net4/wsis/forum/2020/en/Agenda/Session/285.

Yee, Michelle. 2020. "Engaging Older Adults with Digital Health Technology." MedMe, June 25, 2020. https://www.medmehealth.com/blog/engaging-older-adults -with-digital-health.

CHAPTER 5

Designing Integrated Care for an Aging Population: Regulation and Governance for Healthy Aging

Naoki Kondo, Koryu Sato, and Yuiko Nagamine

Key Messages

- Regulation of care systems for older adults is a responsibility of governments.

- Core values for care system regulation include maintaining the dignity and autonomy of older persons and meeting diverse needs in this population.

- Country experiences suggest that care systems for older people work best when leaders adopt a whole-of-government and whole-of-society approach.

- Central, provincial or regional, and local or municipal governments have distinct and complementary roles in overseeing care systems for older adults.

- Both binding regulation and incentives for improving the quality of care are useful governance tools. Preferences will reflect a country's political economy, administrative organization, and the development phase of local care systems.

- Japan and Thailand provide examples of how countries have used governance and regulatory strategies to strengthen community-based care options and improve outcomes for older people.

Core Values in Regulating Primary Health Care for Older People

The remarkable development of health care technologies has enabled humans to live longer than ever before. As people age, however, they start to encounter various chronic diseases as their bodies begin to deteriorate. However, a problem-solving approach that focuses on identifying ailments and resolving them case by case may not meet the ultimate needs of the care recipient.

Although the problem-focused approach is an indispensable part of any good health care system, the central strategy of health care should be to provide support and create environments that add value to people's lives by helping them achieve active, healthy lifestyles.

The overarching goal of primary health care (PHC) for healthy aging, in other words, is not to only heal individual diseases and certainly not to enable people to regain the bodies and minds of their youth, but to create social and community support systems that encourage and empower individuals to realize their intrinsic capacities, optimize their functional abilities, and live meaningful lives. For example, the functional abilities we need to enjoy such lives include the ability to meet basic needs; learn, grow, and make decisions; be mobile; build and maintain relationships; and contribute to society (WHO 2020).

Maintaining the Dignity and Autonomy of Older Adults

Maintaining the dignity and autonomy of older persons is another core value that PHC for older people should seek to uphold. The World Health Organization (WHO) in its constitution affirms that "health is a state of complete physical, mental, and social well-being and not merely the absence of disease or infirmity." However, the completeness of such well-being varies from person to person and should not be determined or imposed by others. Goal setting should include the person needing care with support from family and care providers so that the principles of person-centeredness and autonomy in decision-making are upheld regardless of age. Additionally, because care for older people is usually given by younger providers, health systems should encourage providers to understand older people's physical, mental, and social characteristics and avoid ageism and age discrimination.

Meeting the Diverse Needs of Older People

Having lived through many changes over the decades, older adults are a diverse group; thus, the environment, kinds of assistance, and aids needed to optimize each person's functional abilities are equally diverse. One person may have hearing loss and require a hearing aid. Another may have severe knee joint problems but can move with the help of a cane. Yet another person, living in a remote area without the opportunity to communicate with others, may need access to transportation or internet video calling services to enable them to socialize and engage with others. Often, a single aid or service is not sufficient to achieve these functional abilities. For example, when a health event likely to cause functional disability occurs, such as a stroke, medical care is required during the acute phase, but in the chronic phase, the care needs to shift to maximizing residual intrinsic capacity so that the patient can return to her home community.

Seizing the Opportunity to Introduce New Social Values

The current and projected share of older adults as a proportion of the total global population is unprecedented, which makes the future feel uncertain.

Many policy makers and the public therefore see the aging of society primarily as a problem—a challenge to be overcome. But population aging can also be an opportunity to introduce new social values. Above all, the development of PHC systems for older adults can be a powerful spur to the creation of an inclusive society in which people of all generations have sufficient opportunities to achieve their full potential and participate in society. Several countries that have set up PHC systems for older adults—including Japan, which has the world's most rapidly aging population—have, in addition to learning from failed experiences, developed Community-Based Integrated Care Systems (*chiiki houkatsu kea shisutemu*), that is, regulatory mechanisms that enable older people to continue to work, play a role in the community, speak out, and contribute to society despite their illnesses and disabilities. The systems, originally conceived of and developed to provide care for older people, are now being expanded into inclusive welfare and social security systems for all generations.

Good Governance and Integration among Stakeholders

PHC systems for older adults that meet their diverse care needs on an ongoing basis must have mechanisms to seamlessly link different types of care and ensure continuity of care. Because older people tend to spend much of their time in their home communities, their care will also typically be provided within that community. But often, there are insufficient community resources to provide the necessary care. Diverse stakeholders therefore must work together with those who need care to create and nurture the necessary resources in the community.

Communities are extremely diverse, and local systems need a high degree of regulatory freedom to decide how to use a variety of resources suited to the context of each community. Uniform, top-down regulations applied authoritatively by a central government are not recommended. What is needed instead is the integration of various stakeholders at the national, regional, and local levels, enabling each stakeholder to use local resources to maximize social value (WHO Commission on Social Determinants of Health 2008).

PHC for older adults must be continuous, comprehensive, and integrated with wellness, health care, medical care, and long-term care (LTC). It therefore requires a whole-of-government approach that is based on health perspectives across the policy spectrum—covering government stewardship functions, financing, human resources, and infrastructure development. It must also embrace innovation. Good governance aims to empower all stakeholders in PHC systems, whether individual or organizational, including care planners, providers, government agencies, informal caregivers, and those who need care. The WHO framework for the continuum of LTC proposes that it be rooted in the community and that each community create a dedicated multisectoral coordinating body that works with higher-level organizations to maintain overall governance (WHO 2021) (figure 5.1).

FIGURE 5.1 Dedicated Multisectoral Coordinating Body for the Continuum of Long-Term Care

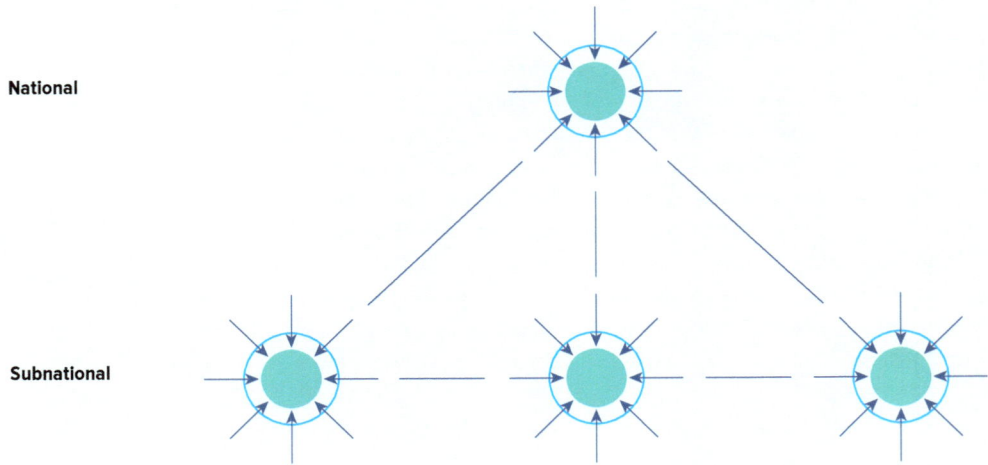

National

Subnational

Source: WHO 2021.

Stakeholders and Their Roles

Integrated care should be delivered to older people in communities, with the goal of maintaining and promoting their well-being. To deliver such care, a community care or community-building perspective is essential. That is, the community should be seen as a team with the goal of providing effective, efficient, and fair care for all older people in the community. Community care also means enhancing the power of the team by fostering good relationships among team members—the stakeholders and actors in the community. Government agencies at the local, regional, and national levels, together with sectors outside the community, can help build the capacity of each community to provide care for older people. In turn, each community should provide information, data, and ideas for improvement to enable the government to effectively operate and regulate the community-based PHC system at each level (figure 5.2). This discussion now looks more closely at the roles of each of the main stakeholders in the community-based PHC system.

Stakeholders and Their Roles in the Community

Care Managers, Coordinators, Planners

Organizations or trained individuals are needed to plan and manage individual care by consulting the person in need, planning care details together, and coordinating and managing the care plan over the long term. These individuals are called "care managers" (*kea-maneijaa*) in Japan, "well-being coordinators" in Singapore, and "link workers" for "prescribing" social activities in the United Kingdom (although it should be pointed out that their roles are not

FIGURE 5.2 Key Stakeholders of a Community-Based PHC System for Older People and Their Roles

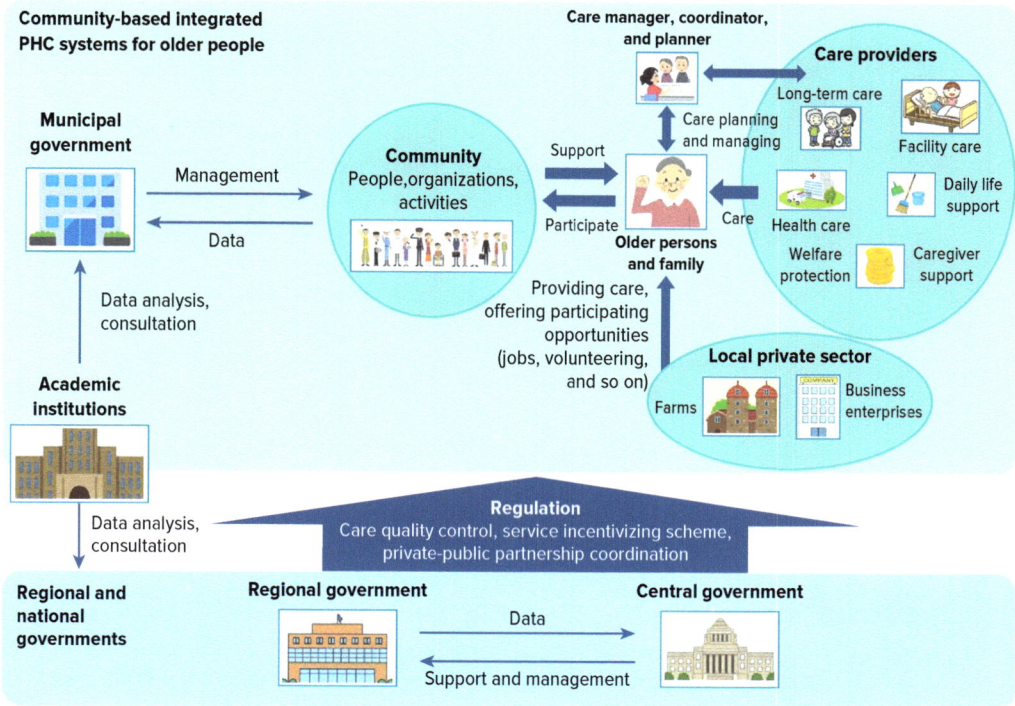

Source: Original figure for this publication.
Note: PHC = primary health care.

entirely identical) (Drinkwater, Wildman, and Moffatt 2019). Various organizations and professionals can play these roles. For example, in Japan, the Community General Support Center is a frontline organization that coordinates individual care for older adults and manages community resources and integrated care activities. Each center has at least one care manager. Large hospitals have medical social workers at the in-hospital community medical liaison office who consult with patients and create care plans to be implemented after discharge from the hospital. Other local offices, such as the welfare office, health post, and health center, can also fulfill these roles after receiving training in Japan's care system, basic interpersonal communication skills, and other necessary skills.

Care Providers

Various organizations participate in PHC systems as care providers. These include organizations that provide LTC, residential care, medical and preventive care, wellness support, support for daily living, and caregiver support. Local people and informal resources (for example, social activities such as hobby groups, citizens' clubs, microfinance loan groups, informal rotating savings associations, and health volunteers) can also provide preventive care and opportunities to participate in society and alleviate social isolation. The roles of local people, and those of informal community resources such as care providers, are critical and can be significant because they live in the same communities as the older people who need care and can serve as effective partners in building their communities.

When an LTC system is being established, informal caregivers such as family members and community health volunteers need special consideration among caregivers because, in many cases, they provide LTC while working, attending school, or performing household chores and are rarely paid for their caregiving labor. Child caregivers are also unlikely to attend school regularly, leading to the creation of a socially disadvantaged group. Regulation and government support for such informal caregivers should be a priority need.

Private Sector

Commercial industries and nongovernmental organizations in various fields are important stakeholders in PHC systems. Because the private sector is responsible for the bulk of the local economy and includes stakeholders that are key actors in the PHC system, it can be especially important as a potential provider of opportunities for social participation for older persons, for example, job opportunities for older people. Some private companies also supply consulting services to local, regional, and central governments in areas such as data analysis, management, and coordination with local stakeholders. Therefore, the government must partner with and monitor the private sector through market mechanisms and regulations.

Role of the Government at the Local, Regional, and National Levels

Municipal government. The government is responsible for regulating and managing PHC systems for healthy aging. At the local level, municipal governments are the frontline agencies that organize and manage community-based PHC systems and the organizations and resources in the regions such systems cover. Municipal governments also control the relationship between care managers, care providers, and the community, with a focus on older individuals. They must therefore develop controls suited to the community's characteristics to help build a system that considers local care needs, the resources available, and the quality of services provided.

Based on local characteristics, municipalities should create a system that facilitates data management by actively collecting and analyzing data from care recipients, care providers, and other actors in the community. Locally appropriate payment schemes for care providers may also be needed, depending on the financing scheme used in national or regional PHC systems.

Because municipal governments provide services directly related to older people and control data on local residents and resources, they are well suited to overseeing the design of care and building care systems based on both individual needs and local characteristics. However, municipal governments tend to be hampered by budget constraints, weak legal authority, limited discretion for creating regulations, and a shortage of individuals with expertise in data analysis and management. They also typically lack access to information on other municipalities, which makes it difficult to benchmark their performance.

Regional government. Given the limitations of municipal governments, a regional or subnational government (such as a province or prefecture) that oversees a broad region consisting of multiple municipalities often plays a key role in supporting municipal governments. The regional government can identify the needs of municipalities, devise plans for regional financing and resource allocation, and help supervise and support municipal governments based on its regional policy. Facilitating information exchange and cooperation among municipalities is also a vital role of regional governments. For example, a regional public health care center under the jurisdiction of a regional government could collect standardized information on older adults and care resources from the municipalities within its jurisdiction. These data can be compiled and compared to provide feedback or advice to municipalities that are struggling to establish or manage care systems.

Central government. The central government determines the overall PHC philosophy for healthy aging and the design, financing, and legal positioning of the nation's PHC system. It develops and manages the national strategy based on the data collected directly and indirectly from municipal and regional governments, using external consulting resources. Any system established by the government in which the public sector provides care and services for older people must be regulated. Standard criteria and evaluation methods must be implemented for the assessment of individuals' physical and mental faculties, and regulations must be developed to monitor the types and quality of services available according to care needs, payment standards, and qualification requirements for service providers. When the private insurance industry is allowed to participate in the PHC system for older people, government intervention is often required to ensure fairness and high-quality care, including by government monitoring of prices and payment standards.

Judicious Use of Researchers and Academic Institutions

For universities and research institutions conducting public health and welfare research, the data collected via the PHC system for older adults represent a treasure trove of information. The establishment of effective and fair models of community PHC systems, and verification of their performance, merit research. Consequently, partnering with researchers from academic institutions that have these interests can produce many benefits, such as better systems management, innovative initiatives, effective use of funds, enhanced fairness, and improved system sustainability (figure 5.3) (Kondo and Rosenberg 2018). Governments, citizens, and researchers can effectively and sustainably build a system of community-based care for older adults by

FIGURE 5.3 A Model of Key Driving Factors for Sustainable Actions for UHC for Older Adults in Japan

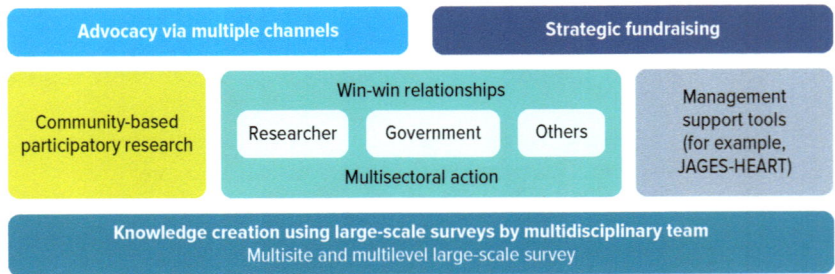

Source: Based on Kondo and Rosenberg 2018.
Note: JAGES = Japan Gerontological Evaluation Study; UHC = universal health coverage.

establishing a win-win relationship in which each actor maintains its independence but also shares knowledge.

Managing Good Governance Mechanisms (Regulatory Devices)

Governments need to listen to the voices of their populations, identify their needs, and establish a regulatory framework to improve services to meet those needs. The framework for service delivery, as outlined by the 2004 World Development Report (World Bank 2004), can be applied to building a system of care for older adults (figure 5.4). The framework includes four actors—citizens/clients, politicians/policy makers, organizational providers, and frontline professionals. In the context of community-based care for older populations, the actors are older adults, the central and regional governments, municipal departments of care for older people, and the individuals providing that care (for example, care managers, physicians, nurses, and formal and informal caregivers). Governments need to match the needs of the demand side (older people) and the services of the supply side (local governments and providers) and make their practices accountable and sustainable. The regulatory devices are explained in detail in World Bank (2004); the discussion below describes some devices specific to community-based care services for older adults.

Regulation

Regulation can be divided into legal regulation by national, regional, and local governments and self-regulation by providers. Legal regulation consists of the laws and ordinances that define the organizational and professional conditions for providing specific care services, service prices, and prohibitions. Self-regulation refers to voluntary rules to maintain fair competition, usually among for-profit providers.

FIGURE 5.4 The Framework of Accountability Relationships

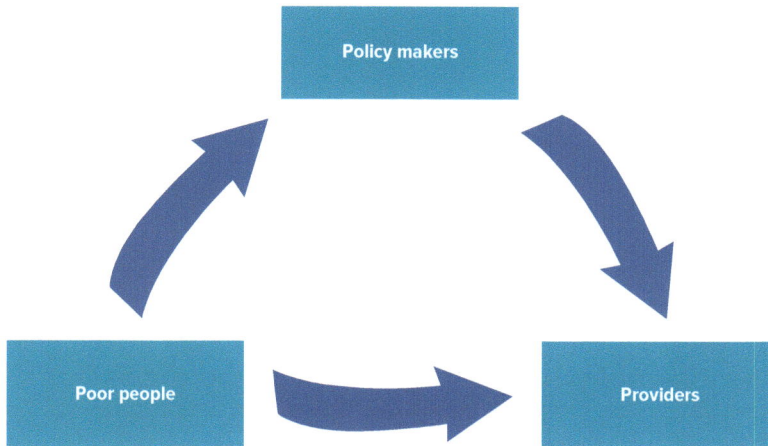

Source: World Bank 2004.

Incentives

Because each provider has its own identity and purpose, not everyone is necessarily focused on the organizational collaboration necessary for the smooth operation of a PHC system for older people. The government can therefore improve the governance of the health system by providing incentives for stakeholders to collaborate. If PHC is financed by insurance or taxes, a system of financial incentives could be created, such as higher prices for more desirable services, or higher payments for the same services if they are provided in a more desirable way.

In Japan, the national government has established a scoring system for prefectures and municipalities based on the status of their activities and offers them incentive grants according to the scores, which are evaluated annually. Activities that should be emphasized can be promoted by changing their scoring. For example, to get more municipalities to create an annual plan to promote integrated care, a paternalistic approach might make such plans mandatory by law. But an alternative approach is to introduce incentives for creating annual plans, such as grants for planning, or disincentives such as financial penalties.

There is no obviously superior approach. The choice between enforcing regulations or promoting incentives should be determined by factors such as the country's political situation, the structure of the administrative organization, and how far along the country is in developing local PHC systems. For example, in the early phases of the process, when municipal-level local systems are not widespread and many municipal governments are unsure of the kind of planning required, a nationwide mandate or a penalty for not making plans would likely cause confusion and generate opposition. In such cases, it might be better to provide positive incentives. On the other hand, even if a system is in the early stages of development, if there are already known best practices that can be applied to various regions, if there is a low probability of adverse events, or if a serious social problem requires urgent measures, it may be appropriate to make such efforts mandatory, while publishing and disseminating sufficient guidance. For example, requiring municipal governments to conduct surveys on abuse of older people and to develop a management plan may be appropriate, or care services whose effectiveness is highly questionable may be prohibited.

Community Organizing

Whether regulations or incentives are adopted, policy makers need a strategy to promote community organizing or to facilitate intersectoral and interorganizational partnerships, based on the well-known program management cycle of plan, do, check, and act. Considering the diverse stakeholders involved, determining who should be responsible for this function can prove challenging. One approach is to have an organization similar to the Community General Support Center in Japan oversee management of the local system while ensuring that participating stakeholders are appropriately involved in the decision-making process. In addition, to facilitate smooth and effective discussions throughout the management cycle, efforts should be made to build solid relationships among stakeholders and increase the social capital—for example, mutual trust and reciprocal norms stemming from interpersonal and organizational ties—of the community.

Below are two practices that aim to foster social capital and that can be applied to many regions regardless of the available resources or the phase of systems development.

Individual Case Review Meetings

Providing integrated and continual care to individuals is not easy. Existing collaborative frameworks for care delivery may not be able to provide an effective care plan for complex and significant challenges such as finances, relationships, and health conditions. In such cases, the use of a multidisciplinary meeting body can be helpful as a form of community care review. Meetings would bring together all the stakeholders involved in care on a regular basis.

The meeting would have two goals—to resolve individual cases and to build relationships among the people and organizations involved. The social capital nurtured in this way can then be applied to other cases as they arise.

PHC Systems Review Meetings

When examining individual cases and determining care, a mechanism is needed to collect and reflect the opinions of a wide range of stakeholders in the implementation of the plan, do, check, and act cycle for the entire system at the regional level. A conference body could be created to review local and regional PHC systems. For example, at the review meeting, municipal governments could convene stakeholders in the area, report on their draft plans, and provide basic data such as care needs and resources, the status of system operations, and issues and opportunities for future improvements.

Use of Professional Facilitators

It would be beneficial to use for-profit organizations (for example, consultation companies), nongovernmental organizations, and citizen organizations that develop and provide services and tools to promote organizational collaboration. Facilitating an effective meeting is not the same as moderating a meeting. The use of professionals who are skilled in designing and managing meetings to develop stakeholder collaboration and mutual trust can improve the performance of PHC systems.

Country Example #1: Japan

Brief Overview

Japan has one of the highest proportions of older adults in the world. In 2020, 28.6 percent of the population were 65 years or older and 14.7 percent were 75 or older (Japan, Ministry of Internal Affairs and Communications 2021). In 2065, the share of people age 65 and older is expected to be 38.4 percent, with people age 75 and older making up 25.5 percent of the population (Japan, National Institute of Population and Social Security Research 2017). In France, it took 114 years (1865 to 1979) for the share of people age 65 and older to double (to 14 percent from 7 percent). It took the United States 69 years (1944 to 2013). In Japan, it took just 24 years (1970 to 1994). Certain Asian countries will see their populations aging at an even faster rate in the future. For example, Singapore's aging rate is expected to double in 19 years (2000 to 2019), the Republic of Korea's in 18 years (2000 to 2018), and Vietnam's in 18 years (2016 to 2034) (UN DESA Population Division 2019).

Overview of National Systems in Japan for Caring for Older People

In April 2000, in response to its rapid population aging, Japan implemented a system of public long-term care insurance (LTCI). In the LTCI system, the level of need of those requiring LTC services is first assessed when they apply to the municipality, based on which a care manager creates a care plan. Insured persons can attend day-care services or receive home-visit care services. The LTCI program also covers home modifications and loans out equipment such as canes and wheelchairs. Insured persons who have difficulty living at home can choose to enter an LTC facility, for which they pay coinsurance for LTC services of 10 percent (20–30 percent for high-income people).

The LTCI scheme was established to socialize LTC. Before this, families took care of older parents at home. LTCI recognizes LTC as a societal issue and provides affordable care financed by taxes and insurance premiums. Article 1 of the Long-Term Care Insurance Law states that benefits are provided for LTC to enable older adults to maintain their dignity and lead independent lives according to their abilities even if they become functionally impaired because of aging. It further states that LTCI is to be established based on the principle of solidarity among citizens.

Unlike Germany, another country with a public LTCI scheme, the Japanese government, after much debate, decided not to provide monetary benefits for family care for several reasons. First, monetary benefits do not always ensure high quality of care, and family members may become bound to family caregiving. Second, monetary benefits can act as an incentive to keep older people dependent at home and to impose an excessive burden of care on the family. And third, there was a need to expand care services by professionals.

Before the LTCI program, in-facility services were provided by either the social welfare system or the medical insurance system. Because of discrepancies in the services provided and differences in cost-sharing arrangements between the two systems, a unified system was needed. Many also felt stigmatized when using the means-tested social welfare system, and users did not like that they could not choose service providers. One reason the LTCI initiative is funded not only by taxes but also by insurance premiums is to dispel stigma by giving users a sense of entitlement to benefits by paying premiums. Because insurance is a targeted financial resource and demonstrates a clear relationship between benefits and burdens, it was also easier to gain public understanding of the new burdens associated with implementation of the LTCI scheme.

Key Regulation Elements and Their Functions

Financing

All persons age 40 or older residing in Japan are required to pay premiums for the LTCI program. Municipalities are the insurers of LTCI because they are the government entity closest to residents. Premiums are set according to income. The average monthly premium is ¥6,014 (approximately US$55) from 2021 to 2023. For those age 40 to 65, the medical insurer collects premiums for the LTCI program, together with medical insurance premiums, on behalf of municipalities. The premium rate is 1.64 percent of payroll (2022) for those enrolled in the Japan Health Insurance Association.

LTCI expenditure is financed 50 percent by taxes, 20 percent by the national government, 17.5 percent by prefectures, and 12.5 percent by municipalities for in-facility services.

Beneficiary Eligibility Regulation and Process

Individuals must be certified by the municipality to receive benefits from the LTCI program for LTC. After a person applies for certification, a caseworker or public-health nurse from the municipality visits the applicant's home to assess his or her physical and mental condition. The certification process has two stages—a computerized decision based on the results of a home-visit survey and a decision by the Certification Committee of Needed Long-Term Care based on the survey and the family physician's written opinion. The committee consists of doctors, public-health nurses, social workers, and other professionals. It examines the person's condition and prognosis for LTC and determines one of eight levels of care—independent, support levels 1 or 2, or care levels 1 through 5. Persons age 40 to 65 are eligible to receive benefits only if one of 16 diseases that occur with aging, such as cerebrovascular disease or dementia in early life, causes the need for LTC. The maximum amount of LTCI services available each month is determined according to the certified level of care needed.

LTCI benefits include home-visit services, day services, short-stay services, residential services, and in-facility services. Municipalities also offer preventive services to persons who have not been certified as needing care. Users pay 10 percent of the total cost of care (20–30 percent for those with high incomes). The national government determines LTC fees and revises them every three years. Fees for in-facility services are paid on a per-day basis; fees for home-visit services are paid on a per-visit basis.

Regulation to Certify Providers

Providers of services covered by LTCI must be designated or given permission by the prefectural governor. Only governments or social welfare or medical corporations can administer LTC facilities; other for-profit companies are not allowed to provide in-facility services. However, for-profit companies can provide other services, including home-visit services, day services, short-stay services, and residential services. Providers must meet personnel, equipment, and operational standards to receive designation or permission, which is then renewed every six years. To help users select quality service providers, prefectures and service providers are required to publicly disclose the content and operation of their LTC services.

Each municipality develops a plan for the provision of LTC services every three years. This plan includes the expected demand for services each year and measures to secure the services needed. A drafting committee is set up to develop the plan, and public hearings are held to solicit the opinions of residents. In addition, prefectures develop support plans for municipal provision of LTC services every three years. The prefectural plan also includes a development plan for facilities given that they must be built to cover a wide area beyond the municipalities. It also determines the required capacity of facilities in the region. To control the number of facilities, prefectural governors may deny designation or permission to construct new facilities if the total capacity of existing facilities exceeds the required capacity.

Opportunities and Challenges

The Japanese government expects LTC expenditure to increase by 2.4 times the expenditure in 2018 by 2040 because of population aging (Japan, Cabinet Secretariat et al. 2018). Various efforts are under way to improve the sustainability of the system while maintaining and improving the quality of care.

Community-Based Integrated Care System

An important concept that has become a pillar of Japan's LTCI program is the Community-Based Integrated Care System (CICS) (figure 5.5). It is defined in the Act for Promoting Comprehensive Measures for Securing Regional

FIGURE 5.5 Conceptual Framework of the Community-Based Integrated Care System in Japan

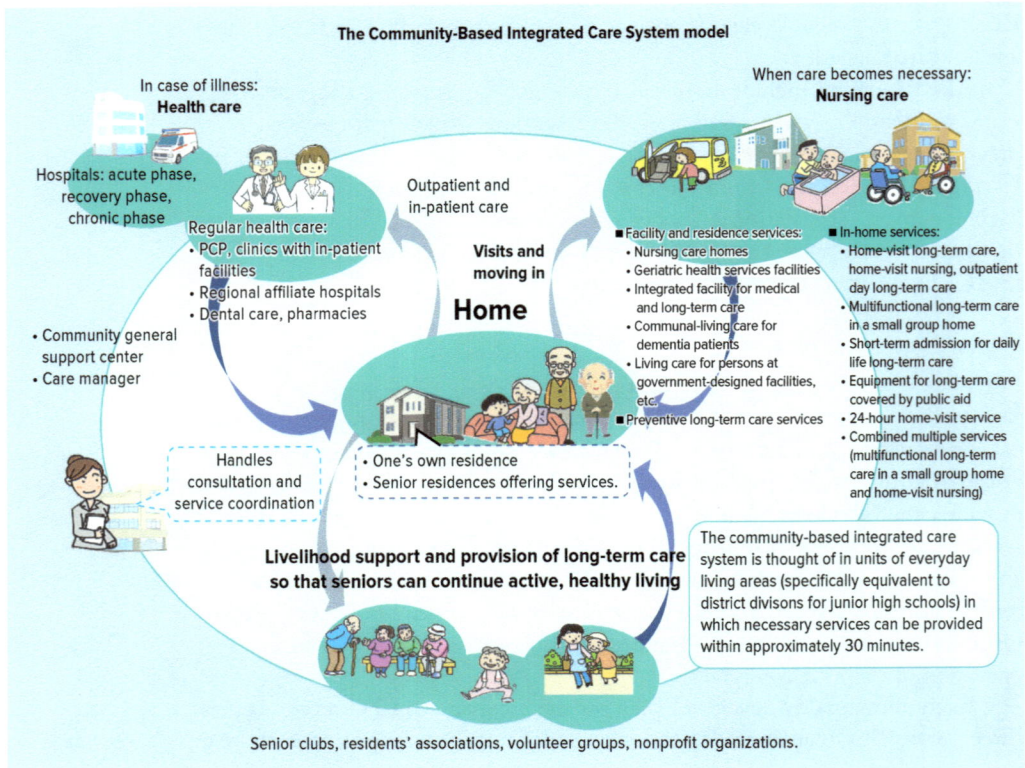

The Community-Based Integrated Care System model

In case of illness:
Health care

When care becomes necessary:
Nursing care

Hospitals: acute phase, recovery phase, chronic phase

Outpatient and in-patient care

Regular health care:
• PCP, clinics with in-patient facilities
• Regional affiliate hospitals
• Dental care, pharmacies

Visits and moving in

■ Facility and residence services:
• Nursing care homes
• Geriatric health services facilities
• Integrated facility for medical and long-term care
• Communal-living care for dementia patients
• Living care for persons at government-designed facilities, etc.
■ Preventive long-term care services

■ In-home services:
• Home-visit long-term care, home-visit nursing, outpatient day long-term care
• Multifunctional long-term care in a small group home
• Short-term admission for daily life long-term care
• Equipment for long-term care covered by public aid
• 24-hour home-visit service
• Combined multiple services (multifunctional long-term care in a small group home and home-visit nursing)

• Community general support center
• Care manager

Home

Handles consultation and service coordination

• One's own residence
• Senior residences offering services.

The community-based integrated care system is thought of in units of everyday living areas (specifically equivalent to district divisons for junior high schools) in which necessary services can be provided within approximately 30 minutes.

Livelihood support and provision of long-term care so that seniors can continue active, healthy living

Senior clubs, residents' associations, volunteer groups, nonprofit organizations.

Source: Ministry of Health, Labour and Welfare, Japan.
Note: PCP = primary care physician.

Medical and Nursing Care as "a system that comprehensively ensures medical care, long-term care, prevention for needing long-term care, housing, and support for independent daily living, so that old persons can enjoy independent daily lives according to their abilities and local conditions in their familiar community as long as possible." The scope of this system extends beyond medical care and LTC to housing and support for daily living, ensuring that these services are comprehensively provided in the community rather than by hospitals or institutions.

Population aging and the increase in chronic diseases has made it a challenge for many people to return to community life after a disease has been completely cured at a hospital. Therefore, the CICS aims to support people living in the community despite their illnesses and disabilities. Given that the number of older people living on their own is increasing, provision of medical care and LTC alone is not sufficient to support community living; person-centered care is also needed. Thus, the system relies on the private sector and residents to provide some services. LTCI covers the costs of social activities organized by community residents, community care meetings, and coordinators who support daily living. Japan aims to extend the system nation-wide by 2025 when the number of people age 75 and over is expected to surge.

Community-Based Integrated Care Visualizing System

To support regional and local governments in the development of community-based integrated care, an easy-to-visualize, graphics-based system has been in operation since 2015 (figure 5.6). The system centralizes information such as the number of people certified for LTC, the benefits provided, the number of medical and LTC facilities and community gathering places, and munici-pal demographic characteristics. The visual information is then depicted on a website in a way that makes it comparable to that of other municipalities. The system therefore makes it easier for local governments to identify issues by analyzing current conditions through intermunicipal comparisons and to develop measures through case studies of municipalities with similar problems.

It also enables staff within a prefecture and municipality to access central-ized information, allowing them to share awareness of issues and facilitate cooperation. In addition, because anyone can access the system, local stake-holders can share problems and encourage efforts to implement community-based integrated care.

FIGURE 5.6 Community-Based Integrated Care Visualizing System

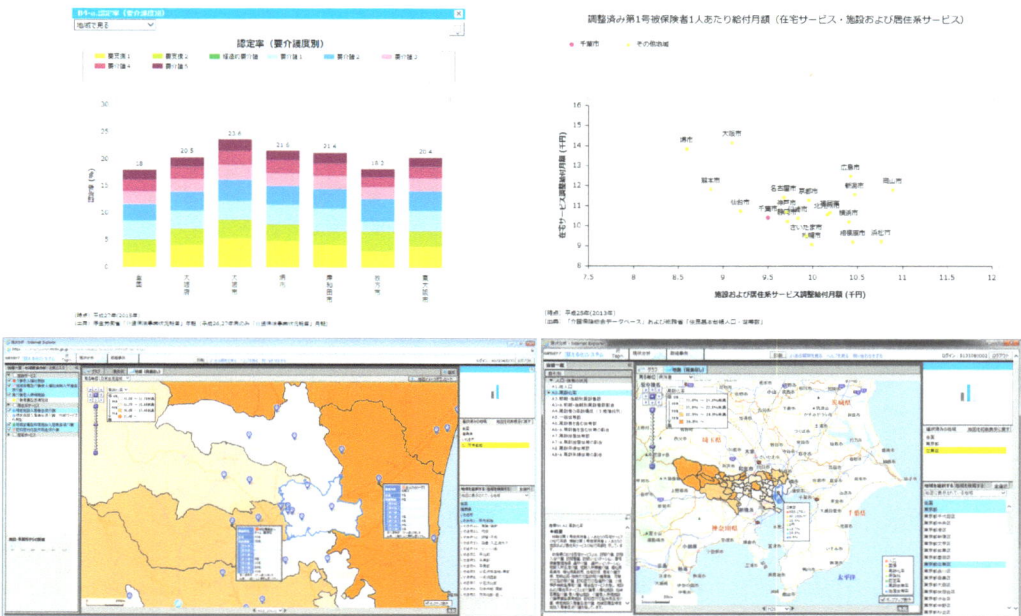

Source: Community-Based Integrated Care Visualizing System (Ministry of Health, Labour and Welfare, Japan).
Note: Once the municipality or indicator to compare has been selected in the system, the results of the analysis are automatically displayed. The upper left shows the results of an intermunicipal comparison of the rate of care required for certification at each level. The upper right shows the relationship between payments for institutional care and home care. The bottom left is a map plotting care providers. The bottom right is an analytical map indicating the percent-age of the older population.

Financial Incentive Scheme for the Prefectures and Municipal Governments

In 2018, the national government launched a scheme to evaluate efforts by prefectures and municipalities to support older people's independence and preventive measures for LTC needs. Performance is assessed on six indicators: (1) strengthening the functions of insurers, (2) improving the quality of care management, (3) activating community-care meetings through collaboration among multiple professions, (4) promoting the fulfillment of LTC needs, (5) promoting moderation in expenditure on LTC, and (6) maintaining or improving conditions for older persons needing LTC. The national government receives the performance results, analyzes them, and reports the results to regional and local governments every year. Based on the evaluation, 40 billion yen (approximately US$364 million) was distributed to regional and local governments in 2021. Researchers can access the data and evaluate the performance of regional and local policies on individual outcomes by linking it to personal information on functional disability, cognitive impairment, and death recorded in the LTCI registry.

Country Example #2: Thailand

Brief Overview

Thailand's population was 66.2 million in 2021. In 2022, the proportion of the population age 65 and over was 13.5 percent, with projections indicating an increase to 25 percent by 2040 (Thailand, Office of the National Economic and Social Development Board 2013). At the same time, the fertility rate has declined dramatically, from 4.9 children per woman in the 1970s to 1.5 in 2021 (TGRI 2016). As a result, although the total population has gradually increased by 0.21 percent per year since 2018, the proportion of the population age 60 and over has risen by 4 percent per year since then.

In 2017, the proportion of Thai people who had difficulty in one or more activity of daily living (ADL) or instrumental activity of daily living (IADL) domains was 35 percent among those 60 years and over (28 percent in one or more IADL domains, 7 percent in one or more ADL domains) (Thailand, National Statistical Office 2018). According to the Department of National Health Insurance, the number of Thais who are bedridden already totals more than 1 million people, and the number continues to grow. In 2017, about 40 percent of older people said their children, spouses, or relatives were their primary source of income, and the old-age pension (Thailand, Ministry of Social Development and Human Security 2003) was the primary source of income for about 20 percent of respondents (Suwanrada, Sukontamarn, and Bangkaew 2018). Consequently, the incomes of one-third of older people in Thailand were below the poverty line in 2016 (TGRI 2016). Like other countries with a large proportion of older people, to tackle the decrease in the number of family caregivers and the increase in older people with care needs, it is critical that an LTC system be established that is suited to the needs of a middle-income country such as Thailand (Mills 2014).

Overview of Thai National Systems for Caring for Older Adults

In Thailand, LTC is defined as "comprehensive care that covers social, health, economic, and environmental dimensions for the elderly who undergo hardships due to chronic illnesses, disabilities, or infirmities and who are partially able or completely unable to help themselves in their routine daily life. Care can be provided formally, by health and social workers, or informally by family members, friends, and neighbors" (Thailand, National Health Commission Office 2009). "Care can also be provided in the family setting, community, or a service establishment" (figure 5.7). (See also Chandoevwit and Vajragupta 2017; Chanprasert 2021; Suriyanrattakorn and Chang 2021.)

Notable Characteristics of LTC in Thailand

The Thai government focuses on strengthening community-based or home-based, rather than facility-based, LTC services. For several reasons, this strategy seems well suited to middle-income countries experiencing rapid increases in their older populations (Chanprasert 2021). First, community- or home-based care can be more cost-effective than facility- or hospital-based care, especially when it comes to chronic or long-term care (Chandoevwit and Vajragupta 2017). Second, LTC services can be operated with community resources, both in big cities and small towns or villages. The services could cover the entire country, with public funding, in collaboration with community and local governments, even considering their limited budgets. Third, the use of a combination of volunteers and trained caregivers to deliver services is also financially beneficial.

Brief History of Community-Based LTC Policy in Thailand

The establishment of Thailand's LTC policy began with the First National Long-Term Plan of Action for the Elderly in 1986, when the share of the population age 60 and over was 6.2 percent (UN DESA Population Division 2019). In Thailand, LTC was established as a community-based, rather than

FIGURE 5.7 Long-Term Care Policy Development in Thailand, 1986–2018

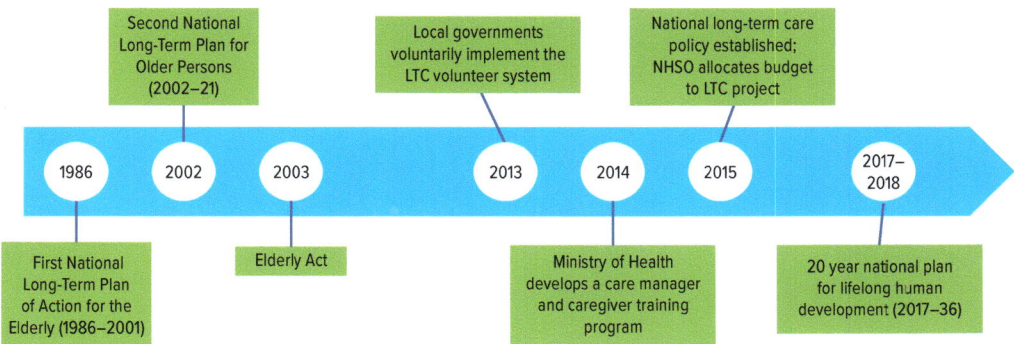

Source: Based on Chanprasert 2021. Timeline on Long-Term Care Development in Thailand. Department of Health, Ministry of Public Health.
Note: LTC = long-term care; NHSO = National Health Security Office.

facility-based, system. In 2008, the community-based project aimed to train LTC volunteers to support bedridden older adults and their families in collaboration with local governments, senior clubs, and other community organizations. Although this project succeeded in expanding the number of LTC volunteers in the community, the scope of services provided by volunteers without specialized training was limited to shopping, cooking, and other daily living tasks. Provision of the physical care that is most needed for bedridden older adults at home was challenging.

In 2013, local governments voluntarily began to implement the LTC volunteer system at the subdistrict level. In 2014, the Ministry of Health developed a care manager and caregiver training program and trained care managers. In 2018, 161,931 older persons in 4,795 subdistricts (66 percent of subdistricts) received LTC services, and 12,817 care managers and 74,833 caregivers were trained.

According to the 20-year plan for lifelong human development drafted in 2016, to use public LTC services, older adults must consult trained care managers for assessment of their care needs based on certain criteria, including ADLs and IADLs. After the assessment, care managers provide the results to the local government, and if certified, applicants are authorized to use public LTC services. Community-based volunteer caregivers were also provided in facilities and communities, in cooperation with senior citizens' families, hospitals, senior clubs, village health volunteers, temples, schools, and community government agencies.

Key Regulatory Elements

Financing and Benefits

Public medical care in Thailand follows what is known as the "30 baht policy." The policy enables individuals to consult doctors or fill prescriptions at public hospitals or clinics at a cost of 30 baht each (approximately US$1). LTC services are also covered by tax-based financing systems. There is no out-of-pocket fee for using public LTC services.

In 2016, the government allocated a budget of US$17.5 million to promote the LTC policy, increased to US$26.2 million and US$33.8 million, respectively, over the following two years. This additional budget, allocated to the National Health Security Office, included not only medical care for older adults but also multiple types of care (for example, nursing services, home visits, community-based volunteers, and provision of some medical aids and equipment). The plan focused on developing data systems for registration, LTC planning, and reimbursement, and ensuring that caregivers are well trained to provide appropriate care to dependent older adults.

Providers

Medical teams consist of the following contributors:

- The family care team (a multidisciplinary team from a community hospital that promotes doctors' visits to older adults at home)

- The community palliative care team (services for those at the end of life, such as cancer patients)
- The district health management system (each district analyzes health problems and prioritizes and resolves them through a district health committee)
- Family doctors (who are trained to work in community hospitals).

The *care manager* assesses the care needs of each older person and manages required services.

In 2018, the government allocated funds in the Ministry of Public Health's budget to train two *caregivers* in every subdistrict implementing LTC, mainly to provide support for homebound, bedridden older adults with severe physical care needs.

Health *volunteers* and LTC volunteers provide daily life assistance for home-based older adults and their families in collaboration with subdistrict hospitals and the local government.

Family members are the primary caregivers providing care to dependent older adults in Thailand.

Governments

Local administration personnel join family care teams to visit dependent older adults at home, act as care managers, and provide devices such as canes that older adults can use at home. In addition, they provide a budget to build community rehabilitation, multipurpose, and quality-of-life development centers; repair homes; and renovate toilets for those with financial difficulties. Some local administrations have residential homes for vulnerable older adults.

Regional inspectors and health personnel from *provincial administrations* (public-health offices) and regional health centers monitor and supervise subdistrict and community LTC through the Ministry of Public Health's inspection system.

The *central government* Department of Health has developed a program to register care managers and caregivers and maintains an LTC reporting system through its Health Data Center. The National Health Security Office allocates funds to train care managers in the community.

Opportunities and Challenges

As a recent opportunity, the Ministry of Public Health plans to achieve 100 percent subdistrict LTC service provision and to develop quality caregivers in every subdistrict in the next few years (Chanprasat 2021). Since the caregivers in Thailand are volunteers at the present time, the ministry is preparing to link LTC data and reports with the National Health Security Office data management system and the local administration to pay and retrain care managers and caregivers. The ministry will also develop an intermediate care model for better care for older adults. After achieving 100 percent coverage of LTC service in the country, one of the next challenges will be planning a long-term preventive care policy to determine additional steps.

References

Chandoevwit, W., and Y. Vajragupta. 2017. "Long Term Care Insurance System: Long Term Care System for Thailand" (in Thai). Thailand Development Research Institute, Bangkok.

Chanprasert, P. 2021. "Long-Term Care Policy and Implementation in Thailand." In *Coping with Rapid Population Ageing in Asia*, edited by O. Komazawa and Y. Saito, 36–44. Jakarta: Economic Research Institute for ASEAN and East Asia.

Drinkwater, C., J. Wildman, and S. Moffatt. 2019. "Social Prescribing." *BMJ* 28 (364): l1285.

Japan, Cabinet Secretariat, Cabinet Office, Ministry of Finance, Ministry of Health, Labour and Welfare. 2018. "Future Prospects of Social Security for the Year 2040." https://www.mhlw.go.jp/stf/seisakunitsuite/bunya/0000207382.html.

Japan, Ministry of Internal Affairs and Communications, Statistic Bureau. 2021. 2020 Population Census. https://www.stat.go.jp/english/data/kokusei/2020/summary.html.

Japan, National Institute of Population and Social Security Research. 2017. "Population Projections for Japan: 2016 to 2065." https://www.ipss.go.jp/pp-zenkoku/e/zenkoku_e2017/pp_zenkoku2017e.asp.

Kondo, Katsunori, and Megumi Rosenberg. 2018. *Advancing Universal Health Coverage through Knowledge Translation for Healthy Ageing—Lessons Learnt from the Japan Gerontological Evaluation Study*. Geneva: World Health Organization.

Mills, A. 2014. "Health Care Systems in Low- and Middle-Income Countries." *New England Journal of Medicine* 370 (6): 552–57.

Suriyanrattakorn, S., and C.-L. Chang. 2021. "Long-Term Care (LTC) Policy in Thailand on the Homebound and Bedridden Elderly Happiness." *Health Policy OPEN* 2.

Suwanrada, W., P. Sukontamarn, and B. Bangkaew. 2018. "Who Supports Intergenerational Redistribution Policy? Evidence from Old-Age Allowance System in Thailand." *Journal of the Economics of Ageing* 12: 24–34.

TGRI (Foundation of Thai Gerontology Research and Development). 2016. *The Situation of Thai Elderly*: Bangkok: TGRI. http://www.dop.go.th/download/knowledge/th1512367202-108_0.pdf.

Thailand, Ministry of Social Development and Human Security. 2003. "The Act on Older Persons B.E. 2546 (2003 A.D.)." Bangkok. https://www.mindbank.info/item/5037.

Thailand, National Health Commission Office. 2009. "Second National Health Assembly Agenda 3.3: Main Document on Development of Long-term Care for Dependent Elderly People." Bangkok. https://en.nationalhealth.or.th/wp-content/uploads/2017/09/3-2009-1.pdf.

Thailand, National Statistical Office. 2018. "Report on the 2017 Survey of the Older Persons in Thailand" (in Thai). Bangkok.

Thailand, Office of the National Economic and Social Development Board. 2013. "Population Projections for Thailand, 2010–2040." Bangkok.

UN DESA Population Division (United Nations Department of Economic and Social Affairs Population Division). 2019. "World Population Prospects 2019, Online Edition. Rev. 1." UN DESA, New York. https://population.un.org/wpp/.

WHO (World Health Organization). 2020. *Decade of Healthy Ageing: Baseline Report*. Geneva: WHO.

WHO (World Health Organization). 2021. *Framework for Countries to Achieve an Integrated Continuum of Long-Term Care*. Geneva: WHO. https://www.who.int/publications/i/item/9789240038844.

WHO Commission on Social Determinants of Health. 2008. *Closing the Gap in a Generation: Health Equity through Action on the Social Determinants of Health*. Final Report of the Commission on Social Determinants of Health. Geneva: WHO.

World Bank. 2004. *World Development Report 2004: Making Service Work for Poor People*. Washington, DC: World Bank.

CHAPTER 6

Evaluating Care of Older Adults in Low- and Middle-Income Countries

Zhanlian Feng, Guadalupe Suarez, and Elena E. Glinskaya

Key Messages

- Researchers often measure care needs in older populations through functional status assessments—a person's ability to perform activities of daily living (ADLs) or instrumental activities of daily living (IADLs). Countries may consider short but validated measurement tools.

- On the supply side, research objectively measuring person-centered care is scant. Some standardized assessment instruments for personalized older adult care have been validated in low- and middle-income countries (LMICs) and show promise.

- As they scale up care systems for older adults, countries can achieve the best results by investing in information, monitoring, and evaluation systems from the start. Evaluation is critical to ensuring that health care and long-term care (LTC) services meet older people's needs equitably and affordably.

Introduction

Although population aging is a global issue, it is occurring at a much faster pace in LMICs than in high-income countries (HICs). With increasing life expectancy and the rising burden of noncommunicable diseases has come an unprecedented demand for health care and LTC services for rapidly aging populations across LMICs, which—like many HICs—are unprepared to meet the needs of this age group.

Meanwhile, amid shifting demographic and cultural trends across LMICs, the erosion of family-based care for older adults—traditionally the mainstay of old-age support and LTC—seems inevitable (Feng 2019). The result is gaps in care for older adults that are increasing as informal (unpaid) care is becoming insufficient, given the changing needs of care for older people and the increased burden they impose on family caregivers. In some LMICs, new forms of older adult care options outside the familial sphere are emerging in the public sector and private market, but both access to, and the affordability of, such formal paid care options remain limited.

Policy responses addressing the challenges of care for older adults vary across LMICs, depending in part on where they are currently situated on the "aging curve." But overall, in most countries, it has not yet been given high enough priority on the national policy agenda (Scheil-Adlung 2015). Many LMICs have just embarked on the process of planning and building basic services for the care of older populations. Others are already exploring innovative care provision and delivery models, either homegrown or drawn from the experiences of other countries, including HICs. But no matter which stage countries are in in developing their systems of care for older adults, it is critical that the features and performance of these emerging systems be evaluated to ensure that they meet the care needs of their aging populations. However, there is a marked deficit of research and empirical evidence on these care policies and practices in LMICs to inform policy planning and evaluation (Lloyd-Sherlock 2014).

This chapter first provides an analysis and synthesis of the findings from a literature review on the current older adult care landscape in LMICs, with a focus on assessing the methods used by researchers to evaluate these care systems on both the demand and supply sides. It then identifies the gaps and barriers to the development of primary health care– (PHC-) driven, integrated, and person-centered older adult care provision and delivery systems in LMICs. Based on this review and drawing on experiences and lessons learned from HICs, the chapter then discusses policy options and provides recommendations for practical approaches to evaluating care systems for older adults in LMICs.

Although the term "older adult care" is used here broadly to cover both medical care and nonmedical aspects of LTC services for older adults, the focus is primarily on LTC services to meet the chronic care needs of older adults with disabilities, as measured by physical or cognitive impairments. Medical care for older adults is discussed mainly in the context of integrating the full range of services on a continuum of care for older adults with disabilities.

The chapter also uses the words "evaluation" and "evaluating" broadly to mean high-level assessment of older adult care provision, organization, delivery system features, and quality performance. Micro-level, technically oriented evaluation of outcomes of specific programs or policy interventions is beyond the scope of this chapter. The analysis and discussions are based on a review of relevant literature, both published and gray, identified through a series of web searches and database searches and English-language national and international policy documents published over the period 2000–21.

Demand-Side Evaluation[1]

Informal, family-based care dominates most older adult care systems in LMICs, where the provision of care and support for older relatives is perceived to be the domain of the family, mostly the women. In some countries, such as China, filial piety is written into law (Feng 2017). Yet long-term demographic and socioeconomic trends—especially urbanization, smaller family size, out-migration, increasing population mobility, and the growth of female labor market participation—are resulting in gaps in caregiving and gradually eroding these traditional, women-provided older adult care systems (Holmes 2021). As these trends continue to evolve and the gap between demand and supply of older adult care widens, the need for LMICs to develop comprehensive LTC systems is becoming ever more imperative (Holmes 2021).

Assessing and Mapping Current Older Adult Care Needs in LMICs

Although a variety of methods can be used to measure needs or disability, the most common method in aging studies is measuring functional status, that is, a person's ability to perform ADLs or IADLs. ADLs include activities such as bathing, dressing, moving from a bed to a wheelchair, and going to the toilet. IADLs include more complex activities a person needs to be able to perform to live independently, such as managing medications, shopping, preparing meals, and performing housework.

The measurement of ADLs has generally been consistent across countries, but the measurement of IADLs has been less so. Surveys to capture IADLs tend to have more variation in domains, reflecting cultural and geographic variations in those activities considered instrumental to daily living (Hu 2012). Comparability in both ADL- and IADL-based disability measures across countries is also hampered by differences in survey questions (for example, wording and types of scales used) and in survey methodology. Cross-country comparisons of ADLs and IADLS in aging study surveys are therefore limited. The lack of standardization in measurements across studies and countries makes the international comparison of functional status and disability rates difficult.

The most well-known comprehensive assessment scale for ADLs is the Katz Index of Independence in Activities of Daily Living, which measures the extent of dependence or independence of a person in six task domains: bathing, dressing, toileting, transferring, continence, and feeding. The level of dependence is categorized by the amount of assistance needed to complete the task (Holmes 2021).

Other common indexes to measure disability include the 10-item Barthel Index (ADLs) and the Lawton Scale (IADLs). Some countries have made their own modifications to these indexes (and others that measure ADLs and IADLs) to measure disability within their aging populations and systems. Researchers in some countries measure disability as the inability to perform at least one ADL without assistance, whereas others categorize difficulties with ADLs and IADLs into different levels of dependency, depending on the level of assistance needed (Holmes 2021). For example, severe disability is often defined as being unable to perform at least three of six ADLs, which is used as the eligibility threshold for government-sponsored LTC insurance benefits in countries such as Singapore (Holmes 2021). Longitudinal surveys with regular waves of data collection that measure ADLs and IADLs can provide data on functional status, the current needs of older people, and the frequency of transitions between different states of the need for care (Holmes 2021).

Table 6.1 summarizes findings from various studies conducted in LMICs, including country, type of ADL or IADL index used to measure functional status, prevalence of disability, underlying population, and source. As shown, the estimates on disability prevalence among older adults, based on either ADL or IADL limitations, vary widely and defy direct comparison across LMICs, depending on the study population and year of data analyzed. The high prevalence of disability among adults age 50 and over, as measured by having difficulty performing at least one ADL, is particularly notable in Ghana (44 percent), the Russian Federation (43.1 percent), and South Africa (38.6 percent) among the 13 countries.

Disability-adjusted life years (DALYs) can be calculated to quantify the burden of a disease, such as dementia, that is associated with severe disability. The Global Burden of Disease report gives dementia a disability weight of 0.67, which is higher than almost any other condition, and signifies a two-thirds loss of healthy life for each year lived with dementia (Kedare and Vispute 2016). It is projected that LMICs will have the largest rise in dementia prevalence by 2050. In 2019, 55.2 million people were estimated to have dementia globally (with more than 60 percent in LMICs), and that number is projected to grow to 139 million by 2050 (WHO 2021b). The estimated prevalence of dementia in Southeast Asia is expected to reach 12.09 million (a 236 percent increase) by 2050 (Dominguez et al. 2021).

One study that assesses the incidence of dementia, DALYs, and cost of care among community-dwelling older Filipinos reports a dementia incidence rate of 16 cases per 1,000 person-years (17 cases per 1,000 person-years for females and 14 for males) and projects 220,632 new cases in 2030, 295,066 in 2040, and 378,461 in 2050 (Dominguez et al. 2021). The study also estimates a dementia-related disease burden of 2,876 DALYs per 100,000 persons and an economic burden of about 196,000 Philippine pesos annually per patient (roughly US$4,070), or 36.7 percent of an average family's annual income (Dominguez et al. 2021).

Issues of timely assessment, diagnosis, and support of people living with dementia are compounded in LMICs that lack the proper infrastructure to provide these services. Additionally, most research on the validity of diagnostic assessments comes from HICs. Cross-country assessments are subject to variance in sensitivity and validity because of the potential of different data collection procedures, diagnostic criteria, and cultural conceptions of the condition (Ferri and Jacob 2017).

TABLE 6.1 ADL- and IADL-Based Measures of Disability among Older Adults in Select LMICs

Country	ADL index or domains	ADL disability prevalence	IADL index or domains	IADL disability prevalence	Population	Source
Argentina	Katz Index	Need assistance with any ADL: 5.8%	Lawton Scale	Need assistance with at least one IADL: 17.6%	3,291 age 65 and over	Encuesta Nacional sobre Calidad de Vida de Adultos Mayores (ENCaViAM, 2012) (Matus-Lopez and Chaverri-Carvajal 2021)
Brazil	Katz Index	Need assistance with any ADL: 11.0%	Lawton Scale	Need assistance with at least one IADL: 35.7%	3,903 age 65 and over	Estudo Longitudinal da Saúde dos Idosos (ELSI-Brasil, 2015/16) (Matus-Lopez and Chaverri-Carvajal 2021)
Chile	Katz Index	Need assistance with any ADL: 8.2%	—	—	31,667 age 65 and over	Encuesta de Caracterización Socioeconómica Nacional (CASEN, 2017) (Matus-Lopez and Chaverri-Carvajal 2021)
China	Bathing, dressing, transferring, eating (including cutting up food), and continence	Difficulty performing at least one ADL: 16.2%	—	—	12,085 age 50 and over	Cross-sectional data from the WHO Study on Global AGEing and Adult Health Wave 1 (2007–2010) (Lestari et al. 2019)
China	Eating, dressing, moving on and off bed, transferring indoors, washing face and brushing teeth, toileting, bathing, and moving upstairs and downstairs	Any ADL limitation: 14.9%	Cooking, washing clothes, cleaning, taking medicine, cutting nails, managing money, making phone calls, getting out in the rain, shopping, and going to a physician	Any IADL limitation: 30.1%	2,195 older adults with mean age of 75.1	Shanghai Longitudinal Survey of Elderly Life and Opinion (2008) (Feng et al. 2013)
Colombia	Katz Index	Need assistance with any ADL: 7.7%	Lawton Scale	Need assistance with at least one IADL: 25.8%	17,134 age 65 and over	Encuesta Nacional de Salud, Envejecimiento y Vejez (SABE, 2015) (Matus-Lopez and Chaverri-Carvajal 2021)
Ghana	Bathing, dressing, transferring, eating (including cutting up food), and continence	Difficulty performing at least one ADL: 44%	—	—	4,057 age 50 and over	Cross-sectional data from the WHO Study on Global AGEing and Adult Health Wave 1 (2007–2010) (Lestari et al. 2019)

(continued)

TABLE 6.1 Continued

Country	ADL index or domains	ADL disability prevalence	IADL index or domains	IADL disability prevalence	Population	Source
India	Bathing, dressing, mobility, feeding, and toileting	Moderate disability: 19%; severe disability: 3%	Preparing a hot meal, shopping for groceries, making telephone calls, taking medications, doing housework, managing money, getting around or finding an address in an unfamiliar place	Moderate disability: 42%; severe disability: 6%	31,464 age 60 and over	Longitudinal Ageing Study of India (LASI, 2017/2018) (Chauhan et al. 2022)
Malaysia	Bathing, dressing and undressing, eating, transferring, and grooming	Difficulty performing at least one ADL: 1.2%	Preparing meals, shopping, managing money, housekeeping, doing laundry, and taking and managing medication	Difficulty performing at least one IADL: 13.6%	2,980 age 60 and over	Mental Health and Quality of Life of Older Malaysians Survey (MHQoLOM) (2003–2005) (Siop, Verbrugge, and Hamid 2008)
Mexico	Katz Index	Need assistance with any ADL: 10.2%	Lawton Scale	Need assistance with at least one IADL: 13.8%	7,909 age 65 and over	Encuesta Nacional sobre Salud y Envejecimiento (ENASEM, 2018) (Matus-Lopez and Chaverri-Carvajal 2021)
Russian Federation	Bathing, dressing, transferring, eating (including cutting up food), and continence	Difficulty performing at least one ADL: 43.1%	—	—	3,422 age 50 and over	Cross-sectional data from the WHO Study on Global AGEing and Adult Health Wave 1 (2007–2010) (Lestari et al. 2019)
South Africa	Bathing, dressing, transferring, eating (including cutting up food), and continence	Difficulty performing at least one ADL: 38.6%	—	—	2,806 age 50 and over	Cross-sectional data from the WHO Study on Global AGEing and Adult Health Wave 1 (2007–2010) (Lestari et al. 2019)
Sri Lanka	Barthel Index	More than one ADL limitation: 16.9%	Lawton Scale	More than one IADL limitation: 39.4%	723 age 65 and over	Community-based cross-sectional study (Wijesiri et al. 2021)
Uruguay	Katz Index	Need assistance with any ADL: 7.0%	—	—	4,042 age 65 and over	Encuesta Longitudinal de Protección Social (ELPS, 2015/16) (Matus-Lopez and Chaverri-Carvajal 2021)

Source: Glinskaya, Feng, and Suarez 2022.
Note: — = not available; ADL = activity of daily living; IADL = instrumental activity of daily living; LMICs = low- and middle-income countries; WHO = World Health Organization.

Evidence of Unmet Needs

Unmet needs occur when health and LTC services are unavailable, inaccessible, or insufficient to meet an older person's needs. Research has shown that older adults with unmet needs have lower quality of life, greater ADL and IADL limitations, more hospitalizations and hospital readmissions, and a higher rate of mortality (Zhu 2015). From January 2021 through June 2022, the World Health Organization (WHO) undertook multicountry, cross-sectional, and longitudinal studies to quantify unmet needs for health and social care among older people. An analysis of unmet health care needs among older persons age 60 or over in 27 countries in the WHO European Region was conducted using cross-national surveys (the Survey of Health, Ageing and Retirement in Europe 2019–2020) (Börsch-Supan 2022). Preliminary results show that about 1 in 10 older persons (12 percent) experienced unmet needs due to affordability barriers. Nearly one-third of older persons in Greece reported unmet health care needs, followed by Bulgaria, Estonia, and Romania, with nearly one in five. The difference between rich and poor people in unmet health care needs ranged from less than 2 percentage points in Croatia, Poland, Slovenia, and Switzerland to more than 20 percentage points in Belgium, Greece, and Romania (WHO and World Bank 2021).

Data on unmet health needs in LMICs are limited, but available studies in select countries reveal substantial unmet needs among older adults. For example, one study in China analyzes 5,166 adults age 65 and older from the 2015 wave of the China Health and Retirement Longitudinal Study (Li et al. 2020). The sample includes the following proportions of older adults: 22 percent without any chronic condition, 27 percent with one chronic condition, 44 percent with multimorbidity, and 7 percent with multimorbidity and functional impairment (Li et al. 2020). The study finds that older adults with both multimorbidity and functional impairment use health care services the most often but still reported the highest level of unmet health care needs (Li et al. 2020).

Another study in China that analyzes the demand and supply of home-based care for older adults finds that approximately 60 percent of older adults needed home visit services, and more than one-third needed psychological counseling or daily care services, although the proportion of these services provided in the community accounted for only 20 percent (Wang 2013). In Greece, 20 percent of older adults had unmet care needs in 2015, rising to 24 percent in 2017. The majority of the population with unmet needs were between 65 and 79 years old, female, living in single households, and had limitations in two or more ADLs (World Bank 2021).

The WHO, in collaboration with the government of India, conducted a cross-sectional, community-based study of the population 60 years and older to identify geriatric health problems in samples drawn from a slum and a village. The study finds a large number of unmet health needs, such as unoperated cataracts, uncontrolled hypertension, and uncorrected hearing impairment (Thakur, Banerjee, and Nikumb 2013).

In summary, policy makers in LMICs must consider regularly evaluating the health and LTC needs of their older adult populations and take steps to address the large gap between the escalating need for care and its limited supply.

Supply-Side Evaluation

This section focuses on the instruments with which to measure and evaluate the service delivery system and outcomes on the supply side. It begins with a brief description of the Donabedian framework for quality assessment and provides examples of existing methods for evaluating the quality of services targeted at older adults, particularly the most vulnerable among them (for example, those of advanced age who are at high risk for functional decline or near the end of their lives). This section also synthesizes the methods for evaluating person-centered care, what it means in different contexts, and finally, current methods developed to facilitate cross-country comparison.

Quality Measures of Care for Older Adults

Quality indicators are standardized, evidence-based measures used to monitor, evaluate, and improve the quality of health care. Originated in the United States, the Donabedian framework has been widely used to measure and evaluate the quality of health care. It organizes quality indicators in three conceptual domains—structure, process, and outcome, as depicted in figure 6.1 (Donabedian 1988, 2005).

Structure indicators involve the elements and attributes of the care setting, such as materials, resources, and staff capacity, and can include organizational and management structures. *Process* indicators refer to the interaction between the individual who uses care and the systems that provide that care, that is, what is done in giving and receiving care. *Outcome* indicators are the results of care and describe the effects on patients' health status (for example, number of patients successfully treated or the level of satisfaction with care) (Joling et al. 2018).

FIGURE 6.1 The Donabedian Framework to Evaluate the Quality of Care

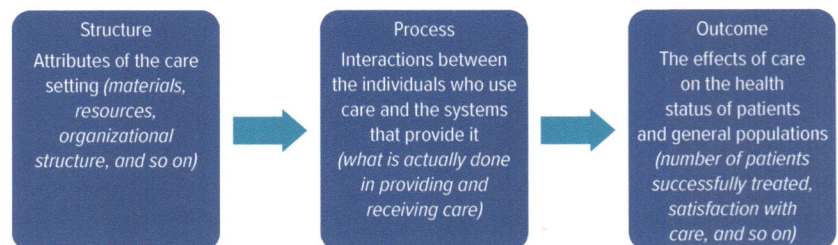

Source: Adapted from Donabedian 1988.

Outcome indicators are typically considered to be the most useful because they assess the effect of health care services on desired outcomes. On the other hand, process indicators are considered to be the most sensitive to differences in the quality of care and can be more straightforward to interpret without extensive risk adjustment (a process that accounts for observable health status and risk factors to make a fair comparison of outcomes among patients) (Joling et al. 2018).

Data collected for quality measurement can be derived from a multitude of sources, including routinely collected administrative data such as medical records or disease-specific registrars, patient or staff surveys, direct observation of physician activities, and chart abstraction. For chart abstraction, if resources and infrastructure are sufficient, information from a patient's medical record can be entered in an electronic medical record. Although electronic medical record systems promote efficiency, adopting them is expensive and maintaining them is time-intensive.

A wide range of existing quality indicators, developed primarily in HIC settings, can inform quality measurement development in LMICs. Within the US health care industry, the National Quality Forum sets standards for quality improvement and reporting. The forum consists of more than 400 member bodies, including consumer organizations, private and public purchasers, hospitals, physicians, certification and accreditation agencies, and other health care stakeholders (Namburi and Lee 2022). The forum's criteria are widely used for evaluating quality indicators with regard to "importance," "scientific acceptability of measure properties," "usability," and "feasibility" (Joling et al. 2018).

A systematic review conducted by Joling et al. (2018) identifies existing quality indicators for community care for older people through a systematic literature review and assesses their methodological quality using the Appraisal of Indicators through Research and Evaluation instrument (Joling et al. 2018). The instrument consists of 20 quality items grouped into four quality domains. The review assesses three of the four domains, including stakeholder involvement, scientific evidence, and additional evidence, formulation, and usage. It identifies 17 quality indicator sets that cover 567 quality indicators. The majority of the quality indicators assess processes of care (80 percent) or measure clinical issues (63 percent) and focus on a specific disease or are applied in a patient group with a particular disease, mostly for people with dementia, followed by several types of cancer and cardiovascular diseases. Of the 17 quality indicator sets, six were found to have high methodological quality on at least two of the three quality domains (Joling et al. 2018). Notable quality indicator sets included the following:

- The Assessing Care of Vulnerable Elders-3 (ACOVE-3) and the Agency for Healthcare Research and Quality (AHRQ) prevention quality indicator sets achieved the highest scores on the domain "scientific evidence." These sets thoroughly describe the methods used to search for scientific evidence and how the evidence was appraised, therefore supporting the selection of the indicators (Joling et al. 2018).

- The interRAI–Home Care quality indicator set scored highest on the domains "stakeholder involvement" and "additional evidence, formulation, and usage." It also provides the best evidence of reliability and discriminative power and uses a rigorous risk-adjustment method (Joling et al. 2018).

Assessing Care of Vulnerable Elders-3

In 2000, researchers at the RAND Corporation developed the first set of quality measures specifically for vulnerable older adults (age 65 or older who are at high risk for functional decline or death), inclusive of comprehensive general medical and geriatric conditions (Askari et al. 2012). Currently in its third phase, the set includes 392 quality indicators, 26 clinical conditions, and 14 different types of care processes and covers four domains of care (screening and prevention, diagnosis, treatment, and follow up and continuity) (RAND Corporation, n.d.). The ACOVE-3 set can be used to evaluate vulnerable older adults at the level of the health system, health plan, or medical group. The indicators can evaluate whether the care being delivered (process measures) meets specified standards that have been developed through evidence and expert opinion (Askari et al. 2012).

A systematic review conducted by Askari et al. (2012) aims to describe studies using the ACOVE-3 quality indicators to reflect how these indicators were used. Regarding data collection, in most studies a combination of patient record review and interviews was used to extract the data; only a few studies used automated data extraction. Three studies (out of 41) reported on the translation of ACOVE-3 quality indicators to another country—Canada to assess the quality of care of older people with cognitive impairment or dementia; the Netherlands to use in general-practice care quality assessment for vulnerable older adults; and the United Kingdom to assess the quality of primary and secondary care for older adults using patient surveys, although not all quality indicators were selected for usage in each country (Askari et al. 2012).

Resident Assessment Instrument

The Resident Assessment Instrument (RAI) was developed in the United States in response to the Nursing Home Reform Act, part of the Omnibus Budget Reconciliation Act of 1987 (Hirdes et al. 2008). Through the Minimum Data Set (MDS, currently in version 3.0), RAI is designed to collect the minimum amount of data to guide care planning and monitoring for residents in LTC settings. The MDS is part of the federally mandated process for clinical assessment of all residents in Medicare- or Medicaid-certified nursing homes and contains items that measure physical, psychological, and psychosocial functioning (Mor 2004).

The interRAI network was established initially through the international collaboration of researchers and practitioners seeking to apply interRAI instruments to nursing-home residents in other countries (interRAI, n.d.). The network currently consists of researchers and practitioners in more than 35 countries. InterRAI instruments are used throughout the world and have been mandated by governments in several economies, including

Belgium; Canada; Finland; Hong Kong SAR, China; Ireland; New Zealand; Singapore; and Switzerland. Member countries also include Brazil, Chile, India, Lebanon, Rwanda, and South Africa. In 2000, interRAI launched a multinational effort to update the entire suite of RAI instruments and develop new instruments for sectors not yet addressed by existing ones (interRAI, n.d.), including the following:

- The Community Health Assessment, which supports the assessment of older and disabled adults living in a range of settings, from independent residences to assisted living
- The Home Care assessment, which evaluates the needs, strengths, and preferences of persons in home and community-care settings
- The Long-Term Care Facilities assessment, which evaluates the needs, strengths, and preferences of persons in chronic-care settings (for example, nursing homes)
- The Palliative Care assessment, which assesses the needs, strengths, and preferences of persons in palliative care or hospices.

Each of these four assessment instruments consists of items common to the other instruments in addition to items exclusive to that instrument. A study conducted by Hirdes et al. (2008) examines the reliability of the items from five interRAI instruments supporting home care, LTC, mental health, palliative care, and postacute care. The study finds that most of the items in these instruments worked very well in multiple service settings and retain reliability when used across care settings.

Currently, the Developing research resources And minimum data set for Care Homes' Adoption and use (DACHA) study is underway in the United Kingdom and aims to generate an MDS by synthesizing existing evidence and data sources with resident data generated from care homes (Burton et al. 2022). From work to date, several early core principles have been developed for an MDS for older adult care home residents that may be of use for stakeholders in LMICs, including the following:

- The MDS must primarily focus on measuring what matters most to support those living in care homes.
- The MDS must reduce data burden and duplication of effort for the care home.
- The MDS requires national infrastructure and integration with existing data systems, including investment in practice development and staff support.

Measurement for Quality Assurance in the United States

Within the United States, various efforts have helped identify outcomes and develop quality indicators and instruments. However, comprehensive health care quality measures for older adults are still needed. The Agency for Healthcare Research and Quality (AHRQ) is a US government agency that supports research to improve the quality of health care. The AHRQ has four quality indicator modules—Prevention Quality Indicators, Inpatient Quality

Indicators, Patient Safety Indicators, and Pediatric Quality Indicators—based on hospital inpatient administrative data that researchers can use to track clinical performance and outcomes (AHRQ, n.d.-b). One drawback is that these indicators are not specifically designed for older, acute-care inpatients. A second drawback is that they include few indicators pertaining to geriatric syndromes (for example, hospital fracture and decubitus ulcer) (Brand et al. 2011).

AHRQ also maintains the Consumer Assessment of Healthcare Providers and Systems surveys, which assess patients' experiences with their health care providers and plans, including hospitals, home health care agencies, hospices, doctors, and health and drug plans (AHRQ, n.d.-a). Within these sets of surveys, the Home and Community-Based Services survey elicits feedback from participants enrolled in state-based government-funded services about their experiences with the provision of services and support (AHRQ, n.d.-c).

The Healthcare Effectiveness Data and Information Set (HEDIS) is a measure set developed and maintained by the National Committee for Quality Assurance to objectively measure, report, and compare quality across health plans. The set includes more than 90 measures across six domains of care, including effectiveness of care, access/availability of care, experience of care, utilization and risk-adjusted utilization, health plan descriptive information, and measures reported using electronic clinical data systems (NCQA, n.d.). The committee develops HEDIS measures through partnerships with representatives from purchasers, consumers, health plans, health care providers, and policy makers (Coordinated Care of Washington, n.d.). However, only a small number of these measures specifically target older people. According to MacLeod et al. (2018), 37 of the 86 specific measures (43 percent) do not apply to Medicare beneficiaries, and only 4 of them (fewer than 5 percent) focus primarily on social issues among older adults (for example, fall risk management and urinary incontinence).

Evaluating Person-Centered, Integrated Older Adult Care

In the field of older adult care, person-centeredness is receiving increasing attention—albeit mostly in HICs. This trend is in conformance with a growing emphasis on aging in place and treating in place, which are increasingly preferred to the frequent, and often disruptive, transition of patients through various care settings and from provider to provider. Person-centered care encompasses care that is planned in response to individuals' personal preferences, values, and goals. It is increasingly important in aged care systems because the prevalence of multimorbidity and long-term health problems increase with age and often require individualized care from multiple providers and a greater focus on patient autonomy and care preferences.

Research objectively measuring person-centered care, including identifying potential instruments of measurement, is presently limited. Given the rapidity with which populations are aging in LMICs, research-based evidence to identify or develop best practices in person-centered care is urgently needed. Through a systematic review of measures of person-centeredness, Wilberforce et al. (2016) identify 11 instruments spanning general and gerontological nursing, rehabilitation and occupational therapy, and palliative care. However, the review is unable to explicitly recommend any measures of person-centeredness for use in older adult care owing to shortcomings in the breadth and methodological quality of research underpinning these measures (Wilberforce et al. 2016).

Yang et al. (2019) conducted a study that explores and compares resident and staff perspectives of the person-centered climate in Chinese nursing homes. The study uses two versions of person-centered climate questionnaires (PCQ), one for residents (PCQ-P) and one for staff (PCQ-S), both originally developed in Sweden. The PCQ-P survey scales comprise three subscales, measuring a climate of safety, everydayness, and hospitality. The PCQ-S comprise three subscales measuring a climate of safety, everydayness, and community.

The study finds that "a climate of safety" and "a climate of everydayness" (an environment enabling positive experiences and a sense of belonging) were rated significantly lower by residents than by nursing staff; "a climate of hospitality" was rated very low by residents; and staff perception of person-centered climate was lower than that reported in Swedish nursing homes.

Overall, in the Chinese nursing homes surveyed, residents and staff ranked the person-centered climate of nursing homes relatively low compared with their counterparts in countries with well-established, residential aged-care systems (for example, Norway and Sweden) (Yang et al. 2019). The authors also note that nursing homes in China experienced higher staff turnover and greater difficulty in retaining staff with experience in aged care, which in turn affected the quality of care and person-centeredness of care for residents (Yang et al. 2019).

Philp et al. (2017) outline how a standardized system for personalized assessment, the EasyCare method, can be implemented in countries at all income levels. The EasyCare method is a person-centered assessment of older people for use in primary care that identifies concerns in health, functional independence, and well-being. The method has been validated in more than 30 countries since its inception in 1994 (Philp et al. 2017). Strong primary care systems are essential to attaining integrated person-centered care because of their broad reach in the older population in the community (Philp et al. 2017). The case studies below detail how this method has been implemented in China, Uganda, and the United Kingdom.

In China, the EasyCare method was first introduced by including it in the 2015 Chinese Longitudinal Healthy Longevity Study, but it was formally implemented in 2016 as an assessment and care-planning tool (Philp et al. 2017). A train-the-trainers workshop was undertaken with participants from Pinetree Care Group (a home-health provider agency), several universities, and the China Association for Gerontology and Geriatrics. Through this workshop, and by implementing the EasyCare method, trainers widened their responses to their clients' identified needs and began partnerships to expand their capacity. Additionally, training in the EasyCare method in China has been updated to include the Pinetree Care approach to restorative care so as to identify and provide interventions for cognitive and physical functions that can still be restored and maintained, align care plans to the goals of the older person, and motivate the person to become an active part of the team (Philp et al. 2017).

In Uganda, EasyCare has been implemented in combination with a community-strengthening approach. This involves a two-step process: issues identified by an EasyCare assessment are first raised at a community meeting and then an action plan is developed to facilitate a supportive environment for older people (Philp et al. 2017). The EasyCare instrument was used for the first time in 2011 by a nongovernmental organization (Health Nest Uganda), a pilot study was conducted, and facilitators were trained to use the tool. In 2012, the government of Uganda accepted the approach as a new way of working with older adult populations (Philp et al. 2017). The use of the EasyCare assessment in Uganda has led to an increase in attendance at community meetings to discuss the needs of older people and created a dialogue between older people, community members, and health service providers.

In the United Kingdom, a local telecommunications company (KCOM in Hull) identified two members to undertake a one-day training course in person-centered care using the EasyCare assessment, and then conduct telephone consultations, face-to-face interviews, and follow-up evaluations. The project then directed the participants to services appropriate for their needs, using a local directory. Among the participants, 90 percent found the assessment helpful in identifying health and care needs important to them that previously would not necessarily have been identified or accessed (Philp et al. 2017). An independent evaluation by the policy group ILC-UK suggested that savings of up to 3.3 billion pounds (roughly US$4.2 billion) could be realized between 2014 and 2030 by adopting this process nationally in the United Kingdom (Philp et al. 2017).

PHC is an important component within an integrated, holistic, person-centered care system and is needed to support healthy aging. Primary care professionals often act as the first point of contact in identifying older people's needs, including physical, psychological, and sociocultural needs, and play a role in preventing disease and managing chronic conditions. Effectively implementing PHC within care systems for older adults requires involvement from national and local governments, service providers, civil society, the private sector, organizations for older people, academia, and older people themselves as well as their families and friends (Giacomin et al. 2021).

A study conducted by HelpAge International in five Asian countries (Cambodia, India, Indonesia, Singapore, and Vietnam) finds that perceptions among older people in relation to access to PHC were predominantly negative (HelpAge International 2008). The study further identifies the following challenges:

- There were insufficient numbers of PHC centers located at reasonable distances for older people. Older people living in rural areas experienced more gaps in the availability and proximity of PHC services than older people in urban areas.

- Health care professionals did not have appropriate training in healthy aging and geriatrics.

- PHC services were largely unaffordable for older people. To alleviate this problem, the study suggests introducing or strengthening cash transfers and other social protection schemes.

International Research to Facilitate Cross-Country Learning

Evaluating country-specific care models for older adults is important for highlighting and developing quality assurance, outcomes, and oversight as well as to inform the development of culturally appropriate policies and practices. LTC policy and practice in LMICs can be informed by comparative international research, but this research is limited by an absence of consensus on how to define, measure, and analyze key concepts, as well as by the lack of comparable multicountry data (Lepore and Corazzini 2019).

Internationally comparable common data elements (CDEs), if developed, could be used to measure essential aspects of LTC in low-, middle-, and high-income countries. The Worldwide Elements to Harmonize Research in Long-Term Care Living Environments (WE-THRIVE) is an international LTC measurement framework consisting of a common set of data elements across countries. It was designed to create consensus in the definition and measurement of key LTC concepts and to strengthen the potential for cross-national research using CDEs. This effort integrates LMICs in the development of international and multicountry data (Lepore and Corazzini 2019).

As part of WE-THRIVE, Lepore and Corazzini (2019) review the literature to examine internationally prioritized LTC measurement concepts in four overarching domains—context (policies, regulations, and financing), workforce and staffing, person-centered care, and care outcomes—with the aim of advancing the identification of CDEs for international LTC research. Also as part of WE-THRIVE, Edvardsson et al. (2019) identify and recommend 12 measures of well-being, quality of life, and personhood as a basis for developing CDEs for LTC outcomes across countries (see table 6A.1 in annex 6A for details). This line of work is ongoing, and no consensus recommendations have yet been identified regarding what elements of LTC domains are relevant to measure, or how best to measure them using CDEs.

Moreover, when it comes to measuring LTC outcomes, deficit-oriented measures such as functional decline in older adults have most often been the focus. But more recently, a shift in LTC practice and research is slowly moving the focus from deficit-oriented measures toward more positive outcomes (Edvardsson et al. 2019). These positive outcomes are evaluated in health-promoting models that implement a salutogenic approach, meaning focusing more on factors that support well-being rather than those that cause disease. Identifying a core set of measures for describing salutogenic attributes of LTC has been a consistent challenge in international research (Edvardsson et al. 2019).

Discussion and Policy Considerations

In most LMICs, health care and LTC policies and service delivery systems tailored to the increasing and complex care needs of aging populations are still in the early stages of development. The review and analysis presented in this chapter highlight the importance for policy makers in these countries of better understanding the needs and unmet needs of older adult care from both the demand and supply sides, while building information, quality monitoring, and evaluation systems. This section discusses potential strategies and pitfalls for policy considerations in these areas.

Older Adult Care Needs—Strengthening Assessment and Quality Measurement

On the demand side, sound evaluation of older adult care needs and the extent of unmet needs starts with assessments to obtain reliable estimates of the number of older people with disability and functional impairments that prevent them from living independently. Numerous variants of needs assessment instruments have been identified in the research literature, most of which are based on measures of an older person's limitations or difficulties in performing ADLs or IADLs. Variations in language and wording, data-collection methods, and the specific data items used to create those measures lead to wide-ranging estimates of disability prevalence rates among older populations in LMICs. As long as such variations reflect careful adaptations that have been made to country-specific contexts, countries can continue using these ADL- and IADL-based assessment tools to gauge older adult care needs, ideally leveraging nationally representative, population-based, and longitudinal surveys of older adults.

Where the costs of frequent and large-scale data collection are a concern, as is common in LMIC settings, researchers and government agencies might consider the use of shortened yet validated instruments such as the Washington Group Short Set on Functioning (WG-SS), developed by the Washington Group on Disability Statistics (Washington Group on Disability Statistics 2020). The WG-SS is designed for use in population censuses, considering the reality that in many countries the decennial census may be the only or most reliable means of collecting population-based data. The brevity of the WG-SS—consisting of just six questions measuring difficulties in seeing, hearing, walking or climbing stairs, remembering or concentrating, self-care, and communication (expressive and receptive)—also makes it well suited for inclusion in larger surveys. Additionally, these questions are calibrated to maximize international comparability in information about difficulties a person may have in undertaking basic functioning activities (Washington Group on Disability Statistics 2020).

On the supply side, evaluation of health care and LTC quality is an important consideration. Research shows that existing quality measures focused on clinical aspects are highly developed compared with those focused on nonclinical measures. Additionally, many current quality assessment methods do not include geriatric conditions and instead focus on a specific process of care or service (for example, bone scans or cardiac stress tests) or a single health condition (for instance, cancer or stroke) (MacLeod et al. 2018). It is also important to note that transferring quality indicators between countries should be done with caution and with input from clinical experts.

The quality of LTC, in particular, is multidimensional and difficult to measure, especially for care and services provided in home- and community-based settings. Even in HICs with well-established data-gathering and quality-measurement development systems, challenges abound. For example, although the European Commission endorses the development of common LTC indicators and organizes cross-country learning activities to facilitate this goal, work is ongoing and progress is slow, hampered to a large degree by the lack of directly comparable data across the 27 European Union member states on the availability of informal and formal LTC services (European Commission 2021).

In the United States, the federal government requires all Medicare- or Medicaid-certified nursing homes (about 15,000 in total) to routinely report detailed resident demographic, health, functioning, and treatment information using the uniform MDS (which ironically contains more than 400 data items) for resident assessment, care planning, payment, and public reporting purposes. Despite the enormous costs of collecting these data as well as developing and maintaining numerous nursing-home quality measures (Mor 2011), the impact of using these data for improving quality and consumer experience is mixed (Davila et al. 2021; Konetzka et al. 2022). In health care more broadly, between 2008 and 2018, the federal government invested more than US$1.3 billion in quality measure development, with approximately 2,300 measures developed, of which 788 (34 percent) are being used in government-mandated quality, reporting, and payment programs (Wadhera et al. 2020). All these quality initiatives entail formidable costs.

In resource-strapped LMICs, policy makers must consider and weigh the costs of setting up information, quality monitoring, and evaluation systems against the intended benefits. Given resource limitations, they should plan to start with and focus on setting up information systems designed to collect a minimal set of data items that are the most essential to support evidence-based policy making (such as data on the availability and mix of LTC services, affordability, accessibility, and regional disparities) and for ensuring minimum quality assurance (such as safety and measures against neglect and abuse).

Even among HICs, there are divergent approaches to LTC quality assurance, and some countries manage to perform well without instituting extensive and expensive quality oversight systems. Sweden stands out as an example. It has a fairly minimal regulatory and quality-monitoring system yet is considered to be one of the few best-performing countries for LTC quality (Dyer et al. 2019).

LMICs can learn from countries such as Sweden that have well-developed yet cost-effective systems for quality control and quality measurement. Policy makers in LMICs can examine existing quality indicators, and then select and adapt them to fit their country-specific context and older adult care system. Doing so would require insight into what indicators are available to measure quality of care specifically for older persons, as well as the extent to which these indicators meet quality requirements.

Some LMICs could also develop their own quality indicators. To do so, it would be advisable for countries to involve a variety of relevant stakeholders. The selected quality indicators should be derived from evidence-based criteria from scientific investigations and rigorous empirical studies. The guidelines derived from empirical studies could be similar to those in HICs but will likely require modification to adapt them to resource constraints as well as the local health care and older adult care landscapes in that LMIC.

Building Information, Monitoring, and Evaluation Systems

There is no one-size-fits-all evaluation approach that is best suited for all older adult care systems in all LMICs. Different approaches have been taken to monitor LTC provision and measure outcomes, and countries vary in the progress of the development of their data and measurement infrastructure. Many countries, especially LMICs, struggle with limited health and social care data sources, poor quality monitoring, and the fragmentation of their health and LTC systems. Data generation from a broad and updated range of sources, including facility-based information systems, public health surveillance systems, and population-based surveys (considering both formal and informal care), as well as monitoring through information systems, are key elements for effectively evaluating LTC system performance (WHO 2021a).

Integrated LTC information systems, made up of both the private and public sectors, help ensure that care is delivered in a nonfragmented way. As suggested in a recent WHO framework, information, monitoring, and evaluation systems are key elements of an integrated continuum of LTC (WHO 2021a).

Below are seven key recommendations that countries should consider, to the extent feasible with available resources, for establishing LTC information, monitoring, and evaluation systems.

- Set up measures of well-being (see table 6A.1 for one list of researcher-recommended measures of well-being, quality of life, and personhood for evaluating LTC outcomes across countries) (WHO 2021a).

- Identify the number and geographic distribution of community social centers, the number of health practitioners delivering LTC services, and the number of people using these services (WHO 2021a).

- Identify the characteristics of the services provided (private vs. public, for profit vs. not for profit, geographic distribution, and quality distribution), including service mix (home care, community based, and institutional) (WHO 2021a).

- When considering a framework for analyzing the quality of LTC in LMICs, because the extent of formal service provision is often much more limited than in HICs, quality assessment should begin with a review of two major inputs: first, the provision and availability of formal LTC services relative to demand, which in turn depends on the number of people with care needs and the capacity of informal provision to meet these needs adequately; and second, the particular mix of LTC services (Lloyd-Sherlock, Penhale, and Redondo 2021).

- Generate reliable data that show utilization rates by service type, and audit the number of LTC facilities, their geographical distribution, number of beds, and number of heath care workers per bed (WHO 2021a).

- Formulate measures for quality assessment such as rates of avoidable hospital admissions, service integration, and clinical outcomes (WHO 2021a). Quality measures can be used to quantify health care processes, outcomes, and patient perceptions. They are needed to assist researchers and regulators in assessing different features of older adult care. On a broader level, quality measures can inform service development and drive the system toward evidence-based practices.

- Generate detailed data on financing, for example, out-of-pocket expenditures for LTC, coverage based on eligibility, and the proportion of care provided by informal caregivers and its costs (WHO 2021a).

Concluding Remarks

This review and analysis reveals evidence of large gaps in numerous LMICs between rising older adult care needs on the demand side, and the availability of formal LTC provision and service delivery systems on the supply side. Informal, family-based older adult care continues to be the norm in these countries, but in the face of long-term trends such as urbanization, increasing mobility, out-migration, smaller family size, and the growing participation of women in labor markets, family-based care alone may no longer be sufficient. Policy makers in LMICs face the challenge of building LTC services while strengthening their existing health care delivery systems to meet the mounting care needs of rapidly aging populations. Such needs are becoming increasingly complex and burdensome because of multimorbidities associated with noncommunicable diseases.

Although building a service infrastructure and enhancing delivery systems could well be justified as the first order of priority, policy makers in LMICs should pay attention to creating an effective information, monitoring, and evaluation system from the outset. It is an important foundational step. Evaluation, in particular, is vital for planning and developing accessible, affordable, and equitable health care and LTC services that meet older people's needs and preferences.

Annex 6A Measures for Long-Term Care Outcomes

TABLE 6A.1 Candidate Measures for Long-Term Care Outcomes of Well-Being, Quality of Life, and Personhood

Concept	Recommended measures
Well-being	ICEpop CAPability Measure for Older people (ICECAP-O): Measures the overall well-being of older people by exploring the capabilities of an individual through five questions related to five different attributes that are associated with well-being (Coast et al. 2008)
	Short Form 36 Health Survey (SF-36): A standardized, self-report survey that measures patient health-related quality of life (Rand Health Care, n.d.; Ware and Sherbourne 1992)
	Patient-Reported Outcomes Measurement Information System (PROMIS): Outcome measures that are person-centered instruments developed to measure physical, mental, and social health (Health Measures, n.d.)
Quality of life	World Health Organization Quality of Life (WHOQOL-BREF/WHOQOL-OLD): A 26-item quality of life assessment measure consisting of four domains: physical health, psychological health, social relationships, and the person's environment (WHO, n.d.)
	EuroQoL—EQ-5D (5L/3L): A standardized, non-disease-specific instrument that measures health status using a visual analog scale and health-related quality of life using a descriptive system (Carr-Hill 1992; EuroQol Research Foundation, n.d.)
	Adult Social Care Outcomes Toolkit (ASCOT): An instrument developed to measure social care-related quality of life (Personal Social Services Research Unit, n.d.)
Dementia-specific quality of life	Health-Related Quality of Life for People with Dementia (DEMQOL): An assessment tool developed to measure health-related quality of life in all stages of dementia, available both as a self-report and as a proxy-report version (Smith et al. 2007)
	Quality of Life in Dementia (QUALIDEM): A proxy-based, dementia-specific quality-of-life instrument available in two versions: a 37-item version for use with people with mild to severe dementia, and an 18-item version for use with those who have very severe dementia (Dichter et al. 2016)
	Dementia Quality of Life Instrument (DQOL): A quality-of-life assessment tool for people with dementia, consisting of 30 items, with five response levels (Brod et al. 1999)
Personhood	Thriving of Older People Assessment Scale (TOPAS): A self- and proxy-rated scale that measures resident thriving in long-term care
	Experience of Home Scale (EOH): A 25-item, self-rated scale designed to measure the strength of meaningful experiences of living in a long-term care home (Molony, McDonald, and Palmisano-Mills 2007)
	Personhood in Dementia Questionnaire (PDQ): Measures staff attitudes toward personhood (Hunter et al. 2013)

Source: Edvardsson et al. 2019.

Note

1. The material included in this section draws heavily from Glinskaya, Feng, and Suarez (2022).

References

AHRQ (Agency for Healthcare Research and Quality). n.d.-a. "About CAHPS." https://www.ahrq.gov/cahps/about-cahps/index.html.

AHRQ (Agency for Healthcare Research and Quality). n.d.-b. "AHRQ Quality Indicator Tools for Data Analytics." https://www.ahrq.gov/data/qualityindicators/index.html.

AHRQ (Agency for Healthcare Research and Quality). n.d.-c. "CAHPS® Home and Community Based Services Survey Database." https://cahpsdatabase.ahrq.gov/HCBSSurveyGuidance.aspx.

Askari, M., P. C. Wierenga, S. Eslami, S. Medlock, S. E. De Rooij, and A. Abu-Hanna. 2012. "Studies Pertaining to the ACOVE Quality Criteria: A Systematic Review." *International Journal for Quality in Health Care* 24 (1): 80–87. doi:10.1093/intqhc/mzr071.

Börsch-Supan, A. 2022. Survey of Health, Ageing and Retirement in Europe (SHARE) Wave 8. Release version: 8.0.0. SHARE-ERIC. Data set. doi:10.6103/SHARE.w8.800.

Brand, C. A., M. Martin-Khan, O. Wright, R. N. Jones, J. N. Morris, C. M. Travers, J. Tropea, and L. C. Gray. 2011. "Development of Quality Indicators for Monitoring Outcomes of Frail Elderly Hospitalised in Acute Care Health Settings: Study Protocol." *BMC Health Services Research* 11: 281. doi:10.1186/1472-6963-11-281.

Brod, M., A. L. Stewart, L. Sands, and P. Walton. 1999. "Conceptualization and Measurement of Quality of Life in Dementia: The Dementia Quality of Life Instrument (DQoL)." *Gerontologist* 39 (1): 25–35. doi:10.1093/geront/39.1.25.

Burton, J. K., A. T. Wolters, A. M. Towers, L. Jones, J. Meyer, A. L. Gordon, L. Irvine, et al. 2022. "Developing a Minimum Data Set for Older Adult Care Homes in the UK: Exploring the Concept and Defining Early Core Principles." *The Lancet Healthy Longevity* 3 (3): e186–e193. doi:10.1016/S2666-7568(22)00010-1.

Carr-Hill, R. A. 1992. "Health Related Quality of Life Measurement—Euro Style." *Health Policy* 20 (3): 321–28; discussion 329–32. doi:10.1016/0168-8510(92)90164-7.

Chauhan, S., S. Kumar, R. Bharti, and R. Patel. 2022. "Prevalence and Determinants of Activity of Daily Living and Instrumental Activity of Daily Living among Elderly in India." *BMC Geriatrics* 22 (1): 64. doi:10.1186/s12877-021-02659-z.

Coast, J., T. J. Peters, L. Natarajan, K. Sproston, and T. Flynn. 2008. "An Assessment of the Construct Validity of the Descriptive System for the ICECAP Capability Measure for Older People." *Quality of Life Research* 17 (7): 967–76. doi:10.1007/s11136-008-9372-z.

Coordinated Care of Washington. n.d. "HEDIS® 2020 Quick Reference Guide." https://www.coordinatedcarehealth.com/content/dam/centene/Coordinated%20Care/provider/PDFs/QI/508-WA-HEDIS-QuickRefGuide.pdf#:~:text=WHAT%20IS%20HEDIS%20HEDIS%20%28Healthcare%20Efectiveness%20Data%20and,measure%2C%20report%2C%20and%20compare%20quality%20across%20health%20plans.

Davila, H., T. P. Shippee, Y. S. Park, D. Brauner, R. M. Werner, and R. T. Konetzka. 2021. "Inside the Black Box of Improving on Nursing Home Quality Measures." *Medical Care Research and Review* 78 (6): 758–70. doi:10.1177/1077558720960326.

Dichter, M. N., T. P. Ettema, C. G. G. Schwab, G. Meyer, S. Bartholomeyczik, M. Halek, and R. M. Dröes. 2016. "QUALIDEM—User Guide." DZNE/VUmc, Witten, Germany.

Dominguez, J., L. Jiloca, K. C. Fowler, M. F. De Guzman, J. K. Dominguez-Awao, B. Natividad, J. Domingo, et al. 2021. "Dementia Incidence, Burden and Cost of Care: A Filipino Community-Based Study." *Frontiers in Public Health* 9: 628700. doi:10.3389/fpubh.2021.628700.

Donabedian, A. 1988. "The Quality of Care. How Can It Be Assessed?" *JAMA* 260 (12): 1743–48. doi:10.1001/jama.260.12.1743.

Donabedian, A. 2005. "Evaluating the Quality of Medical Care." *Milbank Quarterly* 83 (4): 691–729. doi:10.1111/j.1468-0009.2005.00397.x.

Dyer, S. M., M. Valeri, N. Arora, T. Ross, M. Winsall, D. Tilden, and M. Crotty. 2019. *Review of International Systems for Long-Term Care of Older People*. Adelaide, Australia: Flinders University.

Edvardsson, D., R. Baxter, L. Corneliusson, R. A. Anderson, A. Beeber, P. V. Boas, K. Corazzini, et al. 2019. "Advancing Long-Term Care Science through Using Common Data Elements: Candidate Measures for Care Outcomes of Personhood, Well-Being, and Quality of Life." *Gerontology and Geriatric Medicine* 5: 2333721419842672. doi:10.1177/2333721419842672.

European Commission. 2021. *Long-Term Care Report: Trends, Challenges and Opportunities in an Ageing Society*. Volume I. Luxembourg: Publications Office of the European Union.

EuroQol Research Foundation. n.d. "EQ-5D." https://euroqol.org/eq-5d-instruments/.

Feng, Q., Z. Zhen, D. Gu, B. Wu, P. W. Duncan, and J. L. Purser. 2013. "Trends in ADL and IADL Disability in Community-Dwelling Older Adults in Shanghai, China, 1998–2008." *Journals of Gerontology. Series B, Psychological Sciences and Social Sciences* 68 (3): 476–85. doi:10.1093/geronb/gbt012.

Feng, Z. 2017. "Filial Piety and Old-Age Support in China: Tradition, Continuity, and Change." In *Handbook on the Family and Marriage in China*, edited by X. Zang and L. X. Zhao, 266–85. Cheltenham, U.K.: Edward Elgar Publishing.

Feng, Z. 2019. "Global Convergence: Aging and Long-Term Care Policy Challenges in the Developing World." *Journal of Aging and Social Policy* 31 (4): 291–97. doi:10.1080/08959420.2019.1626205.

Ferri, C. P., and K. S. Jacob. 2017. "Dementia in Low-Income and Middle-Income Countries: Different Realities Mandate Tailored Solutions." *PLOS Medicine* 14 (3): e1002271. doi:10.1371/journal.pmed.1002271.

Giacomin, K. C., P. J. F. Villas Boas, M. A. R. da Costa Domingues, and P. A. Wachholz. 2021. "Caring throughout Life: Peculiarities of Long-Term Care for Public Policies without Ageism." *Geriatrics, Gerontology and Aging* 15: e0210009. doi:https://doi.org/10.5327/Z2447-21232021EDITESP.

Glinskaya, E., Z. Feng, and G. Suarez. 2022. "Understanding the "State of Play" of Long-Term Care Provision in Low- and Middle-Income Countries." *International Social Security Review* 75 (3–4): 71–101. doi:https://doi.org/10.1111/issr.12308.

Health Measures. n.d. "Intro to PROMIS®." http://www.healthmeasures.net/explore-measurement-systems/promis/intro-to-promis.

HelpAge International. 2008. "Primary Healthcare for Older People: A Participatory Study in 5 Asian Countries." HelpAge International, Chian Mai, Thailand.

Hirdes, J. P., G. Ljunggren, J. N. Morris, D. H. Frijters, H. Finne Soveri, L. Gray, M. Bjorkgren, and R. Gilgen. 2008. "Reliability of the interRAI Suite of Assessment Instruments: A 12-Country Study of an Integrated Health Information System." *BMC Health Services Research* 8: 277. doi:10.1186/1472-6963-8-277.

Holmes, W. 2021. "Projecting the Need for and Cost of Long-Term Care for Older Persons." Sustainable Development Working Paper 74, Asian Development Bank, Manila.

Hu, J. 2012. "Old-Age Disability in China: Implications for Long-Term Care Policies in the Coming Decades." Pardee RAND Graduate School, Santa Monica, CA.

Hunter, P. V., T. Hadjistavropoulos, W. E. Smythe, D. C. Malloy, S. Kaasalainen, and J. Williams. 2013. "The Personhood in Dementia Questionnaire (PDQ): Establishing an Association between Beliefs about Personhood and Health Providers' Approaches to Person-Centred Care." *Journal of Aging Studies* 27 (3): 276–87. doi:10.1016/j. jaging.2013.05.003.

interRAI. n.d. "About interRAI." https://interrai.org/.

Joling, K. J., L. van Eenoo, D. L. Vetrano, V. R. Smaardijk, A. Declercq, G. Onder, H. P. J. van Hout, and H. G. van der Roest. 2018. "Quality Indicators for Community Care for Older People: A Systematic Review." *PLOS ONE* 13 (1): e0190298. doi:10.1371 /journal.pone.0190298.

Kedare, J., and C. Vispute. 2016. "Research Priorities for Cognitive Decline in India." *Journal of Geriatric Mental Health* 3 (1): 80–85. doi:10.4103/2348-9995.181923.

Konetzka, R. T., H. Davila, D. J. Brauner, J. F. Cursio, H. Sharma, R. M. Werner, Y. S. Park, and T. P. Shippee. 2022. "The Quality Measures Domain in Nursing Home Compare: Is High Performance Meaningful or Misleading?" *Gerontologist* 62 (2): 293–303. doi:10.1093/geront/gnab054.

Lepore, M., and K. Corazzini. 2019. "Advancing International Research on Long-Term Care: Using Adaptive Leadership to Build Consensus on International Measurement Priorities and Common Data Elements." *Gerontology and Geriatric Medicine* 5: 2333721419864727. doi:10.1177/2333721419864727.

Lestari, S. K., N. Ng, P. Kowal, and A. Santosa. 2019. "Diversity in the Factors Associated with ADL-Related Disability among Older People in Six Middle-Income Countries: A Cross-Country Comparison." *International Journal of Environmental Research and Public Health* 16 (8): 1341. doi:10.3390/ijerph16081341.

Li, C., R. Zhou, N. Yao, T. Cornwell, and S. Wang. 2020. "Health Care Utilization and Unmet Needs in Chinese Older Adults with Multimorbidity and Functional Impairment." *Journal of the American Medical Directors Association* 21 (6): 806–10. doi:10.1016/j.jamda.2020.02.010.

Lloyd-Sherlock, P. 2014. "Beyond Neglect: Long-Term Care Research in Low and Middle Income Countries." *International Journal of Gerontology* 8 (2): 66–69.

Lloyd-Sherlock, P., B. Penhale, and N. Redondo. 2021. "Evaluating the Quality of Long-Term Care Services in the City of La Plata, Argentina." *Ageing & Society* 41 (1): 208–30.

MacLeod, S., K. Schwebke, K. Hawkins, J. Ruiz, E. Hoo, and C. S. Yeh. 2018. "Need for Comprehensive Health Care Quality Measures for Older Adults." *Population Health Management* 21 (4): 296–302. doi:10.1089/pop.2017.0109.

Matus-Lopez, M., and A. Chaverri-Carvajal. 2021. "Population with Long-Term Care Needs in Six Latin American Countries: Estimation of Older Adults Who Need Help Performing ADLs." *International Journal of Environmental Research and Public Health* 18 (15): 7935. doi:10.3390/ijerph18157935.

Molony, S. L., D. D. McDonald, and C. Palmisano-Mills. 2007. "Psychometric Testing of an Instrument to Measure the Experience of Home." *Research in Nursing and Health* 30 (5): 518–30. doi:10.1002/nur.20210.

Mor, V. 2004. "A Comprehensive Clinical Assessment Tool to Inform Policy and Practice: Applications of the Minimum Data Set." *Medical Care* 42 (4 Suppl): III50–9.

Mor, V. 2011. "Cost of Nursing Home Regulation: Building a Research Agenda." *Medical Care* 49 (6): 535–37. doi:10.1097/MLR.0b013e31821f7f56.

Namburi, N., and L. S. Lee. 2022. "National Quality Forum." StatPearls Publishing, Treasure Island, FL.

NCQA (National Committee for Quality Assurance). n.d. "HEDIS and Performance Measurement." https://www.ncqa.org/hedis/.

Personal Social Services Research Unit. n.d. "Adult Social Care Outcomes Toolkit." https://www.pssru.ac.uk/ascot/.

Philp, I., K. Tugay, Z. Hildon, S. Aw, Y.-H. Jeon, M. Naegle, J.-P. Michel, A. Namara, N. Wang, and M. Hardman. 2017. "Person-Centred Assessment to Integrate Care for

Older People." In *Global Consultation on Integrated Care for Older People (ICOPE)— The Path to Universal Health Coverage*. Geneva: World Health Organization.

RAND Corporation. n.d. "Quality Indicators—ACOVE 3." https://www.rand.org /health-care/projects/acove/acove3.html.

Rand Health Care. n.d. "36-Item Short Form Survey (SF-36)." https://www.rand.org /health-care/surveys_tools/mos/36-item-short-form.html.

Scheil-Adlung, Xenia. 2015. "Long-Term Care Protection for Older Persons: A Review of Coverage Deficits in 46 Countries." Working Paper 50, International Labour Office, Geneva.

Siop, S., L. M. Verbrugge, and T. A. Hamid. 2008. "Disability and Quality of Life among Older Malaysians." Presentation at Population Association of America 2008 Annual Meeting, New Orleans, LA, April 17–19, 2008.

Smith, S. C., D. L. Lamping, S. Banerjee, R. H. Harwood, B. Foley, P. Smith, J. C. Cook, et al. 2007. "Development of a New Measure of Health-Related Quality of Life for People with Dementia: DEMQOL." *Psychological Medicine* 37 (5): 737–46. doi:10.1017/S0033291706009469.

Thakur, R., A. Banerjee, and V. Nikumb. 2013. "Health Problems among the Elderly: A Cross-Sectional Study." *Annals of Medical and Health Science Research* 3 (1): 19–25. doi:10.4103/2141-9248.109466.

Wadhera, R. K., J. F. Figueroa, K. E. Joynt Maddox, L. S. Rosenbaum, D. S. Kazi, and R. W. Yeh. 2020. "Quality Measure Development and Associated Spending by the Centers for Medicare & Medicaid Services." *JAMA* 323 (16): 1614–16. doi:10.1001 /jama.2020.1816.

Wang, L. 2013. "A Study on the Demand, Supply and Utilization of Home-Based Care Services for the Elderly Based on the Theory of 'Services Chain.'" *Population Journal* 35: 49–59.

Ware, J. E., Jr., and C. D. Sherbourne. 1992. "The MOS 36-Item Short-Form Health Survey (SF-36). I. Conceptual Framework and Item Selection." *Medical Care* 30 (6): 473–83.

Washington Group on Disability Statistics. 2020. "The Washington Group Short Set on Functioning (WG-SS)." Washington Group on Disability Statistics, Hyattsville, MD.

Wijesiri, H. S., S. K. Maliga, S. Wasalathanthri, S. H. De Silva Weliange, and C. N. Wijeyaratne. 2021. "The Prevalence and Correlates of Activity Limitations among the Elderly in Informal Caregiving Settings in Colombo District, Sri Lanka: A Community Based Cross-Sectional Study." *International Journal of Caring Sciences* 13 (3): 1568–77.

Wilberforce, M., D. Challis, L. Davies, M. P. Kelly, C. Roberts, and N. Loynes. 2016. "Person-Centredness in the Care of Older Adults: A Systematic Review of Questionnaire-Based Scales and Their Measurement Properties." *BMC Geriatrics* 16: 63. doi:10.1186/s12877-016-0229-y.

WHO (World Health Organization). 2021a. *Framework for Countries to Achieve an Integrated Continuum of Long-Term Care*. Geneva: WHO.

WHO (World Health Organization). 2021b. *Global Status Report on the Public Health Response to Dementia*. Geneva: WHO.

WHO (World Health Organization). n.d. "WHO Quality of Life-BREF (WHOQOL-BREF)." WHO, Geneva. https://www.who.int/substance_abuse/research_tools /whoqolbref/en/.

WHO (World Health Organization) and World Bank. 2021. *Tracking Universal Health Coverage 2021 Global Monitoring Report: Conference Edition*. Geneva: WHO.

World Bank. 2021. "Technical Report with an Assessment of Demand for and Supply of Elderly Care in Greece Part I: Overview of Demand for and Supply of Home-Based

Care in Greece: An Empirical Investigation Based on Survey of Health, Ageing and Retirement in Europe (SHARE)." Unpublished, World Bank, Washington, DC.

Yang, Y., H. Li, L. D. Xiao, W. Zhang, M. Xia, and H. Feng. 2019. "Resident and Staff Perspectives of Person-Centered Climate in Nursing Homes: A Cross-Sectional Study." *BMC Geriatrics* 19 (1): 292. doi:10.1186/s12877-019-1313-x.

Zhu, H. 2015. "Unmet Needs in Long-Term Care and Their Associated Factors among the Oldest Old in China." *BMC Geriatrics* 15: 46. doi:10.1186/s12877-015-0045-9.

CHAPTER 7

Community-Based Integrated Care in Japan

Japan International Cooperation Agency (JICA),
summarized by Risa Nakayama and Xiaohui Hou

Key Messages

- Japan's Community-Based Integrated Care System (CICS) aims to provide integrated care in the community to maintain the dignity of older people and support their independence. The roots of the CICS reach back several decades in Japan, and it has been progressively integrated into national legislation, insurance, and care delivery.

- CICS core principles include (1) collaborating to optimize regional resources, (2) enhancing self-support and mutual support among older adults and across the community, (3) enabling dignified lives, and (4) adapting to local contexts.

- Three detailed local examples showcase important operational features of the CICS, including integrated medical care, long-term care, and comprehensive living-support services.

- The CICS experience may hold lessons for developing countries. Key among them is the importance of designing comprehensive older adult care policies and programs from a long-term perspective that is not restricted to medical care.

- Fostering communities where older adults can live with dignity means moving toward a social model. Some developing countries have distinctive strengths for this approach, including traditions of community solidarity and mutual support.

Historical and Institutional Background of Japan's Community-Based Integrated Care System

As the population of Japan rapidly ages, improving the legal system to better support the health and welfare of older people has become more important. Various measures have been developed to address this challenge. Figure 7.1 shows the population composition and transition of the aging rate—the proportion of the population that is made up of people age 65 and older—from 1950 to 2019.

In 1961, Japan's social health insurance and pension insurance programs attained universal coverage. Until then, social health insurance and pension programs had mainly been for employees and civil servants. Even as late as the mid-1950s, about one-third of Japanese citizens were not covered by health insurance programs. Those not covered were primarily the self-employed; microenterprise employees; agriculture, forestry, and fisheries workers; and their families. Informal sector workers and nonworkers also had no pension program. In response to the need to enhance social security, health insurance, and pension insurance, coverage was extended to every citizen at a relatively early stage in Japan's economic development.[1]

Until the early 1960s, welfare policies for older people had mainly targeted those in financial distress as part of an effort to alleviate poverty. But as the population composition, socioeconomic environment, and family structures changed, it became necessary to implement measures that would respond to the mental and physical difficulties commonly encountered by older adults. The Welfare Act for the Elderly was enacted in 1963 to address the welfare

FIGURE 7.1 Trends in Population Composition and Aging Rate, Japan, 1950–2019

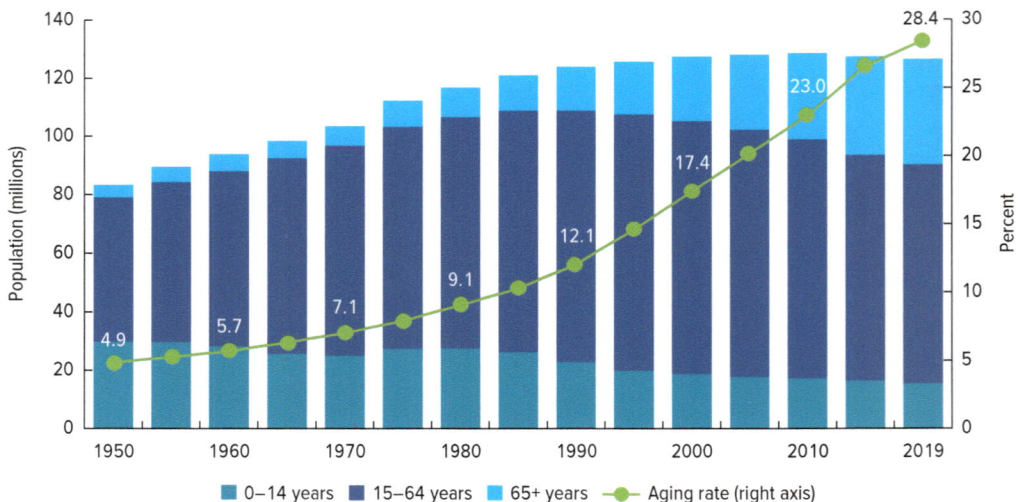

Source: Based on Ministry of Health, Labour and Welfare 2020.

of older adults in a widespread and comprehensive way. Specific measures of the act included creating special nursing homes, giving the visiting caregiver program legal standing, and conducting health checkup services.

Although universal health coverage was achieved, there was an institutional disparity in the differing copayment rates depending on the program in which one was enrolled. Because older people often have multiple illnesses, medical expenses were an economic burden for them, especially because many did not have high incomes. In response, with Japan attaining an aging rate of 7.1 in 1970, the Welfare Act for the Elderly was revised in 1973, implementing free medical care for older persons. By World Health Organization criteria, an "aging society" is any society with an aging rate exceeding 7 percent. Under the revised act, persons age 70 or older had their out-of-pocket medical expenses paid by public funds from the national and local governments. The result was that older people's visits to doctors were no longer suppressed for financial reasons, improving their access to medical services.

With respect to income security for older people, the legal bases for the Employee's Pension Insurance and National Pension Insurance programs were both revised in 1973. To maintain real benefits against inflation, an index was introduced to revise benefit amounts if inflation rose to more than 5 percent. In addition, a reevaluation of the standard remuneration that forms the basis for the calculation of an employee's health insurance benefits ensured that benefits reflected increases in wage levels associated with economic growth. National Pension benefits were also raised significantly.

After the introduction of free medical services for older people, hospitalization and consultation rates increased significantly (figures 7.2 and 7.3). In addition to the treatment of illnesses, prevention and early-detection services became more important. These uses, however, put new pressure on the

FIGURE 7.2 Trends in Hospitalization Rates, by Age Group, Japan, 1965–2020

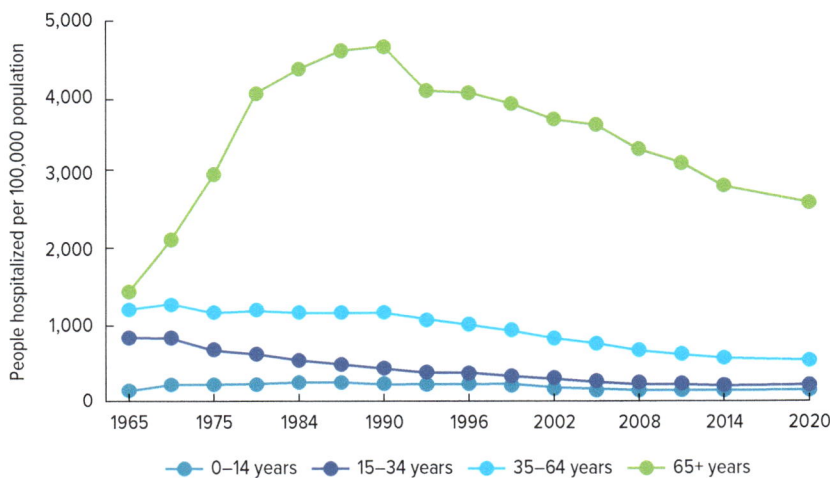

Source: JICA 2022, based on Ministry of Health, Labour and Welfare Patient Survey.

FIGURE 7.3 Trends in Outpatient Consultation Rates, by Age Group, Japan, 1965–2020

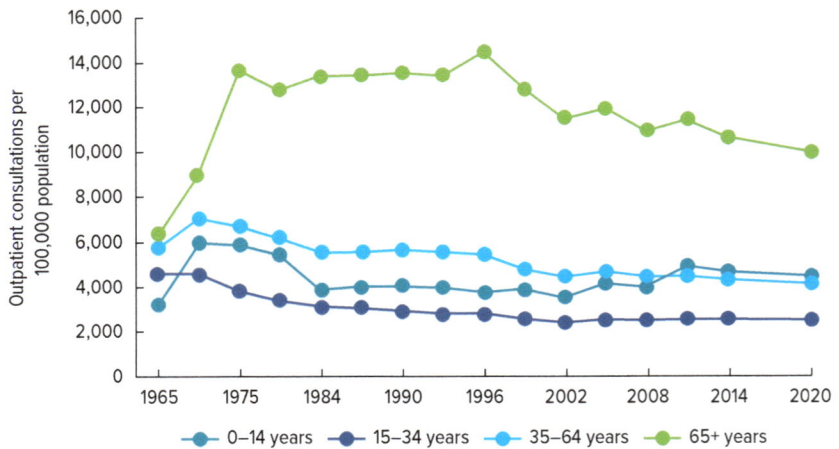

Source: JICA 2022, based on Ministry of Health, Labour and Welfare Patient Survey.

finances of the National Health Insurance Program, which had a particularly significant share of older people in the covered population.

The Health and Medical Services Act for the Elderly, enacted in 1982, abolished the free medical care program for older persons and reinstated copayments for patients age 70 and over, encouraging self-care and proper consultations for staying healthy.

In 1986, the Health and Medical Services Act for the Elderly was revised, and Health Service Facilities for the Aged were established as intermediate facilities between hospitals and home. Health Service Facilities for the Aged provided nursing care, long-term care, and functional training for older people whose medical conditions were relatively stable.

In the 1980s, measures for home medicine and home care began to be implemented, and the Ten-Year Strategy to Promote Health Care and Welfare for the Elderly (the Gold Plan) was formulated in 1989. The Gold Plan established goals for the decade starting in 1990 for home-, community-, and institution-based services, with particular attention to the promotion of home- and community-based services.

In addition, the Welfare Act for the Elderly was revised in 1990, establishing a system in which the responsibility for implementing welfare services for older adults was unified with municipalities. Municipalities and prefectures were mandated to create older people's health and welfare plans. This reform required municipalities, which are the closest to residents, to provide home- and community-based and institution-based welfare services in a unified and planned manner.

Five years after the formulation of the Gold Plan, in 1994, when Japan reached an ageing rate of 14.1 percent—formally becoming an "aged society"—a new Ten-Year Strategy to Promote Health Care and Welfare for the Elderly (the New Gold Plan) was formulated. The New Gold Plan revised the second five years of the original plan and addressed care for the subsequent five years. It was aimed at the further enhancement of the long-term care infrastructure ahead of the enactment of the forthcoming Long-Term Care Insurance Act.

In 1997, the Long-Term Care Insurance Act was enacted, and the associated long-term care insurance program came into effect in April 2000. It provided a mechanism for all citizens to support the long-term care of older people, considering older adults to be equally entitled, bona fide members of society.

To enforce long-term care insurance, the Direction of Health and Welfare Policies for the Elderly over the Next Five Years (Gold Plan 21) was formulated as a continuation of the New Gold Plan. In addition to development of the care service infrastructure, the aim was to create a participatory society in which older adults stayed healthy and had a sense of purpose, ensuring their dignity and supporting their independence by promoting frailty prevention and providing everyday living support and other services.

In 2003, a report developed by the Elderly Long-Term Care Study Group,[2] *Toward the Establishment of Elderly Long-Term Care and Care to Support the Dignity of the Elderly in 2015* (Ministry of Health, Labour and Welfare 2003), became the first government document to articulate the idea of a "community-based integrated care system." The report found that many older people faced real challenges in continuing to live at home, and presented the idea of a CICS.

Following the report, this new system was clearly positioned under the Long-Term Care Insurance Act and related laws. Also, for health service provision, there was a transition from the hospital-centered model, which aimed at complete recovery from illnesses followed by discharge, to a community-based model that maintains and supports life in the community while people sometimes coexist with illness. That prompted the development of a medical care provision in the CICS (see figure 7.4).

The Philosophy of Long-Term Care

Long-term care for older adults is now a universal need in Japan, and a mechanism to provide it required the support of society as a whole. See table 7.1 and figure 7.5 for the broad outlines and operations of Japan's system.

The Long-Term Care Insurance Act specifies that the purpose of this system is to "provide necessary health care services and welfare service benefits" for people in need of long-term nursing care so as to "maintain dignity and independence according to their abilities in their daily lives."

However, following the introduction of long-term care insurance, further challenges related to the health and welfare of older adults emerged and needed to be addressed. Because many older people wanted to continue living in their own familiar community, each individual's challenges became a focus—from living with dementia, to living alone, to long-term care needs, and so on. It became difficult to meet every need of every older person under long-term care insurance alone, including maintaining and, going beyond that, improving their physical and mental health.

FIGURE 7.4 Timeline of Health Care Development in Japan, 1961–2017

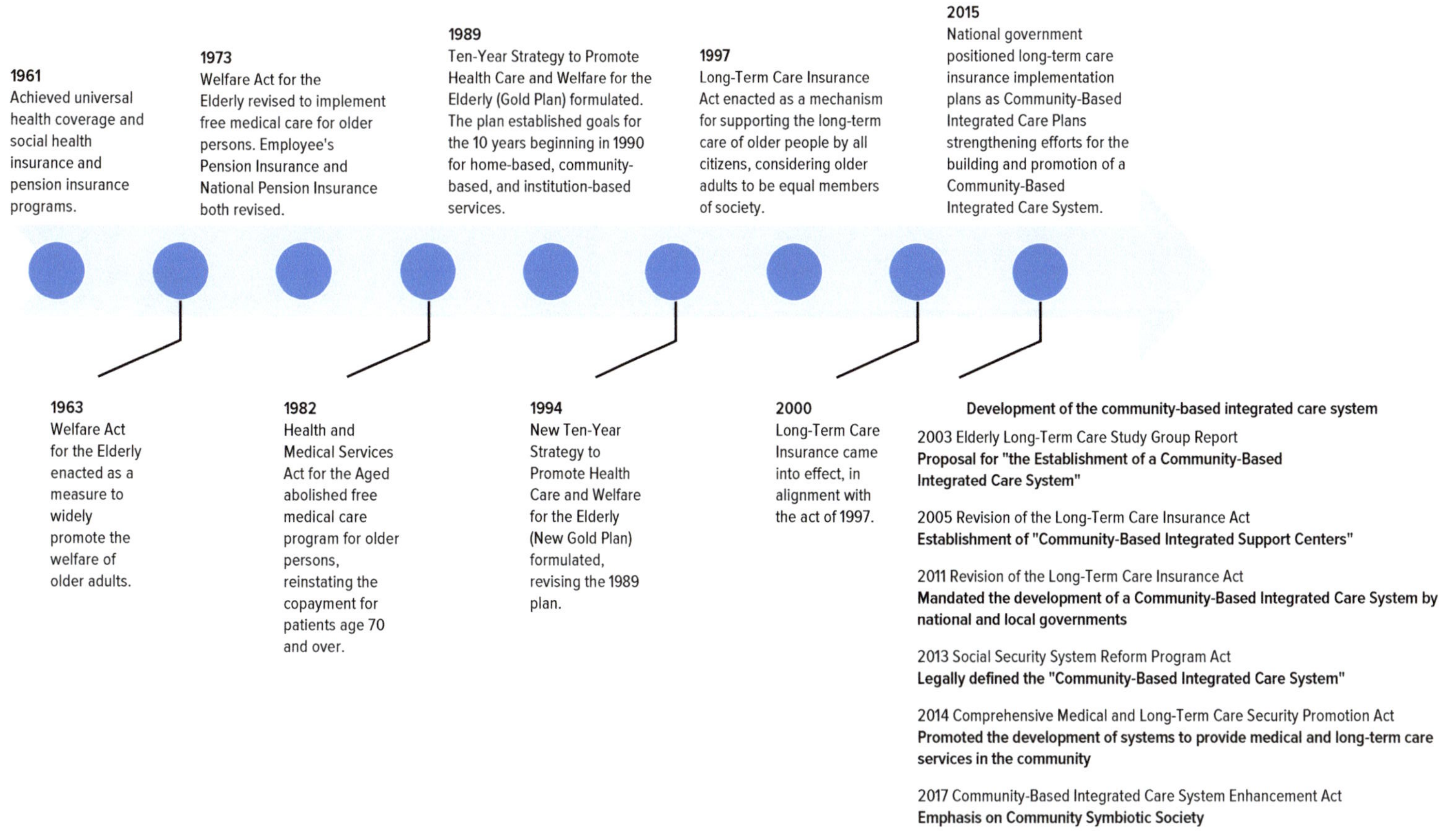

1961
Achieved universal health coverage and social health insurance and pension insurance programs.

1963
Welfare Act for the Elderly enacted as a measure to widely promote the welfare of older adults.

1973
Welfare Act for the Elderly revised to implement free medical care for older persons. Employee's Pension Insurance and National Pension Insurance both revised.

1982
Health and Medical Services Act for the Aged abolished free medical care program for older persons, reinstating the copayment for patients age 70 and over.

1989
Ten-Year Strategy to Promote Health Care and Welfare for the Elderly (Gold Plan) formulated. The plan established goals for the 10 years beginning in 1990 for home-based, community-based, and institution-based services.

1994
New Ten-Year Strategy to Promote Health Care and Welfare for the Elderly (New Gold Plan) formulated, revising the 1989 plan.

1997
Long-Term Care Insurance Act enacted as a mechanism for supporting the long-term care of older people by all citizens, considering older adults to be equal members of society.

2000
Long-Term Care Insurance came into effect, in alignment with the act of 1997.

2015
National government positioned long-term care insurance implementation plans as Community-Based Integrated Care Plans strengthening efforts for the building and promotion of a Community-Based Integrated Care System.

Development of the community-based integrated care system

2003 Elderly Long-Term Care Study Group Report **Proposal for "the Establishment of a Community-Based Integrated Care System"**

2005 Revision of the Long-Term Care Insurance Act **Establishment of "Community-Based Integrated Support Centers"**

2011 Revision of the Long-Term Care Insurance Act **Mandated the development of a Community-Based Integrated Care System by national and local governments**

2013 Social Security System Reform Program Act **Legally defined the "Community-Based Integrated Care System"**

2014 Comprehensive Medical and Long-Term Care Security Promotion Act **Promoted the development of systems to provide medical and long-term care services in the community**

2017 Community-Based Integrated Care System Enhancement Act **Emphasis on Community Symbiotic Society**

Source: JICA 2022.

TABLE 7.1 Outline of Long-Term Care Insurance in Japan

Financial resources	Premiums (50%), tax (50%)	
Insurers	Municipalities, special wards (Tokyo—23 wards)	
Insured	Primary insured	Secondary insured
Eligible persons	Persons age 65 or older	Health insurance subscribers between 40 and 64 years old
Eligibility for benefits	People requiring long-term care (bedridden, in a condition requiring long-term care due to dementia, and so forth) People requiring support as needed for daily life	Persons requiring support or long-term care because of specific disease caused by aging
Collection of premiums	Collection by municipalities (persons with a certain pension amount have pension deductions)	Collection by health insurers with health insurance premiums
Benefits	Long-term care benefits and prevention benefits (benefit in kind: reimbursements are sent to service providers for users)	
User copay	10–30% copay, depending on income	

Source: Based on Ministry of Health, Labour, and Welfare materials.

FIGURE 7.5 Long-Term Care Insurance Operating Mechanism in Japan

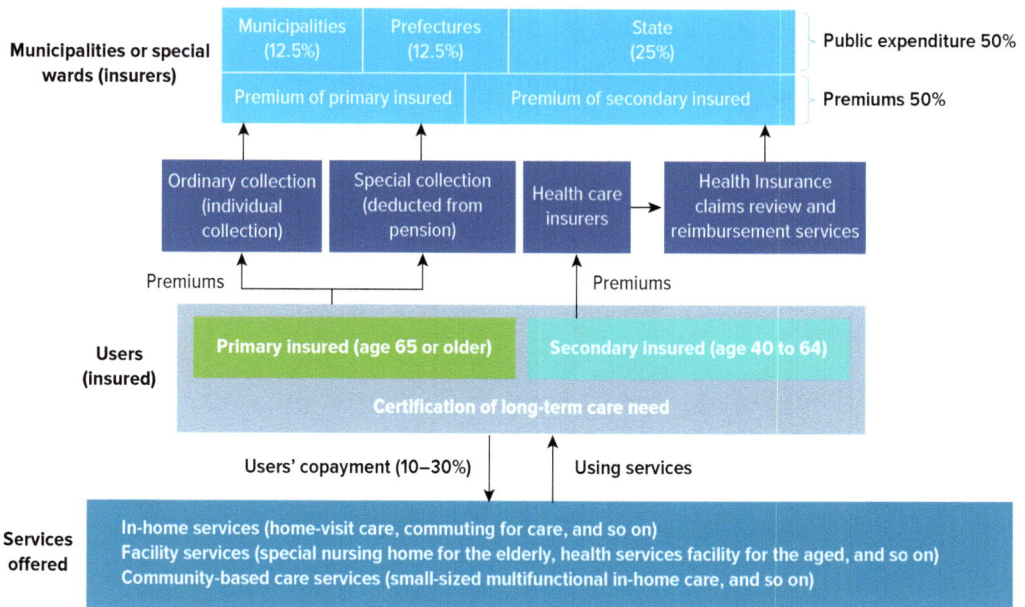

Source: Based on Ministry of Health, Labour, and Welfare materials.

And in a broader context, with the aging of the nation's population, chronic illnesses and degenerative diseases such as cancer, heart disease, and dementia increased, as did the number of older persons living alone, introducing new challenges not only in concrete care issues but also in medical thinking, health values, and the values of patients. These challenges concerned not only curing illnesses but securing and improving the quality of people's lives while they lived with illness. In this context, the aim now was to realize a community-based model of providing medical care that took characteristics of hospitals and clinics and shaped them to support the lives of patients in the community and to guarantee needed medical care in cooperation with the entire community (National Commission on Social Security).

The Ministry of Health, Labour, and Welfare defines the CICS as "a system providing integrated support and services in the community to maintain the dignity of elderly people and support their independence, so that they can continue to live, to the extent possible, in their own way in the communities to which they are accustomed to the end of their lives."

Creating and maintaining such a system requires the following actions.

Coordinate All Community Resources

Older people have a diverse range of living needs associated with specific illnesses, their level of physical independence, family structure and level of support, and particular ways of life. Communities have many resources and actors that support older people's daily living, including governments and medical institutions, long-term care service providers, nongovernmental organizations, families, volunteers, and others. However, there was no coordination mechanism for such resources, and as a result they were fragmented. For services ranging from medical and long-term care to everyday living support to be provided in a continuous and integrated way, it was necessary to coordinate and encourage the cooperation of all community resources, and this needed to be done from the perspective of the older people themselves.

Enhance Self-Support and Mutual Support

Although the preventive benefits of long-term care insurance were aimed at reducing care dependence through the use of preventive services, this aim was not completely fulfilled, and the numbers of older adults who needed mild support in long-term care were increasing. It was important for older people themselves to work toward promoting health and preventing frailty, and to decrease as much as possible the period for which they would require long-term care. In addition, as the number of healthy older people in a community rises, they themselves often build a support system in which they become active participants. Enhancing self-support and mutual support, alongside institutionalized mutual assistance services such as long-term care insurance, medical insurance, and so on, can mutually enhance the effectiveness of both.

Maintain the Dignity of Life

As specified in the Long-Term Care Insurance Act, the basic philosophy behind long-term care is to maintain the dignity of older persons. Even when older persons require long-term care, it is vital that they are still able to continue to live life in their own way and to make their own decisions. In supporting older people, it is important that experts and nonexperts such as local volunteers support the decision-making of the older person and that they serve and respect their decisions, making it possible for older people to live with dignity.

Respond to the Increasing Diversity of Local Contexts

The aging of communities differs between urban and rural areas, and even among rural areas, and these differences are expected to grow. In addition, the generation that is about to become the older population is expected to have even more diverse needs than the current one, having experienced the period of high economic growth and having diverse values. As the characteristics of various communities and the images of older persons diversify, measures that are suited to those communities and to the individuality of their residents need to be developed.

Practicing Community-Based Integrated Care in Japan: Three Cases[3]

This section discusses three case examples covering (1) integrated medical care, (2) long-term care, and (3) comprehensive living-support services under the CICS developed in Japan. These cases, which may have useful implications for developing countries, are the following:

- Komagane, Nagano: Self-management support for stroke patients
- Fujisawa, Kanagawa: Example of an urban area
- Higashiomi, Shiga: Example of a rural area

Komagane

Basic Information

The city of Komagane belongs to the Kamiina District secondary medical area (map 7.1). Showa Inan General Hospital, the main hospital in this area, provides emergency and other acute care. Ina Central Hospital is responsible for tertiary emergency care. Komagane is divided into three residential areas, each with a municipal community-based integrated care center.

- Area: 165.86 square kilometers
- Total population (2015): 32,759
- Proportion of the population age 65 and over (2015): 29.2 percent
- Proportion of those age 65 and over who need long-term care or support (2020): 14.1 percent

MAP 7.1 Secondary Medical Area (Kamiina District), Japan

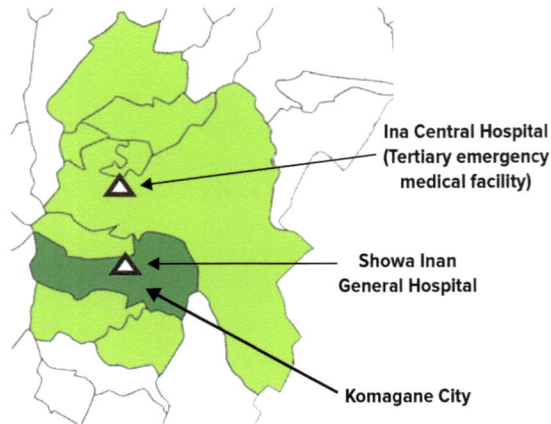

Source: Based on Nagano Community Medical Care Concept, Kamiina Secondary Medical Area, and core hospitals.

Background

In Komagane, stroke is the second most common causative disease among those requiring long-term care, after dementia. The mortality rate due to stroke is 15 times higher than the national average, and the municipality recognized this problem. In response, Showa Inan General Hospital, which is responsible for emergency medical care, conducted a survey of cases at the hospital. The result showed that about 20 percent of hospital admissions for stroke were recurrent, and there were many cases of recurrence within a year after discharge.

Activities

To prevent the recurrence of stroke, the municipality and Showa Inan General Hospital cooperated to establish a system to support the self-management of patients from admission to discharge and during their lives at home. Follow-up consultations are held on a regular basis to help patients better understand the risk of recurrence and self-management.

Increasing understanding of recurrence risk and self-management. On admission, the hospital advises patients about the risk of recurrence and the importance of self-management. Throughout a patient's hospital stay, the nurses in charge of the ward provide preventive education to the patients to increase their understanding of the high risk of recurrent stroke and the importance of self-management.

Developing a self-management plan. During the hospital stay, accompanying persons (a community-based integrated care center staff member and an in-home care manager) develop a self-management plan based on the patient's preferences and information from the hospital.

Providing hospital discharge support. At discharge, the accompanying persons develop a final self-management plan based on the patient's preferences and information from the hospital.

Creating accompanying support for self-management. After discharge, the accompanying persons visit the patient and the family on a quarterly basis to follow up on implementation of the self-management plan. The accompanying persons, hospital staff, and municipal staff hold monthly case conferences. Based on the progress of the patient's self-management, they discuss how to support the patient.

Results

Impact on health care. A support system has been established among hospital professionals, the local government, and the community-based integrated care center. The rates of recurrence and readmission among stroke patients have declined.

Impact on patients. Integrated medical care and long-term care services are now available. Maintaining good health and being able to continue living at home have been proven to be realistic and achievable outcomes.

Future Direction

Self-management support for other diseases will be developed. Consultation services for health promotion and prevention of long-term care by the municipality will be established in private fitness clubs to improve the health of citizens.

Fujisawa

Basic Information

The city of Fujisawa is divided into 13 districts (map 7.2). One or two community-based integrated care centers (*iki* support centers) are located in each district, with a total of 19 in the city.

- Area: 69.57 square kilometers
- Total population (2015): 423,894
- Proportion of the population age 65 and over (2015): 23.4 percent
- Proportion of those age 65 and over who need long-term care or support (2020): 18.4 percent

Background

Because of urbanization and an increase in small nuclear families rather than large extended families, more and more people lack relationships with their local communities, making it increasingly difficult for those in need of long-term care to continue living in the community. In addition, issues such as poverty, child care, and long-term care are becoming more diverse and complex in nature.

MAP 7.2 Fujisawa City's 13 Districts (Areas), Japan

Source: JICA 2022.

For older adults requiring long-term care, the services are becoming a more central part of their lives, further dividing them from their communities. In addition, older adults are likely to be viewed negatively as people in need of being looked after, and thus support for them to live with dignity and autonomy is limited.

Activities

Municipality Promotes Fujisawa-style CICS for all Generations
Promoting measures to realize an "inclusive society" based on the community for mutual support. In each of the 13 districts community social workers are assigned to provide consultation support and community development based on the needs of each area.

Engawa project. This project provides a place for multigenerational interaction open to all, including older adults, persons with disabilities, and children.

Community-Based Integrated Care Center: Aoi Care

At Aoi Care, older people are encouraged to play active roles and take initiative by identifying their strengths and special skills from their life experiences. Aoi Care provides an environment where they can put these skills into practice. Instead of being a "special place to receive care," the Aoi Care facility is designed to be more like an ordinary place within the community, a comfortable environment where everyone gathers.

Community-Based Integrated Care Center: Grundtvig

Based on the principle of "making the community one big family," the Grundtvig example highlights the use of a vacant housing complex to be tailored to multigenerational needs. It not only includes a home-visit nursing station for older adults, but also offers space for a diverse range of generations to gather and interact. Acting as an intergenerational hub designed to revitalize the local community, Grundtvig takes a person-centered, holistic approach to physical, mental, social, and cultural strengths so that people can recover their physical and mental functions in the community.

Results

Impact on the community. The philosophy and concept of community-based integrated care has, over time, become more common. Shifting to person-centered care for older adults, relationships are formed among people who provide informal support.

Impact on older people. Older people are able to live their lives with greater dignity and autonomy, with a more active role in the community and stronger relationships with the community.

Future Direction

As Japan moves toward an even more aged society by 2040, efforts will be made to further promote community-based integrated care. A multigenerational apartment building will be operated where young people and older adults live together, supporting each other. The community of mutual support will be expanded into neighboring areas beyond the residential complexes.

Higashiomi

Basic Information

- The rural city of Higashiomi belongs to the Higashiomi secondary medical area (map 7.3). The city is divided into 13 districts, with Eigenji district located in the most eastern part of Higashiomi.
- Area: 388.37 square kilometers
- Total population (2015): 114,180
- Proportion of the population age 65 and over (2015): 24.6 percent
- Proportion of those age 65 and over who need long-term care or support (2020): 15.7 percent

Background

Hospitals and related organizations in the communities had no structure for cooperation when patients were transferred from in-hospital care to home-based care, and the modest cooperation that did exist was complicated. There was not a good level of collaboration between hospitals and the relevant organizations that were involved in home care, which made it difficult to follow up

MAP 7.3 Higashiomi City and Eigenji District, Japan

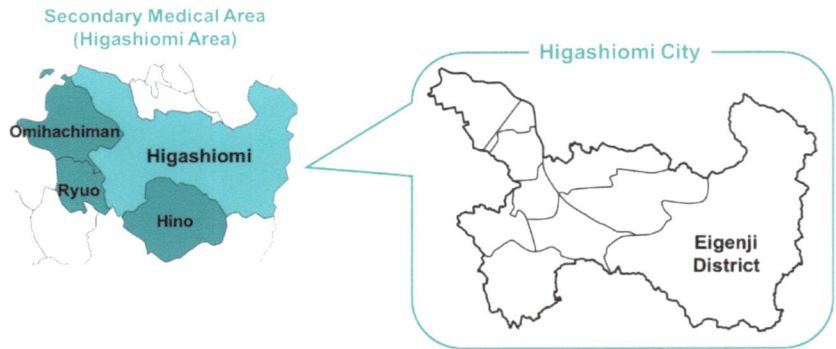

Source: JICA 2022, based on Shiga Prefecture Health and Medical Care Plan, Higashiomi City Elderly Health and Welfare Plan, and Long-Term Care Insurance Plan.

on the patient's condition after discharge. It was difficult to support patients' lives at home, which often relied on informal services after formal medical intervention.

Activities

The Higashiomi Community Medical Collaboration Network Study Group (or the Good for Everyone Study Group) was launched in the Higashiomi Secondary Medical Area to build a medical collaboration system that would cover patients from inpatient medical care to home medical care. With stroke as a model case, a critical pathway for regional cooperation was developed, and since then monthly study meetings have been held among members concerned with medical and long-term care. Team Eigenji, which is active in the Eigenji District of Higashiomi, initially held case meetings at the Eigenji Clinic, but as an outgrowth of this is now positioned as a Community-Level Good for Everyone Study Group. Various people involved in the local community meet regularly as members of Team Eigenji to address issues in the community and discuss what each person can do to resolve them.

Good for Everyone Study Groups

Development of a community collaborative critical pathway for stroke. Using a stroke case, the actual pattern of a series of services from hospital admission to home care was identified, clarifying the functions of each hospital (acute, recovery, and maintaining), allocating them roles, and creating a system of cooperation.

Sharing patients' information in a Good for Everyone Handbook. The hand-book is purchased and owned by the patients who use the critical pathway. Hospitals and long-term care service providers also enter information into the handbook about treatment, rehabilitation, drugs, other diseases managed, and so on, in order to share this information.

Building face-to-face relationships. Once a month, a study group is held with the participation of many professionals involved in medical and long-term care. Learning sessions and case studies are held on a variety of themes. To build face-to-face relationships, the meetings use a variety of features, such as self-introductions, sitting in a circle, active listening, maintaining punctuality out of respect for one another's time, and rotating the venue.

Team Eigenji

Regular study sessions are held with a variety of local stakeholders, primarily medical and long-term care professionals and nonprofessionals. Originally, only the medical profession held case meetings about patients, but this has evolved into multidisciplinary study sessions that connect people involved in mutual support with medical professionals in the form of social solidarity support, based on the realization that medical treatment alone is not sufficient to support patients' lives.

Results

Changes in formal services and the community. The average length of stay shortened in both acute and rehabilitation hospitals. Emergency patient transfer rates improved, and the number of patients receiving end-of-life care at home increased.

Impact on local people. Patients became able to move into rehabilitation at an earlier stage, live at home, and therefore continue living in environments more familiar to them.

Future Direction

The number of participants in the network will be increased. Good practices in each community will be disseminated to other communities through the Sanpo Yoshi Study Group, and they are expected to spread throughout the city of Higashiomi and Shiga Prefecture.

Key Lessons from the Three Cases

Life Values Realized through the CICS

Continuing to live in the community to which people are accustomed (aging-in-place). As the aging of Japanese society progresses, it will be a challenge for older people to continue to live in the communities to which they are accustomed—particularly those people who need long-term care, have dementia, or live alone. The creation of an integrated system that aims for such a society is under way in many communities in Japan. Such a system would provide comprehensive care, including medical and long-term care, as well as prevention and daily living support, in a form that is firmly rooted in the community.

- *Komagane.* Self-management support is helping people maintain their health and improve their motivation for life, reducing stroke recurrence and rehospitalization.

- *Fujisawa.* The creation of mutually supportive relationships is promoting the social participation of older adults and enabling them to continue living in the community with informal support.

- *Higashiomi.* Through the development of a community collaborative pathway, the provision of care with a view to living at home is being realized. Professionals and nonprofessionals are working together on community development, and relationships of mutual support are being created.

Preserving dignity and autonomy. The vision of the CICS is that, in everyday living in familiar communities, the dignity and autonomy of each older adult is valued. Autonomy means "determining for yourself what kind of life you want to live." As people age, even if their physical and cognitive functions decline, they can still maintain their dignity and live their own lives, making everyday decisions for themselves and having a role in society by interacting with people in the community.

Each of the three communities studied, through their activities, exemplifies this level of care and approach:

- *Komagane.* Older adults who are involved in their own medical management can take ownership of their own lives and lifestyles.

- *Fujisawa.* Support is provided so that each individual can act autonomously, focusing on what they like and what they are good at.

- *Higashiomi.* Emphasis is placed on dialogue with the person concerned, and care is provided to realize his or her preferences and goals.

System Values Realized through Integrating Community Characteristics

The environments surrounding older people, the challenges they face, and the resources available to them differ from community to community. The understanding of what self-support and mutual support mean, and the associated values each community brings, may also differ from community to community. Therefore, for older people to be able to continue to live at home, it is important to provide care in an integrated manner, including housing, medical care, long-term care, preventive care, and daily living support, but the methods by which this care is provided, and the local capacity for providing such care, will differ from community to community. In all three cases, rather than seeking first to have a top-down model of care provided to the community, and then making up for what is lacking, the communities themselves held—and continue to hold—ongoing discussions with relevant parties and community stakeholders. In short, they have developed their plans collaboratively and organically. With this process, it is possible to make use of the diverse resources, people, and strengths within each particular community and build a care system that suits that community, because one size does not fit all.

Figure 7.6 shows a community that has realized its enhanced functions as a result of establishing a CICS.

Rather than offering fragmented, discontinuous medical and long-term care, a CICS is "focused on the individual," "enhancing self-support and mutual

FIGURE 7.6 Community Targets in Community-Based Integrated Care

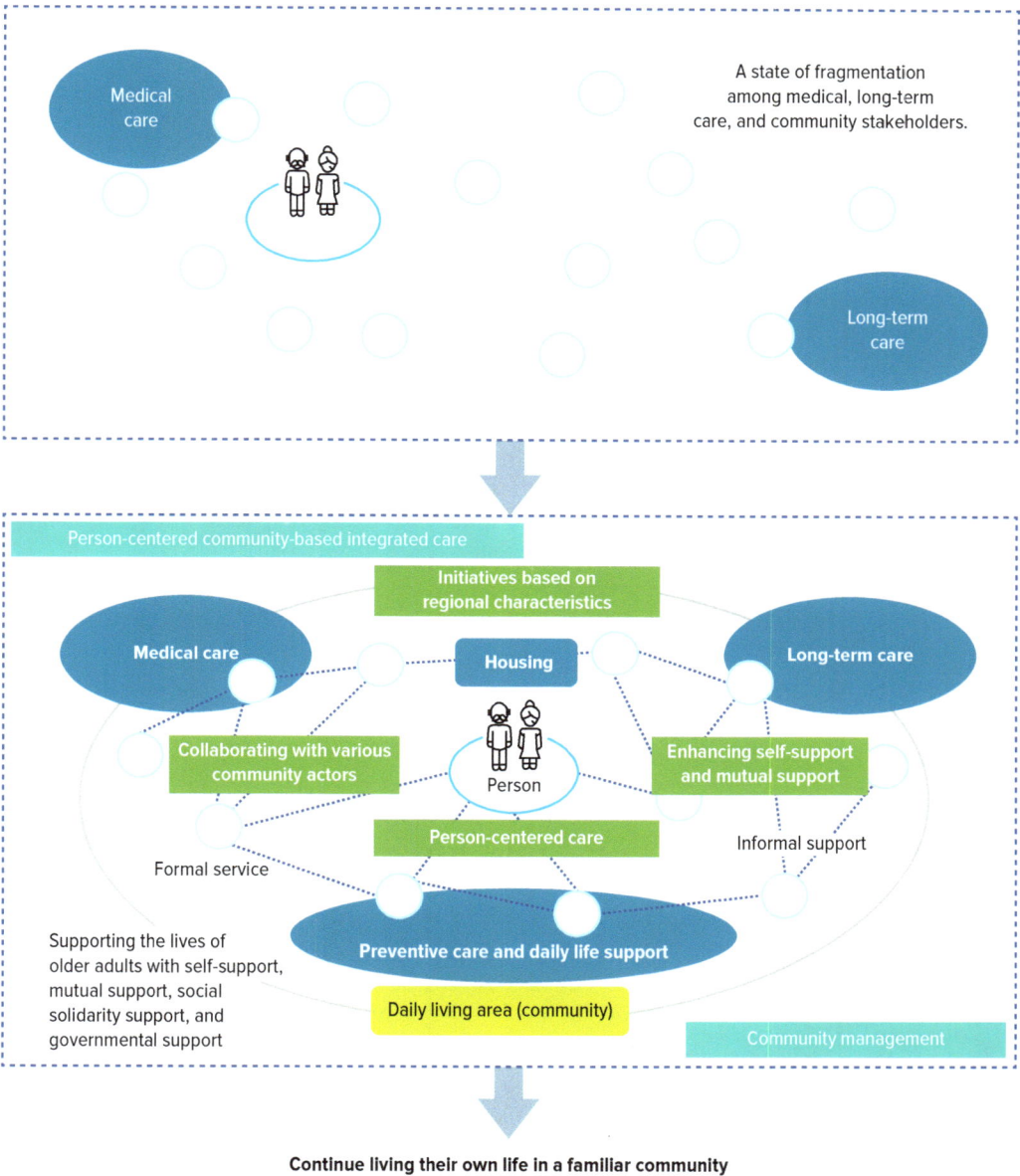

A state of fragmentation among medical, long-term care, and community stakeholders.

Medical care

Long-term care

Person-centered community-based integrated care

Initiatives based on regional characteristics

Medical care

Housing

Long-term care

Collaborating with various community actors

Person

Enhancing self-support and mutual support

Person-centered care

Informal support

Formal service

Supporting the lives of older adults with self-support, mutual support, social solidarity support, and governmental support

Preventive care and daily life support

Daily living area (community)

Community management

Continue living their own life in a familiar community

Source: JICA 2022.

support," "collaborating with various community actors," and coordinating "efforts based on the characteristics of the community." By deploying these values and goals of older adults, it is possible to provide integrated care focused on the individual and rooted in the community so that older adults can continue living in the communities with which they are accustomed.

Lessons Learned and Recommendations

Developing countries face diverse age-related challenges, but they are also home to many relationships of mutual support in their communities and have many sources of strength for the promotion of community-based integrated care. Lessons from Japan may help them address their challenges and harness their strengths. The following recommendations are drawn from the three case studies in this chapter.

Design Comprehensive Older Adult Care Policies and Programs from a Long-Term Perspective

As nuclear (rather than extended) family life and women's participation in the workforce increase, it will likely become more difficult for families alone to take care of their older members. Japan's experience has shown that reliance on medical-oriented systems and policies for an aging population hinders the dignity and autonomy of older adults and, additionally, is financially inefficient. It is important to look ahead to the conditions and challenges in an aging society from a long-term perspective so as to consider how to provide older adults with comprehensive care that does not rely solely on traditional medical intervention.

Design Communities Where Older Adults Can Live with Dignity (Move toward the Social Model)

To realize a life with dignity for older adults, which can be obtained by making decisions for themselves and living with autonomy (self-care), relationships with people in the community and mutual support are as essential as specialized services such as medical care and long-term care. To foster this kind of self-care and mutual support, a shift to a social model is required. It is necessary for developing countries to take advantage of their strengths, such as a strong sense of community solidarity and mutual support, and design communities where self-care and mutual support can be fostered.

Work on Community Development as an Evolving Process

Japan's approach to community-based integrated care can be described as a long-term, democratic, evolving process of community development based on the active participation of and dialogue with diverse actors. The conditions, needs, challenges, and resources of each community and each era must be considered afresh. Strong leadership is needed to manage such a consensual, dialogue-based process of community development. Capturing and using resources that are already widely available in the community, rather than limiting solutions to the fields of medical care and welfare, can be an effective strategy.

See Older People Not as People Who Need to Be Supported by Others, but as Supporters of Themselves and Others

As in developed countries, the disease pattern is shifting from infectious diseases to noncommunicable diseases, and the length of medical treatment is expected to increase in developing countries as populations age. Proactively adopting self-care initiatives, including self-management of support and preventive care, will be important.

Create a Mechanism for Providing Medical Care that Aims to Help Older People Return to Live at Home and Continue to Live There

When the aim is to return a patient to his or her home, coordination of medical care and services from the time of hospitalization to the time of discharge can improve the consistency of medical management and the quality of home life, and reduce the risk of readmission or becoming bedridden. In developing countries, public medical institutions are often responsible for the health care of the population, which can be an advantage in providing seamless care.

Design Administrative Systems Consistent with Community-Based Integrated Care

In some countries, decentralization of health services is promoted, but there are also cases in which local governments are not clearly provided with the authority they need, including over the use of the budget, to respond to community needs. In addition, when medical services are provided by the central government and social services are provided by local governments, the capacity levels of the implementing bodies often differ. In Japan, in the past, the various authorities for implementing systems related to older adult care were dispersed among levels of government,[4] and there were multiple programs for the same purpose,[5] hindering the delivery of integrated services. Because the conditions of older adults and that of communities, and the values and goals of people, differ from community to community, it is important to empower the local authorities that implement systems related to older adult care and respond to the diverse priorities in each community.

It is also important that community-based integrated care not be limited to older people but be made available to an inclusive society. In the Japanese experience, strictly and exclusively reserving programs and budgets for each target group can be a hindrance when dealing with cross-targets. Designing programs so that they can respond flexibly to similar needs, regardless of the target, is useful.

Build a Strong Foundation

It should be noted that when aiming for a society in which older people are able to live with dignity in their own communities, the approach of building and promoting community-based integrated care *on its own* has limitations.

It cannot all by itself grant the dignity older people deserve. In many developing countries, for example, medical and income security are not yet mature, or they are fragile, yet good health care and income security are essential parts of realizing a dignified life. The foundation for creating and promoting a CICS is the development of basic public services.

Notes

1. Persons receiving welfare benefits, however, are excluded from applying for National Health Insurance because medical care is provided for most of them through the medical assistance aspect of welfare public assistance.
2. The Elderly Long-Term Care Study Group was a group of experts appointed by the director-general of the Health and Welfare Bureau for the Elderly of the Ministry of Health, Labour, and Welfare.
3. In this chapter, all care provided under the CICS is referred to as "Community-Based Integrated Care."
4. The levels of administrative organization were different in Japan before 1990, with facility services overseen by prefectures and home-based services overseen by municipalities.
5. Until the introduction of the Long-Term Care Insurance Act in 2000, even where the content of the service was the same, medical care was provided by medical insurance, and welfare was provided by the social welfare system, making it a complicated system for users.

References

JICA (Japan International Cooperation Agency). 2022. "Community-based Integrated Care in Japan—Suggestions for Developing Countries from Cases in Japan." Tokyo. https://openjicareport.jica.go.jp/pdf/1000048192.pdf.

Ministry of Health, Labour and Welfare. 2003. *2015 nen no Koreisha Kaigo* (in Japanese) (*Toward the Establishment of Elderly Long-Term Care and Care to Support the Dignity of the Elderly in 2015*) Elderly Long-Term Care Study Group Report. https://www.mhlw.go.jp/topics/kaigo/kentou/15kourei/2.html.

Ministry of Health, Labour and Welfare. 2020. "Annual Health, Labour and Welfare Report 2020." Tokyo. https://www.mhlw.go.jp/english/wp/wp-hw13/index.html.

National Commission on Social Security. 2008. *Interim Report of the National Commission on Social Security Second Subcommittee: Service Guarantees—Medical, Long-term Care, and Welfare*. 2008. Tokyo: National Commission on Social Security Second Subcommittee. https://www.mhlw.go.jp/shingi/2008/06/dl/s0619-6o.pdf.

CHAPTER 8

Conclusions and Policy Takeaways

Xiaohui Hou, Jigyasa Sharma, Feng Zhao, and Alexander Irwin

Introduction

In Malawi, Rwanda, Uganda, and Zimbabwe, the number of people age 60 and over is expected to quadruple by 2050, among the fastest rates of older adult population growth in the world (UN DESA 2017). Once seen only in the richest societies, rapidly rising populations of older adults now characterize every global region and the large majority of countries. Longevity gains reflect hard-won progress in human development. However, aging populations are driving an upward spiral in health service needs and costs that will test health systems everywhere.

This book argues that, by acting now, countries can grasp population aging as an opportunity to accelerate progress toward key health and development goals, notably universal health coverage. To take advantage of this opportunity, countries will need to develop integrated care systems for older people centered on primary health care (PHC). Anchored in communities, PHC is the component of health systems closest to people's daily lives, characterized by first contact, accessibility, longitudinality, and comprehensiveness (Starfield 1992). Strong PHC improves people's health at all ages through disease prevention and health promotion, protects patients and families financially, builds public confidence in health systems, and lowers system costs (Baris et al. 2021; National Academies of Sciences, Engineering, and Medicine 2021).

But to meet the needs of aging populations, PHC itself must evolve. With its tragic toll on older people, the COVID-19 (coronavirus) crisis has underscored that most countries' PHC systems are not ready for the complex challenges posed by growing numbers of vulnerable older adults, many with chronic comorbidities.

Financing, innovation, regulation, and evaluation—the four pillars of the FIRE framework this book sets forth—are priority levers that all countries can use to strengthen PHC-centered, integrated care for aging populations.

Policy actions across multiple health system domains will be needed to improve care for older people. But the FIRE components are foundational arenas in which countries at all income levels can act to strengthen service delivery, improve patient outcomes, and rein in surging costs.

Financing: Managing Resources for PHC-Led System Change

Countries advancing toward universal health coverage need robust mechanisms to pool resources across population strata: young and old, rich and poor, and the formal and informal employment sectors. Policy makers in each country face hard decisions about who to cover, for what services, and for how much, given real-world economic and political constraints.

Meeting the care needs of aging populations will require additional health investments in most countries. Importantly, though, research and country experience show that population aging is a significant driver not only for increased health spending, but also for a stronger public role in financing health care services. As a population ages, a window of opportunity can open for increased public financing—through political demand driven by older people's rising vote share, as well as economic resources generated by countries' demographic dividend. Thus, as a country develops economically and its population matures, policy makers have the opportunity to redirect resources so as to increase the share of health spending that flows through efficient pooling mechanisms, rather than being paid out of pocket by individuals and families when they need care (the least equitable and least efficient form of health financing). Investing new public funds strategically—in PHC-led care systems—can help contain health system costs. The shift to more robust public financing can also strengthen equity in health care access, improve care quality and value for money, and benefit all generations (Fan and Savedoff 2014).

Recent analyses in countries such as Japan underscore the importance for financing of a long-term perspective on population aging that incorporates—but also looks beyond—medical care, engaging whole-of-government and whole-of-society strategies. Important cost-saving opportunities will stem from policies and programs that offer comprehensive care for older adults not solely reliant on medical care (Song and Tang 2019). Lower-income countries that act now can secure long-term savings, increase efficiency, and improve outcomes by learning from the approaches—and the mistakes—of high-income societies where population aging is already advanced, and where initial approaches to the aging challenge were disproportionately medicalized, resulting in missed opportunities (Saito et al. 2019).

This book highlights the following policy pathways in health financing:

- *Leverage financing to strengthen PHC gatekeeping and care coordination.* The integration and coordination of PHC services with referrals to secondary care and long-term care (LTC) is a key policy objective for countries, linked to PHC's gatekeeping function. PHC's success in promoting care coordination often depends on the configuration of two system-level features:

first, the organizational architecture of the health system, that is, the specific relationships between the health payer or payers and health provider organizations; and second, the robustness of primary care providers' gatekeeping function within the system (Roberts et al. 2008; Sripa et al. 2019). Canada and the Netherlands are examples of countries that have successfully enforced gatekeeping as part of their health insurance programs.

• *Use universal coverage rather than age cutoffs to improve outcomes for older adults.* A life-course perspective emphasizes that people's health at older ages depends on their health earlier in life. A specific age cutoff for covering older people with health services is not recommended. Avoiding age cutoffs enables the health system to address needs among older adults more equitably and reinforce disease prevention and health promotion, preempting many costly health problems before they start. Countries including Canada, Colombia, the Netherlands, and Saudi Arabia have developed promising models that provide universal mandatory coverage regardless of age. In contrast, in the United States, an age threshold of 65 years for publicly funded care has been in place for decades, despite evidence of the cutoff's negative impacts on population health. Such experiences confirm an important lesson: long after a policy has been introduced, a residual level of "stickiness" in the policy design may continue to hamper change.

• *Align financing strategies with health system architecture.* Although the means of financing—through general revenues or payroll taxes—may be a central focus of policy reform, it is just as important for decision-makers to consider overall system architecture: how the system as a whole is organized, including publicly provided services and the referral system, as well as regulations governing provider networks in systems that involve insurance. Countries where public provision is dominant need to be cautious as private sector care expands, managing system change to accommodate private sector growth through an appropriately regulated insurance model. Recent experiences in China, Colombia, and Saudi Arabia suggest that robust health insurance models can help balance access and benefits for system users, while providing incentives for care coordination and efficient referrals within provider networks.

• *Seize reform windows based on country demographics, macroeconomic conditions, and political resources.* Population aging can be a crucial part of a country's economic development, as demonstrated by extensive work on the demographic dividend. As reductions in mortality followed by drops in fertility transform countries' population age structure, windows of opportunity can emerge, enabling policy makers to implement universal-coverage programs for health insurance and even long-term care insurance. Japan and the Netherlands are examples of countries that have introduced mandatory LTC insurance. Uncertainty around economic resources implies that windows of opportunity may be brief for countries to implement health policy reforms to cover more people and offer more benefits. Timely action to seize political openings is critical.

Innovation: New Tools for the Aging Challenge

As health systems navigate demographic change, multiple forms of innovation will be needed to improve outcomes in older populations while controlling costs. Some countries have leveraged innovative care delivery models to advance toward person-centered, PHC-driven, and integrated care systems encompassing the full range of acute, postacute, and LTC services in a continuum. Person-centeredness entails the delivery of care at or near the place where older people live, consistent with the preference for aging in place and (when feasible) treating in place.

To date, innovative holistic service provision models remain rare in low- and middle-income countries (LMICs). However, experiences in countries such as Ghana, Kenya, and Tanzania show that some policy makers and practitioners in LMICs are already aiming high, testing local delivery systems that incorporate desirable system features from high-income settings, while adapting to local resource profiles and cultural preferences (Petsoulas 2019). In Ghana, for example, the Care for Aged Foundation provides individualized care plans developed in collaboration with older people and their families. Young volunteer workers deliver personalized services and receive free health care in exchange. The model incorporates the traditional local care structure, in which the young assist older adults, so home-care services are provided in a manner that is culturally acceptable, though questions of sustainability persist for models reliant on volunteers (Petsoulas 2019). Aided by cross-country learning and a growing knowledge base from international health care and LTC research, more and more countries can grasp opportunities to "leapfrog" by adapting international best practices.

Digital health innovations have the potential to transform PHC for older populations and solve stubborn health system challenges. However, significant barriers to uptake tend to discourage the investments needed, especially but not only in LMICs. Principal among these barriers are affordability, the lack of digital skills (particularly among the most at-risk and low-income populations), and the shortage of user-friendly features. A senior-centric design approach is necessary for better use of digital technology in older adult care. Country experiences to date show concrete steps health leaders can take to accelerate and apply digital health innovation for better care. Conducting assessments to understand the challenges, bottlenecks, preferences, and capabilities of local older adult populations should be the first step. Based on a nuanced situation assessment, regulation can be designed to promote innovation while avoiding potential risks or harms to users.

Successful countries are exploring new business models to enhance digital health innovation, including public-private partnerships. Coordination with the private sector is essential, given that most digital health innovation stems from that source. Financial incentives and an enabling ecosystem can foster the creation of local start-ups and expand market access. Reimbursement policies may also increase affordability and uptake. Meanwhile, to understand the extent of benefits provided by digital health for older adults, more research and evaluation studies are needed. A shortage of evidence persists around digital health technologies (Ienca et al. 2021). Economic evaluation tools, including measures of cost-effectiveness, can help prioritize interventions and show the way forward.

The following policy directions hold promise in innovation:

Integrated Care Delivery

- *Use individualized care assessments and care planning to optimize home- and community-based services.* Home- and community-based services allow older people with significant physical and cognitive limitations to remain integrated within the community by living at home, or in a home-like setting. Such approaches are increasingly welcomed by older adults and their family members, particularly in the post-COVID-19 era. Promising models for lower-resource settings include the personalized, multidimensional support package for low-income older adults that HelpAge International tested in Tanzania from 2014 to 2017 under the Better Health for Older People in Africa program (Petsoulas 2019).

- *Use care management models to strengthen integrated service delivery.* In Thailand, an LTC pilot program managed by the National Health Security Office and local authorities operates through an innovative care-management system. Launched in 2016, the program provides two to eight hours of home-based care support a week, depending on clients' needs. Social services such as assistance with housework and activities of daily living and obtaining assistive devices are provided to older persons who meet eligibility criteria. Medical services are also available through the program and Thailand's universal health coverage package (ADB 2020).

- *Engage multidisciplinary teams to deliver personalized LTC.* In Kenya, a private nursing agency provides individualized in-home care to paying clients and those whose medical insurance covers home-based care (Petsoulas 2019). Services include personal care, specialized home health care, nutritional advice, psychosocial support, and disease management services. Diverse, multiskilled teams of health professionals work with patients to create personalized care delivery plans. Although this type of private sector–driven model is growing in popularity, older individuals without insurance may face gaps in access. To build and deploy multidisciplinary care teams at scale, many LMICs will need to invest in human resources. Policy makers can boost education and training to upgrade skills among current LTC workers and expand the multidisciplinary care workforce, incorporating geriatricians, therapists, dietitians, nurses, social workers, case managers, and LTC facility administrators (Feng et al. 2020).

- *Draw on older people's knowledge, skills, and networks to implement community-based LTC.* In Cambodia, China, India, Indonesia, Myanmar, Nepal, the Philippines, Sri Lanka, and Vietnam, Older People's Associations (OPAs)—membership organizations led or managed by older people—often facilitate activities and deliver services for older adults. By partnering with government service providers, OPAs provide an added layer of support for older persons' well-being that complements existing medical service delivery mechanisms with social and community engagement.

Digital Health for Older Adults

- *Prioritize digital health interventions based on local people's preferences and capabilities.* Conduct systematic local assessments to understand older adults' preferences, capabilities, and challenges with digital health. Based on findings, a comprehensive program can be devised to upgrade digital skills among older adults and their care providers. Set priorities for digital health interventions through a consultative process that engages local older adults and other stakeholders. Road maps for implementation need to be drawn up early. Decision-makers can harness proven evaluation tools to assess costs and benefits and measure impact as programs roll out.

- *Craft regulatory frameworks to foster digital health innovation while protecting users.* A strong regulatory framework is needed to ensure older adults' privacy and data security, promote equity of access, and tackle digital divides. Balanced regulation will also aim to nurture each country's digital health ecosystem and facilitate uptake of senior-focused technologies. Committed participation by the ministry of health is essential to achieving a balanced framework. Comprehensive regulations encompass legal measures; the privacy and security of data; evidence-based assessment of medical devices, technologies, and algorithms; medical liability; compliance to secure value-based care; and partnerships and collaboration between the supply side (for example, technology companies and start-ups) and the demand side (for example, ministries, patients, and providers) (Bresnick 2019).

- *Grow digital health ecosystems and explore new partnerships.* Burgeoning interest in digitally enabled technology for older adults has fueled an increasing number of start-ups and funding for home health care and old-age care as part of the "silver economy." This is occurring in areas such as in-home services (telemedicine, home testing, self-examination), loneliness (social networks), and support to caregivers. This trend is more prominent in middle- and high-income countries, where regulations and incentives are often in place to spur growth in local ecosystems. In LMICs, technology hubs and other supportive structures can nurture innovation and attract investment. New business models, including public-private partnerships, hold promise in some settings.

- *Engage caregivers as allies in design and implementation.* Governments, payers, medical organizations, and technology companies seeking to develop and encourage the use of digital health by older adults can speed progress by engaging caregivers. In many cases, the caregiver is a family member and a significant source of support for the older person. If caregivers are treated as integral to technology design—and engaged as key users—the result will be increased awareness, adoption, and compliance: in short, better outcomes.

Regulation: Leveraging Older Adult Care to Advance Health System Stewardship

Regulation and governance offer crucial levers with which to strengthen care provision and outcomes for older adults. These gains can yield benefits for the wider health system and service integration across sectors. Regulation of care systems is the responsibility of governments. Central, provincial or regional, and local or municipal governments have distinct and complementary roles in overseeing care systems for older adults. Typically, local governments are the frontline authorities regulating community-based PHC systems, while the central government determines the broad structures and philosophy of a national healthy aging strategy and establishes the design, financing, and legal positioning of PHC-led care. Regional governments can play a key role in supporting local and municipal authorities. Regional governments can track changing needs across municipalities in their jurisdiction, devise plans for regional financing and resource allocation, and supervise and support local actors.

Country experience underscores the challenges of implementing whole-of-government and whole-of-society approaches to care governance—but also the benefits of these models for older populations. Policy makers need a deliberate strategy to promote inclusive community engagement in older adult care solutions and facilitate intersectoral and interorganizational partnerships. A practical approach is to have a single designated organization oversee the management of the local system. Japan's Community General Support Center structure provides an example. It coordinates local resources for care of older adults and ensures that all local stakeholders are appropriately involved in decision-making processes at each phase of care quality improvement cycles.

Specific mechanisms have shown promise in building solid relationships among care stakeholders and increasing social capital across the community. These include (1) regular individual case review meetings that bring together all players involved in care processes for older adults and (2) PHC system review meetings convened by municipal governments that create a higher-level forum for stakeholders to share plans, implementation strategies, and results; jointly assess care needs and resources; and identify emerging issues and opportunities. Both of these mechanisms foster social capital within the care community and can be applied in lower-income settings.

The track record of regulation and governance in HICs—including their failures—may offer important lessons and leapfrogging opportunities for PHC-centered older adult care in developing economies. A crucial require-ment is seeing age-responsive community development not as a "one-off" action but as an evolving process. Japan's current approach to community-based integrated care offers a strong example. It can be described as a democratic and evolving process of community development based on the participation and dialogue of diverse actors. The conditions, needs, challenges, and resources of each community are considered, while recognizing that all of these factors change over time. Strong leadership is needed to manage dynamic community development processes. Japan's experience suggests that countries can get the best results by harnessing the full range of social resources in the community, not limited to medical care and formal welfare systems.

The analysis in this book highlights the following policy directions in regulation and governance:

- *Adopt a whole-of-government approach.* Care systems for aging populations work best when they adopt a whole-of-government and whole-of-society strategy that advances health and well-being for older adults across multiple policy domains. Priority action areas include government stewardship, financing, human resources, and infrastructure. A key stewardship task is facilitating the appropriate engagement of local communities and the private sector in older adult care. A robust whole-of-government model leverages the strengths of national, regional, and local governments. Appropriately supported local actors are positioned to shoulder crucial delivery and care coordination tasks.

- *Ensure regulatory flexibility to foster local decision-making and innovation.* Communities are diverse, and local systems need a high degree of regulatory freedom to decide how to use resources in the ways best suited to each community. Uniform, top-down regulations applied by a central government bring limited benefits. Best results come with the integration of stakeholders at the national, regional, and local levels, enabling actors to use local resources to enhance social value (WHO Commission on Social Determinants of Health 2008). The World Health Organization's (WHO's) recent LTC framework proposes that each community create a dedicated multisectoral coordinating body that works with higher-level organizations to exercise LTC governance (WHO 2021).

- *Balance "hard" regulations and "soft" incentives.* Regulation can be divided into legal regulation by governments and self-regulation by players. For the former, laws and ordinances may define the organizational and professional conditions for providing specific care services, set prices and standards, and define violations and sanctions. Self-regulation refers to voluntary rules, usually among for-profit providers. The government can often improve system governance by providing incentives for collaboration and good performance among players. For example, financial incentives can be created, such as higher prices for more desirable services, or higher payments for the same services if they are provided in a more desirable way. Choices between "hard" regulation and the use of incentives in specific cases will reflect factors such as the country's political traditions and administrative organization and the development stage of local PHC systems.

- *Prioritize home- and community-based LTC to boost flexibility and control costs.* Thailand's community-based LTC approach may provide lessons for other countries. The Thai government focuses on strengthening community-based or home-based LTC services, rather than facility-based care. For several reasons, this strategy may be especially well suited to middle-income countries experiencing rapid increases in their older adult populations (Chanprasert 2021). First, community-based or home-based care can be more cost-effective than facility-based or hospital-based care, especially for

LTC (Chandoevwit and Vajragupta 2017). Second, community-based or home-based LTC services have the flexibility to accommodate local conditions. Such services operate using community resources and can function in urban settings, smaller towns, or rural villages, meaning they can cover the entire country, in collaboration with community and local governments, even where budgets are tight. Additionally, the Thai model's combined approach to service delivery, using both volunteers and professional caregivers, helps control costs. Japan's Community-Based Integrated Care System for older adults also supports delivery of a full range of services for older adults in the community, rather than primarily through hospitals or institutions. The system bolsters local stewardship capacity to coordinate LTC, medical care, and health promotion for older adults, along with housing and support for independent daily living.

- *Look beyond medical care to foster stewardship with a social lens.* A key governance lesson is the importance of starting early to design comprehensive older adult care policies and programs from a long-term perspective that is not restricted to medical care. Japan's experience, for example, has shown that the country's early, medically oriented systems and policies for the aging population did not optimally promote the dignity and autonomy of older adults. They also proved to be financially inefficient. Designing communities where older adults can live with dignity implies shifting to a social model. In this respect, some emerging economies may have important advantages, such as cultural values of community solidarity and mutual support, enabling these countries to promote communities where self-care and mutual support can be fostered.

Evaluation: Better Measurement Fuels Efficiency

Evaluation and measurement are key to understanding older people's care needs and ensuring that the supply of services matches demand. Today's care landscape for older adults in LMICs is marked by deficits in research, validated tools, and empirical evidence relevant to evaluation. This book's treatment of evaluation synthesizes findings from a literature review on older adult care across LMICs, placing a strong focus on LTC.

Good measurement tracks both the demand and supply sides of the care equation: on the one hand, older adults' care needs and preferences and, on the other, the composition, distribution, accessibility, and quality of health and LTC services to meet those needs. On the demand side, countries need to start by obtaining reliable estimates of the number of older people with disabilities that prevent them from living independently. Standard assessment tools for this purpose measure people's ability to carry out activities of daily living (for example, bathing and dressing) and instrumental activities of daily living (for example, managing money).

On the supply side, robust evaluation strategies address both the availability of health and LTC services for older adults and their quality. The quality of LTC, in particular, is multidimensional and difficult to measure, especially for care and services provided in home- and community-based settings. A variety of tools have been developed, mostly in HICs, to measure LTC care quality and person-centeredness. Some streamlined instruments are beginning to be validated in LMIC settings. Given the speed of population aging in many LMICs, additional evidence to define best practices in person-centered care is urgently needed.

Based on the literature review and drawing on potentially relevant experiences and lessons learned from HICs, this book recommends practical strategies for assessing older adult care needs, service availability, and care quality in LMICs, and for building the information, monitoring, and evaluation systems that countries need to improve health and well-being for older adults. Although policy makers understandably prioritize investments in infrastructure and service delivery, countries working to upgrade their older adult care systems also have an interest in creating effective information, monitoring, and evaluation systems from the start. Doing so is the best way to ensure that investments in older adult care remain cost-effective while delivering the benefits that citizens want.

The following policy directions and implementation strategies show promise for improving care for older adults through better measurement:

- *Obtain regular, reliable estimates of the number of older people with disabilities that prevent them from living independently.* To gauge care needs for older adults, countries can deploy assessment tools that measure people's ability to carry out activities of daily living and instrumental activities of daily living. Where possible, these efforts should leverage nationally representative, population-based, longitudinal surveys of older adults. Where the costs of frequent large-scale data collection are a concern, researchers and government agencies can consider shortened yet validated instruments such as the Washington Group Short Set on Functioning (Washington Group on Disability Statistics 2020).

- *Use streamlined tools to measure health care and LTC availability and quality.* Given resource limitations, LMIC policy makers can opt for information systems designed to collect a minimal set of data items that are the most essential for supporting evidence-based policy making (for example, data on the availability and mix of LTC services, affordability, accessibility, and regional disparities) and for minimum quality assurance (for example, patient safety and measures against neglect and abuse). LMICs can learn from countries such as Sweden that have well-developed yet cost-effective systems for quality measurement and control. Policy makers can assess existing quality indicators and adapt them to LMIC contexts and care systems.

- *Harness diverse data sources for more robust evaluation.* Data generation from a broad range of sources tends to strengthen evaluation. Useful sources include facility-based information systems, public health surveillance systems, and population-based surveys (considering both formal and informal care), as well as routine monitoring through information systems. Integrated LTC information systems, encompassing both the public and private sectors, can help ensure that care is delivered in a nonfragmented way (WHO 2021).

- *Use evidence-based operational steps to build and reinforce LTC evaluation systems.* Expert groups and normative agencies, notably the WHO, have developed updated recommendations for countries working to establish LTC information, monitoring, and evaluation systems. Action steps for decision-makers and implementers include the following:

  - Choose country-relevant measures of well-being, quality of life, and personhood for evaluating LTC outcomes

  - Identify the characteristics of services provided (private vs. public, for profit vs. not for profit, geographic distribution, and quality distribution), including service mix (home care, community based, and institutional)

  - Generate data that show utilization rates by service type, and audit the number of LTC facilities, their geographic distribution, number of beds, and number of heath care workers per bed

  - Formulate measures for quality assessment, such as rates of avoidable hospital admissions, service integration, and clinical outcomes

  - Generate detailed data on financing, for example, out-of-pocket expenditures for LTC, coverage based on eligibility, and the proportion of care provided by informal caregivers and its costs (WHO 2021).

Summary of Policy Recommendations

Table 8.1 organizes the top-line policy messages emerging from the FIRE analysis. These recommendations address policy makers, their advisers, and implementers at the country level.

Success in the approaches highlighted depends on incorporating the voices of older people themselves in policy design and delivery, through inclusive partnerships engaging civil society and communities, together with multilateral agencies, the private sector, academic researchers, faith-based organizations, and others. Strategies for broad stakeholder engagement and participation in healthy aging are advancing through the UN Decade of Healthy Ageing agenda,[1] the work of the WHO,[2] and regional efforts such as the Asia Health and Wellbeing Initiative.[3]

Additional operational recommendations for policy and implementation, especially in LMICs, will be profiled in a forthcoming companion volume of country case studies on integrated, PHC-centered care for older adults.

An Ongoing Learning Agenda

Even as it presents policy and implementation recommendations for countries based on available evidence, this volume identifies numerous gaps in knowledge to be addressed by future research. Accelerating the learning agenda around integrated services for older adults will be crucial to enabling countries to continuously improve PHC-centered care systems for older people as needs, resources, and contextual conditions change.

TABLE 8.1 Policy and Implementation Takeaways in the FIRE Domains

FIRE component	Policy and implementation pathways
Financing	– Leverage financing to strengthen PHC gatekeeping and care coordination – Use universal coverage rather than age cutoffs to improve outcomes for older adults – Align financing strategies with health system architecture – Seize reform windows based on country demographics, macroeconomic conditions, and political resources – Leverage population aging trends to boost public financing of health services and reduce out-of-pocket health spending by patients and families
Innovation (care delivery)	– Use individualized care assessments and care planning to optimize home- and community-based services – Use care management models to strengthen integrated service delivery – Engage multidisciplinary teams to deliver personalized LTC; invest in diversified human resources – Draw on older people's knowledge, skills, and networks to implement community-based LTC
Innovation (digital health)	– Prioritize digital health interventions based on local people's preferences and capabilities – Craft regulatory frameworks to foster digital health innovation while protecting users – Grow digital health ecosystems and explore new partnerships – Engage caregivers as allies in design and implementation
Regulation	– Adopt a whole-of-government approach – Ensure regulatory flexibility to foster local decision-making and innovation – Balance "hard" regulations and "soft" incentives – Prioritize home- and community-based LTC to boost flexibility and control costs – Look beyond medical care to foster stewardship with a social lens

Evaluation	– Obtain regular, reliable estimates of the number of older people with disabilities that prevent them from living independently
	– Use streamlined tools to measure health care and LTC availability and quality
	– Harness diverse data sources for more robust evaluation
	– Use evidence-based operational steps to build and reinforce LTC evaluation systems:
	  ○ Choose country-relevant indicators
	  ○ Characterize available services (for example, private vs. public)
	  ○ Generate core utilization and facility data
	  ○ Formulate context-appropriate measures for quality assessment
	  ○ Generate detailed data on financing (for example, out-of-pocket expenditures for LTC)

Source: World Bank.
Note: FIRE = financing, innovation, regulation, and evaluation; LTC = long-term care; PHC = primary health care.

Country-level research will constitute an especially important strand of this learning work. As noted, a companion volume to this book, currently in preparation, will contribute to this agenda. That volume will present a series of regional and country case studies detailing how countries at different income levels and stages of health system development have taken action to strengthen PHC-centered integrated care delivery, leverage opportunities for efficiency gains, bolster measurement and evaluation, and improve outcomes for older adults.

The Way Forward: Systems Integration for the Silver Age

By activating the FIRE levers, along with other entry points for health system reform, countries can turn the aging-population challenge into an opportunity to drive long-awaited system transformation and build more inclusive and productive societies.

Health leaders have long known that integrated, person-centered PHC is the best way to deliver quality and affordable clinical services and comprehensive care for healthier living—not just for older people, but for all (International Conference on Primary Health Care, Alma-Ata, USSR, 1978; WHO 1978; see also WHO and UNICEF 2018). However, although the value of integrated, PHC-based care models is recognized, their implementation has lagged. Care fragmentation has continued to mark the structure of health systems and the experiences of many patients within them, especially but not only older adults with multiple chronic comorbidities (MacLeod et al. 2018). The promise of person-centered PHC has remained partially fulfilled, at best, and until recently most countries seemed inclined to continue postponing bold investments in PHC-driven health system transformation (Baris et al. 2021; OECD 2020).

Coupled with the shock of COVID-19, the global demographic transformation now underway has changed that calculus for good. Today, as populations of older adults surge in virtually all countries, the demand for comprehensive, age-responsive care is rising at a pace that countries literally cannot afford to ignore (Levy et al. 2020). To keep their health systems solvent and their economies productive, countries need to deliver PHC-centered care reforms swiftly and at scale. Doing so involves fundamental action to enhance PHC, strengthen coordination among care providers at all levels, and integrate quality clinical services into broader models of lifelong care and community-led social support. As they advance this agenda, countries will improve health for all their people. By expanding care access and ensuring financial protection for older adults and their families, countries will take bold steps on the road toward health equity and universal health coverage—with substantial benefits for their human capital, productivity, and competitiveness (World Bank 2019, forthcoming).

Engaging the knowledge and creativity of older people in defining priorities and designing solutions will be crucial to this process. Older adults are the experts in their own health and in the care models that will work best to facilitate the dignified lives they want. The countries that have achieved the strongest results in comprehensive care for older people have done so by listening to their voices. They have engaged older people as actors for their own health, as innovators, and as problem solvers. Such approaches have paid rewards in health outcomes, but also in other ways that may be equally important. Countries choosing this path have begun to model the more inclusive and productive societies to which all aspire, in which people of all generations reach their full potential, lead satisfying lives, and contribute to their communities at every life stage. Accelerating demographic transformation means the chance—and the obligation—to tap this vast potential everywhere.

This book shows how core policy levers—including health financing, innovation in care delivery and digital technology, regulation, and evaluation—will help countries achieve the goal. The ultimate result will be more integrated care systems that link different facets of people's health and well-being across the life course. By advancing this agenda, countries have an opportunity to repair the fragmentation that mars health systems today. Such fragmentation has fueled chronically suboptimal care quality for older adults. It has also weakened health outcomes for other population groups and sharply exacerbated the health and economic consequences of health emergencies, notably COVID-19 (World Bank 2022). Building integrated, person-centered PHC for older populations provides countries with a powerful means to advance the broader agenda of systems integration. The practical measures described in this book can support countries in bridging siloed financing and care-delivery mechanisms and providing integrated, person-centered care for older people and for all.

Notes

1. "Decade of Healthy Ageing: The Platform," https://www.decadeofhealthyageing .org.
2. World Health Organization, "Aging," https://www.who.int/health-topics/ageing #tab=tab_1.
3. Asia Health and Wellbeing Initiative, "About AHWIN," https://www.ahwin.org /about-ahwin/.

References

ADB (Asian Development Bank). 2020. *Country Diagnostic Study on Long-Term Care in Thailand*. Manila: Asian Development Bank. doi:http://dx.doi.org/10.22617 /TCS200373-2.

Baris, Enis, Rachel Silverman, Huihui Wang, Feng Zhao, and Muhammad Ali Pate. 2021. *Walking the Talk: Reimagining Primary Health Care after COVID-19*. Washington, DC: World Bank.

Bresnick, Jennifer. 2019. "Apple Floats Idea of Subsidizing Watches for Medicare Advantage." *HealthPayerIntelligence Private Payers News*, January 17, 2019. https:// healthpayerintelligence.com/news/apple-floats-idea-of-subsidizing-watches-for -medicare-advantage.

Chandoevwit, Worawan, and Yos Vajragupta. 2017. "Long Term Care Insurance System: Long Term Care System for Thailand" (in Thai). Thailand Development Research Institute, Bangkok.

Chanprasert, Puangpen. 2021. "Long-Term Care Policy and Implementation in Thailand." In *Coping with Rapid Population Ageing in Asia,*" edited by Osuke Komazawa and Yasuhiko Saito, 36–44. Jakarta: Economic Research Institute for ASEAN and East Asia (ERIA).

Fan, Victoria Y., and William D. Savedoff. 2014. "The Health Financing Transition: A Conceptual Framework and Empirical Evidence." *Social Science & Medicine* 105: 112–21.

Feng, Zhanlian, Elena Glinskaya, Hongtu Chen, Sen Gong, Yue Qiu, Jianming Xu, and Winnie Yip. 2020. "Long-Term Care System for Older Adults in China: Policy Landscape, Challenges, and Future Prospects." *The Lancet* 396 (10259): 1362–72.

Ienca, Marcello, Christophe Schneble, Reto W. Kressig, and Tenzin Wangmo. 2021. "Digital Health Interventions for Healthy Ageing: A Qualitative User Evaluation and Ethical Assessment." *BMC Geriatrics* 21 (1): 412. https://doi.org/10.1186/s12877-021 -02338-z.

Levy, Becca R., Martin D. Slade, E-Shien Chang, Sneha Kannoth, and Shi-Yi Wang. "Ageism Amplifies Cost and Prevalence of Health Conditions." *Gerontologist* 60 (1): 174–81. doi:10.1093/geront/gny131.

MacLeod, Stephanie, Kay Schwebke, Kevin Hawkins, Joann Ruiz, Emma Hoo, and Charlotte S. Yeh. 2018. "Need for Comprehensive Health Care Quality Measures for Older Adults." *Population Health Management* 21 (4): 296–302.

National Academies of Sciences, Engineering, and Medicine. 2021. *Implementing High-Quality Primary Care: Rebuilding the Foundation of Health Care.* Washington, DC: National Academies Press.

OECD (Organisation for Economic Co-operation and Development). 2020. *Realising the Potential of Primary Health Care.* OECD Health Policy Studies. Paris: OECD.

Petsoulas, Christina. 2019. "Thinking about Long-term Care in a Global Context—A Literature Review." Green Templeton College, Oxford University, Oxford, U.K.

Roberts, Marc, William Hsiao, Peter Berman, and Michael Reich. 2008. *Getting Health Reform Right: A Guide to Improving Performance and Equity.* New York: Oxford University Press.

Saito, Junko, Maho Haseda, Airi Amemiya, Daisuke Takagi, Katsunori Kondo, and Naoki Kondo. 2019. "Community-Based Care for Healthy Ageing: Lessons from Japan." *Bulletin of the World Health Organization* 97 (8): 570–74. doi:10.2471/BLT.18.223057.

Song, Peipei, and Wei Tang. 2019. "The Community-Based Integrated Care System in Japan: Health Care and Nursing Care Challenges Posed by Super-Aged Society." *BioScience Trends* 13 (3): 279–81. doi:10.5582/bst.2019.01173.

Sripa, Poompong, Benedict Hayhoe, Priya Garg, Azeem Majeed, and Geva Greenfield. 2019. "Impact of GP Gatekeeping on Quality of Care, and Health Outcomes, Use, and Expenditure: A Systematic Review." *British Journal of General Practice: The Journal of the Royal College of General Practitioners* 69 (682): e294–303. https://doi.org/10.3399/bjgp19X702209.

Starfield, Barbara. 1992. *Primary Care: Concept, Evaluation, and Policy.* New York: Oxford University Press.

UN DESA (United Nations Department of Economic and Social Affairs Population Division). 2017. *World Population Ageing 2017.* New York: UN DESA.

Washington Group on Disability Statistics. 2020. "The Washington Group Short Set on Functioning (WG-SS)." Washington Group on Disability Statistics, Hyattsville, MD.

WHO (World Health Organization). 1978. "Declaration of Alma-Ata. International Conference on Primary Health Care, Alma-Ata, USSR, 6–12 September 1978." World Health Organization (Alma-Ata, USSR). https://www.who.int/teams/social-determinants-of-health/declaration-of-alma-ata.

WHO (World Health Organization). 2021. *Framework for Countries to Achieve an Integrated Continuum of Long-Term Care.* Geneva: WHO.

WHO Commission on Social Determinants of Health. 2008. *Closing the Gap in a Generation: Health Equity through Action on the Social Determinants of Health.* Final Report of the Commission on Social Determinants of Health. Geneva: WHO.

WHO and UNICEF (World Health Organization and the United Nations Children's Fund). 2018. "Declaration of Astana." WHO and UNICEF. https://www.who.int/docs/default-source/primary-health/declaration/gcphc-declaration.pdf.

World Bank. 2019. *High-Performance Health Financing for Universal Health Coverage: Driving Sustainable, Inclusive Growth in the 21st Century.* Washington, DC: World Bank.

World Bank. 2022. "Change Cannot Wait: Building Resilient Health Systems in the Shadow of COVID-19." World Bank, Washington, DC.

World Bank. Forthcoming. *Promoting Healthy Longevity and Enhancing Human Capital by Tackling Noncommunicable Diseases: Findings from the World Bank Healthy Longevity Initiative.* Washington, DC: World Bank.

www.ingramcontent.com/pod-product-compliance
Lightning Source LLC
Chambersburg PA
CBHW060759270326

41926CB00002B/31